making waves

Mark Davies & Tina Catling

CAPSTONE
be inspired! ™

contents

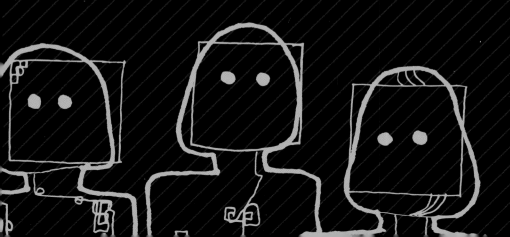

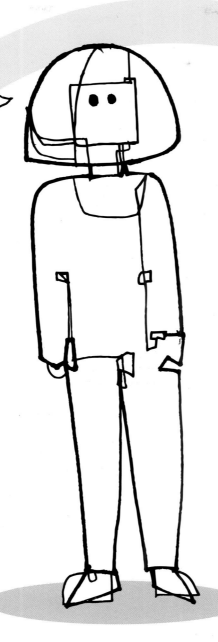
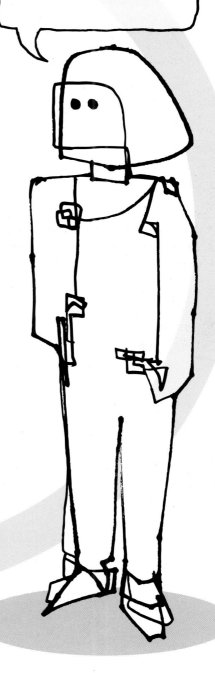

120

Website
Design

140

Search Engine
Optimisation

152

Paid Search
Marketing

162

Social Media

176

Testing

190

And Finally...

making waves

The world of marketing is a turbulent place, moving at an incredible pace as technology and attitudes change. **Making Waves** rides the chaos and sets free the power of the masses.

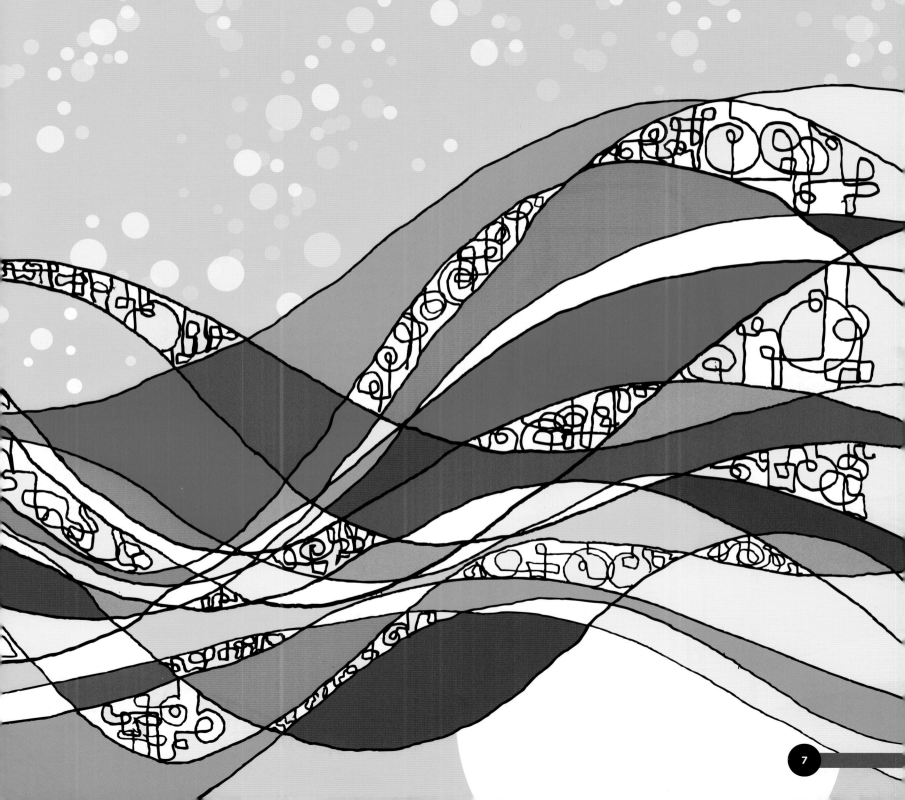

From guerilla warfare in the Ryvita Inch War campaign of the seventies, to a gorilla outdoing Phil Collins on drums for Cadbury at the end of the noughties, big disruptive creative ideas have been the hallmark of all that is great in advertising. However, a big idea can't produce even the tiniest ripple on the public consciousness by itself. To really make waves, an idea needs to be delivered to its audience through the right channels, and these days, the channels themselves are just as important, varied and exciting as the ideas they deliver.

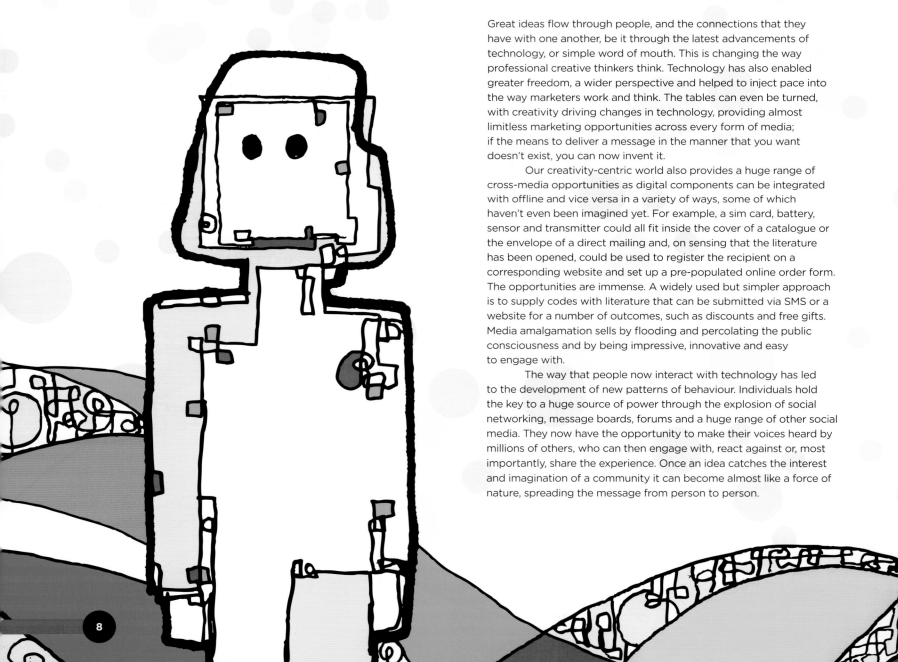

Great ideas flow through people, and the connections that they have with one another, be it through the latest advancements of technology, or simple word of mouth. This is changing the way professional creative thinkers think. Technology has also enabled greater freedom, a wider perspective and helped to inject pace into the way marketers work and think. The tables can even be turned, with creativity driving changes in technology, providing almost limitless marketing opportunities across every form of media; if the means to deliver a message in the manner that you want doesn't exist, you can now invent it.

Our creativity-centric world also provides a huge range of cross-media opportunities as digital components can be integrated with offline and vice versa in a variety of ways, some of which haven't even been imagined yet. For example, a sim card, battery, sensor and transmitter could all fit inside the cover of a catalogue or the envelope of a direct mailing and, on sensing that the literature has been opened, could be used to register the recipient on a corresponding website and set up a pre-populated online order form. The opportunities are immense. A widely used but simpler approach is to supply codes with literature that can be submitted via SMS or a website for a number of outcomes, such as discounts and free gifts. Media amalgamation sells by flooding and percolating the public consciousness and by being impressive, innovative and easy to engage with.

The way that people now interact with technology has led to the development of new patterns of behaviour. Individuals hold the key to a huge source of power through the explosion of social networking, message boards, forums and a huge range of other social media. They now have the opportunity to make their voices heard by millions of others, who can then engage with, react against or, most importantly, share the experience. Once an idea catches the interest and imagination of a community it can become almost like a force of nature, spreading the message from person to person.

Consider the potential of all of these in an explosive cocktail. It's a combination of creative prowess, rich expertise in traditional techniques and the ability to tap the force of online communities. The 'pass it on', ripple-like, nature of this social phenomenon put us in mind of a giant digital Mexican wave, and the unpredictable flooding and flowing that takes place led us to only one possible label for these powerful and fluid events: **Waves.**

Now we can make waves of a much bigger kind, creating big disruptive ideas which gain massive momentum. In next to no time, a ripple becomes a roaring forty, using the audience itself as the most effective medium yet.

The Benefits

ROI

The huge efficiencies that occur both through the greater-than-the-sum-of-their-parts media combinations and the fact that it is promoted primarily through the public, free of charge leads to a fantastic Return on Investment. Making waves leads to a greater, faster and cheaper awareness than any other method that exists today.

Feedback

The sheer scope for feedback that a campaign can achieve through the ability to enter into conversations on a massive scale is astounding. Making waves is not simply one-way, but can create a dialogue where response and criticism are encouraged and facilitated. Feedback is an incredibly valuable commodity in the marketing world and, if properly nurtured, a campaign can harvest a wealth of data on which it can then feed and grow.

Loyalty

Because of its interactive nature, a campaign that makes waves can create a stronger bond between brand and audience, often to the point where brands are perceived as trusted friends rather than remote corporate assets. A course of relevant and considerate marketing activities could capture the heart and the mind of a customer and generate a high level of personal loyalty and attachment to the brand – or completely repel them if it's not done well!

Wave marketing is far from being an exact science and its chaotic nature can cause no end of headaches, but a well planned campaign should minimise possible difficulties and provide the kinds of returns that would be difficult to sustain through any other means.

The Splash

To start a wave, you need to create a splash. This can be a big budget, multi-channel marketing push or the tiniest of nudges in the right direction, but whatever it is, it has to be both relevant and original as relevance combats disposability while originality makes a message more memorable and shareable.

As we mentioned above, the ideal process should not be restricted by the available media; there will be a point in the strategic process where the question of what is achievable needs to be asked – have a look at the **Consolidation** section of our **Strategy** chapter – but in the first stages there should be no such concerns. The focus should be entirely on creating the most original and relevant ideas and then appropriating, manipulating or even inventing media to fit it. The **Explosion** segment of our **Strategy** chapter provides in-depth guides on how to achieve original and relevant ideas.

After creating a big idea, the next step is to identify the right place to make the splash, and this requires a good strategy. Every strategy should start with a period of **Absorption**, where a huge range of the aspects of a company/brand and its surrounding environment – customers, competition, etc. – are studied in as much detail as possible, and it is from this in depth research that the answer to the question of where a campaign should start will be found.

Who to Splash…

A large part of finding the right place to start a wave is deciding who to engage with and establishing how likely they are to take the message and pass it on. Within every target audience there are individuals who are predisposed to search out and share interesting and entertaining media, who revel in the act of discovery. The best way to engage with them is to leave small and inconspicuous titbits, puzzles or breadcrumbs for them to follow. Usually the challenge is its own reward, but providing prizes can inspire further motivation for people to join in.

A far larger group are much happier letting the message come to them and will utilise websites that compile all of the best media that the previous individuals discovered, or will rely on their social networks to provide links to interesting videos, articles or events both online and offline. This group can then be divided across a spectrum depending on how likely they are to share media and how large their networks are, but generally, the best way to connect with them is to find the places that they are getting their information from and ensure that there are references and links to the campaign positioned on them. For example, if a target demographic is mothers, then mentions on sites such as **mumsnet.com** or their homophonic rivals **netmums.com** will do a great deal to start spreading the word.

Bloggers and journalists are the most useful of all groups. Their raison d'être is to spread the word and attracting their attention gives any wave a phenomenal kick-start.

But what of the passives – those to whom sharing in the context of social media is anathema? Depending on the audience, this group can be both large and critical to campaign success. They are receptive to traditional direct marketing techniques and should be targeted with direct mail and emails.

...And How?

The development of an effective media strategy should be as creative as the big idea itself. Our limitless approach to the development of a campaign is made possible because we can appropriate, manipulate or even invent the media through which we communicate. The audience, its sensitivities, its viewing, listening, reading and digital behaviours determine the optimum nature and blend of media.

It is important to provide people with what they actually want rather than what they say they want. The biggest splash comes from presenting people with something that they didn't even realise that they wanted as surprise and discovery are a great catalyst for a recipient's desire to share; providing them with a 'look what I found' moment. If you investigate deeper into target audiences by trawling through their message board comments – filtering programs can be employed for this as they can identify when specific key words have been used – and starting conversations, you will gain far more honest opinions than can be garnered by questionnaires or focus groups, and with that information it should be possible to ascertain what it is that people want, both in a product/service and the marketing that promotes it.

After performing the customer analysis, the next step is to research the media – reading this book is a good start – so that you have an understanding that will allow you to use them to their full potential. Each media has its strengths and weaknesses and can be combined with others to both emphasise the positives and counteract the negatives. The key is to achieve relevance of media as this is just as important as relevance of message. To do this, look at the target audience to determine how they are used to receiving their information and which media channels best reflect them. For instance, a trendy company with ecological aspirations and a young demographic may be best suited to a campaign based around younger magazines, relevant TV programs, social media, emails, websites and concise mailers printed on recycled materials rather than one that uses half a rainforest's worth of catalogues.

A great way to make an impact is to create an experience for the public to become involved in and want to share with their peers. This can be as simple as a funny video, picture or article or it can be a huge event with light shows and fireworks; the trick is to provoke a response that propels the brand out of the mess of marketing messages that flood everyday life, and into a person's conscious. This is why physical media – such as direct mail and catalogues – retain their importance as, although the internet is a great facilitator for fast and inexpensive marketing, until it can tickle the senses with sensory stimulation through touch, taste and smell, the greatest impact will always be created through a campaign that involves something that the consumer can physically engage with.

The Long Wave

'...word-of-mouth marketing will forever be the most powerful way of persuading customers to join us."
Richard Branson. The Future of Marketing [The Marketing Society]

If a wave is started in the right place and imbued with a sufficient amount of originality and relevance, much of the input to spreading the wave is taken on by the public, but at no point will a campaign become completely self-perpetuating; it will always require enlivening by a series of supporting initiatives, such as a well timed surge in social media presence, to give it the push it needs to get back to the forefront of the public consciousness. There is no point making a big splash, only to watch it quickly fade into obscurity. This is another great reason for using a combination of media as they all have very different response times: a TV advertisement or eshot will have a huge peak of activity in response, but die quickly while catalogues, door drops and even press will have less of an immediate peak but will draw responses over a much longer time period.

The reason for the importance of word of mouth is that, in general, we as a species of consumers are pack animals and we crave reassurance from those around us. Our money is hard earned and any purchase is usually preceded with a mental calculation of **Value** – found through the multiplication of **Quality** and **Benefit** divided by **Price** – versus the **Time** and **Effort** that it took to make the money required. A problem can arise with this process if certain values are unknown due to a lack of experience with the product, service, brand, etc. For instance, the quality of a product could be poor but

> The development of an effective **media strategy** should be as **creative** as the big idea itself

the retailer isn't going to promote it as such and so the potential customer becomes uncertain; reassurances are, therefore, going to have to be provided before the purchase can be completed. Before the internet, the foremost method of obtaining reassurance was in brand recognition because it stood to reason that a brand that could afford advertising must have a large number of customers, and if they are receiving media coverage then they must be important to, and favoured by, a large number of people. In short, brand recognition was so powerful because there is safety in numbers.

In those decades where brand recognition was key, word of mouth worked best for niche or elite brands – such as Branson's **Virgin Atlantic** – where their customer community was small, discerning and well connected. However, the internet changed this as, above every other advancement that it provided the marketing world – speed, value or potential for targeting – its allowance for a huge number of people to make their voices heard by the rest of that huge number of people, turned word of mouth marketing from a niche approach to a mass market one. As such, peer recommendations and reviews have become the way to sell as they are incredibly accessible and add an extra level of reassurance; they reassure the potential customer that the reassurance is genuine. The product is no longer championed by a faceless mass of populace, but by Dave from Bristol who, as a real person, inspires far more trust. The reassurance relationship has, therefore, advanced from a primitive pack mentality to a civilised dialogue between individuals and it is this dialogue that needs to be at the forefront of marketing activities. A good example of this is **Trip Adviser**, where people who have been on holiday post reviews of the trip online for others to see.

It follows then, that to sustain a wave a company must amass customers who then go on to spread the word about the magnificence of their product and there are five key stages to achieve this:

1. Win the customer
The first of these is the traditional goal of marketing and it remains incredibly important to meet customers' needs.

2. Impress them
To impress a customer, a marketer needs to engage with the product or service and ensure that the communication has integrity; that what you are saying can be substantiated. Otherwise, ultimately, it will fail.

3. Take care of them
To meet customer needs you have to understand that, in the world of waves, loyalty is worth more than novelty. There used to be a divide in marketing: current customers on one side and prospective customers on the other. Businesses that wanted to expand would have to win new customers and this took massive investment, often to the detriment of the existing customers. The thought seemed to be that once all of the wooing and promising had persuaded an individual to

make a number of purchases, those individuals were already in the bank and could be relied on to continue to spend with the brand with minimal marketing input while other conquests were sought out.

However, there is an ever growing movement of people investigating whether there are greener pastures elsewhere and, once again, the availability of a vast array of reviews and comparisons makes it likely that if a better service exists, they will find it. This Lothario-esque approach can, therefore, no longer work. Not only will the customer find somewhere else to spend their money, they will also take their potential as wave makers. To combat this marketers have to pay just as much attention and use just as many resources on current customers as they do on the potential ones. Why, after all, should a new customer get a discount, while the loyal customer gets nothing? Those loyal customers will see that they are being treated unfairly – and it really is quite unfair – and move on.

4. Provide them with sufficient means and motivation to tell the world
This stage requires a variety of channels to be set up for customers to leave public feedback. This can be accomplished through online social media, where it is easy for people to both leave and read comments. We cover the specifics in more detail in our **Social Media** chapter, but the general aim of advertising the means by which customers can publicly query, praise or complain is to make it as easy as possible to spread the word and also to reinforce the honesty and customer engagement of a brand.

Once a means by which customers can share their views has been established, it is important to engage with the reviewers and get involved in the reviewing platform. Look through the comments and reviews and turn them into conversations by responding. The response needs to be dynamic, targeted reinforcement of customer importance, so thank an individual for a good review and address the concerns of a negative reviewer. By taking an interest on the human level, even bad reviews can become opportunities to show how a brand holds the customer's concerns above all else.

5. Cultivating the Why
Most companies market themselves based on **What** they do and **How** they do it – "we make the best cars using the newest technology" – but they rarely say **Why** they do what they do. Loyalty can be triggered by the **Why**, as it creates a set of values with which the customers can identify and engage with. For instance, staying with our car example, telling people that, "we make cars because the world is a fascinating place and we want you to be able to get there," informs the customers of what a brand stands for. What it believes in. And, in doing so, attracts individuals who have the same beliefs or values. It turns the act of purchasing, from a simple acquisition, to a vote, a pledge or an enrolment.

Bad Waves

Wave marketing isn't without its problems. Its power is generated in a natural, chaotic, almost Darwinian environment and, as such, there is far less control of how a message is received and reacted to. There will, therefore, be times when obstacles – a bad press review for instance, or a disgruntled customer – will present themselves, determined to derail a campaign's wave building initiative. The trick is to learn from others' mistakes and aim for a preventive approach rather than a reactionary one, as the very nature of wave marketing makes it difficult to implement any counter measures after a campaign has been introduced into the public domain and produced a negative reaction.

One of the potential problems that can scupper a campaign is delivering the message to the wrong audience. **Apple** learnt this when they made the UK version of their 'I am Mac, I am PC' adverts. The ads had the comedians Robert Webb and David Mitchell claiming to be a Mac and a PC, respectively, and meant to present the PC as unreliable and boring while the Mac was cool and fun. There were two problems with these adverts: one was that the vast majority of those viewing them were PC users who weren't going to be won over by being called boring; and the other was that the PC character actually had the best, funniest lines and came across as far more likeable than the smug Mac character. It was so counter-productive, in fact, that **Microsoft** appropriated the 'I'm a PC' slogan in their own marketing.

Another common crisis occurs when claims and promises made in the marketing literature are not supported by strong products or services as it quickly becomes evident that the reality doesn't live up to the marketing and any positive wave will, at best, dissipate and, at worst, turn into a wave of negativity.

One of the most famous examples of this, which has become something of a legend, told to young marketers as a cautionary tale, is **The Great Hoover Flight Fiasco of '92**. **Hoover** had a backlog of vacuum cleaners and washing machines and had the ingenious idea of offering two free return flights to Europe when a customer spent £100 on any Hoover products. Word spread quickly and the response was massive, with a huge number of people taking Hoover up on its incredibly generous offer. The problem was that it was too generous and the travel agents struggled with the demands for free flights. To make matters worse, Hoover were seemingly oblivious to the trouble that they were in and launched another promotion, this time offering flights to the USA. Inevitably, the demand grew beyond Hoover's means and they were unable to deliver. Consumer watchdogs and the media became involved – further publicising, and driving demand for, the offer – and, after a prolonged series of lawsuits, the final cost to the company was £48m, accompanied by job losses for those involved and a big hit to the brand's reputation. In the end, Hoover had made a massive wave but was unprepared and paid a heavy price for their mistake.

These types of event aren't hugely common, though, and if a campaign does attract negative comments it is not worth panicking. A certain amount of criticism is only to be expected as it is impossible to please everybody. Customers are aware of this and tend, therefore, to base their decisions on a range of feedback rather than being completely turned off by one bad review.

Wave goodbye and start again

Every wave has its own natural lifespan and begins to dissipate when interest subsides and its energy is expended. If a campaign is based on a promotion or competition, the length of the wave is predetermined, adding urgency to response. If this element is absent, the audience activity around the campaign should be closely monitored throughout to provide an indication of when it is time to move on. The wave-maker should be succeeded in a timely way by a new campaign that capitalises on the impact of its predecessor.

Creating a New Wave

To summarise, when it comes to starting a new wave remember:

- Make sure that the idea is big, strong, relevant, exciting and interesting as most individuals suffer from a sales message overload and this means that an idea needs to **stand out** if it is to be passed on.

- Most companies can take advantage of a **variety** of direct, targeted marketing media channel.

- No matter the means that are decided on to spread a campaign's message, there needs to be one constant if it is going to create the largest, longest running and most prevalent wave: the **human** component.

- Ensure that the product or service and after-purchase support lives up to the marketing and that there are plenty of channels for customers to spread the word. That what you are communicating has **Integrity**.

- Give it a big start and **know when to finish**; you can even have a cut off point as this lends urgency, creates more interest and drives you to create the next campaign.

Throughout the rest of this book we have aimed to help you to generate the ideas, create the strategies and choose the best combination of media and techniques – for example, traditional direct mail techniques are now being used in the creation of websites – to really make waves. We have captured for you some of the best tips to use in direct response media, the sort of media that allow you to measure their impact easily. However, keep in mind that these are only guidelines and that the best marketing is based on creativity and that any of these guidelines can, and should, be broken rather than get in the way of innovation. As Thomas Eddison once said, "Hell there are no rules here. We're trying to accomplish something."

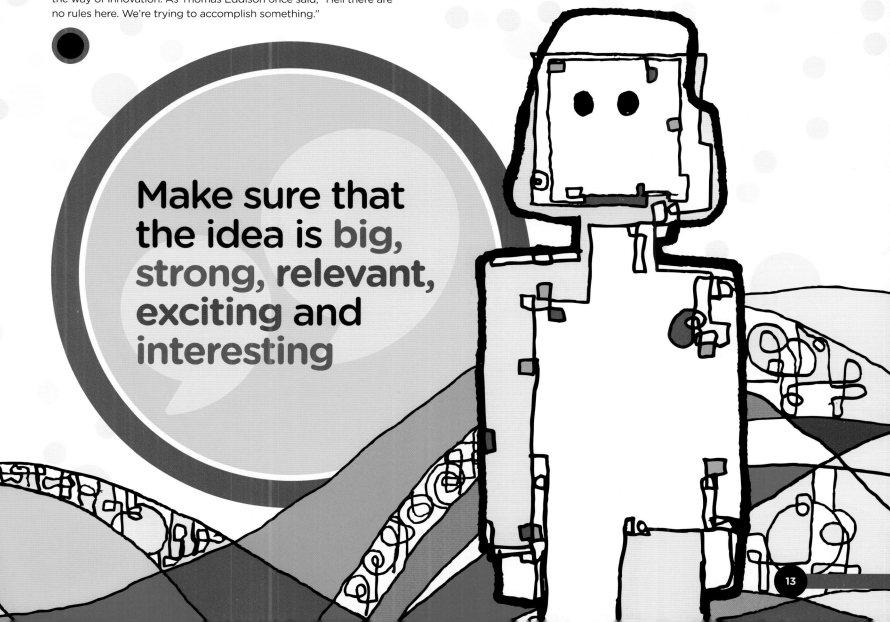

Make sure that the idea is big, strong, relevant, exciting and interesting

marketing strategy and planning

Concentrate your resource on the greatest opportunities

Marketing Strategy is the management process responsible for identifying, anticipating and satisfying customer requirements.

This customer-centric activity results in the delivery of the right product, in the right place, at the right time and at the right price. Then we need to make the right communication to the right people in order to stimulate demand and make sales.

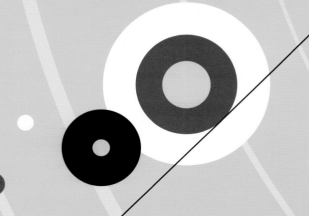

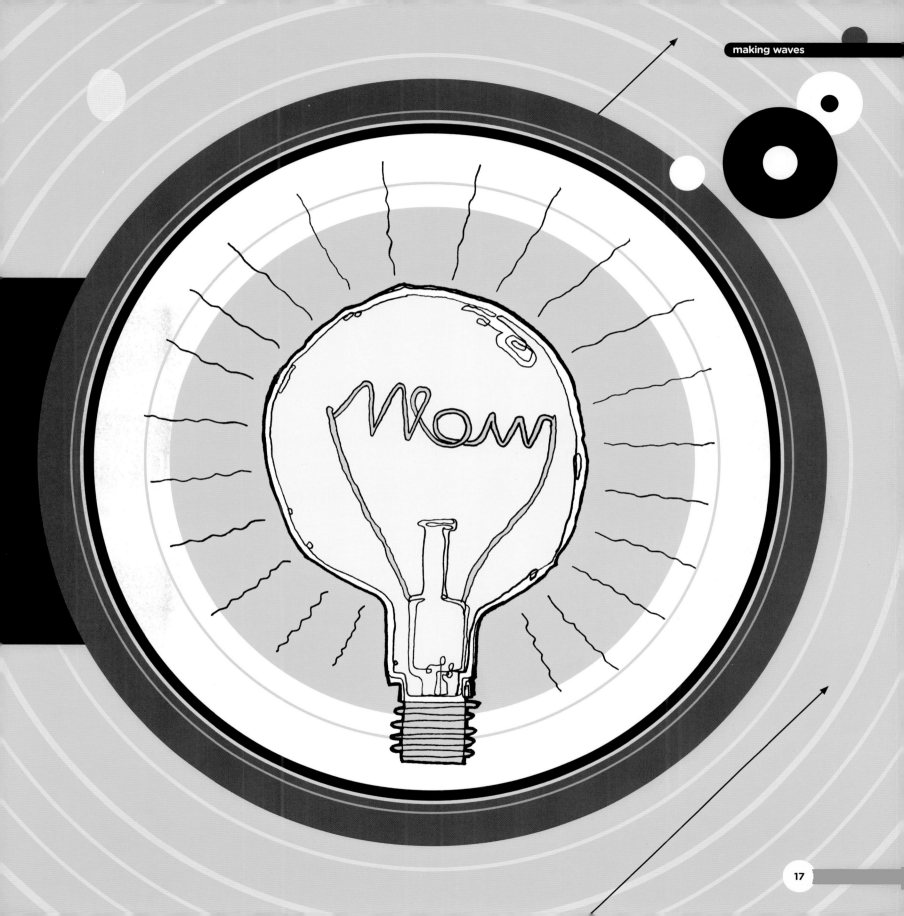

Fail to plan and you'll plan to fail

Whilst at **outside the box** we love nothing more than to generate outstanding ideas, we have to concede that they can only exist in an environment where the correct foundations have been laid. Unbridled, chaotic creativity is of little use if there is no product relevance or if your campaign is badly targeted.

We use a range of tools to build the necessary foundations, boundaries and objectives. They can be tangible tools such as tables, formulae and matrices, or they can be processes; a checklist of actions to be taken. They can even be the right state of mind, and the techniques to get there. The emergent marketing plan and communication plan is the key to success.

If a product or service, or indeed a company, is to fare well in its competitive environment we need to understand the relevance of its current status, define marketing objectives, plan and develop accordingly. Classically, there are seven key areas that are examined and to make it easy, they all begin with the letter **'P'** which is quite strange if you think about it.

how will you know if **the idea** you run with is the **best idea**?

1. Product
Is it relevant to the audience? Does it differentiate itself from similar products?

2. Price
Is the product/service competitively priced, would it benefit from premium pricing?

3. Place
Where is it sold? Is it accessible?

4. People
Do you have the right team to fulfill your marketing plan?

5. Positioning
What messages reflect your product/service/company and differentiate you?

6. Packaging
How should you package your product, your people and your company? (this is really about your brand, but brand doesn't start with a 'P')

7. Promotion
What is the best way to communicate your message to your audience(s)?

These seven 'P's are at the heart of sound Marketing Strategy. The first four deliver a set of marketing objectives critical to the development of a robust Marketing Plan. The Plan's outputs, and ultimately its success, are based on five key criteria:

- Fact-based, not assumption-based
- Provision of distinctive direction
- Matching of resources to market opportunities
- Informing and directing the business
- Maximisation of revenue and profits to meet the business plan

'P's 5, 6 and 7, which are all about Communication Strategy and Promotional Planning, enable us to promote our defined product/service by targeting the right people with the right message in the right way.

The Big Plan

For the development of promotional campaigns, **outside the box** has created a process, involving a number of techniques, which never fails to deliver innovative solutions and significant results. It is a perpetual cycle, with one round of activity feeding learnings into the next.

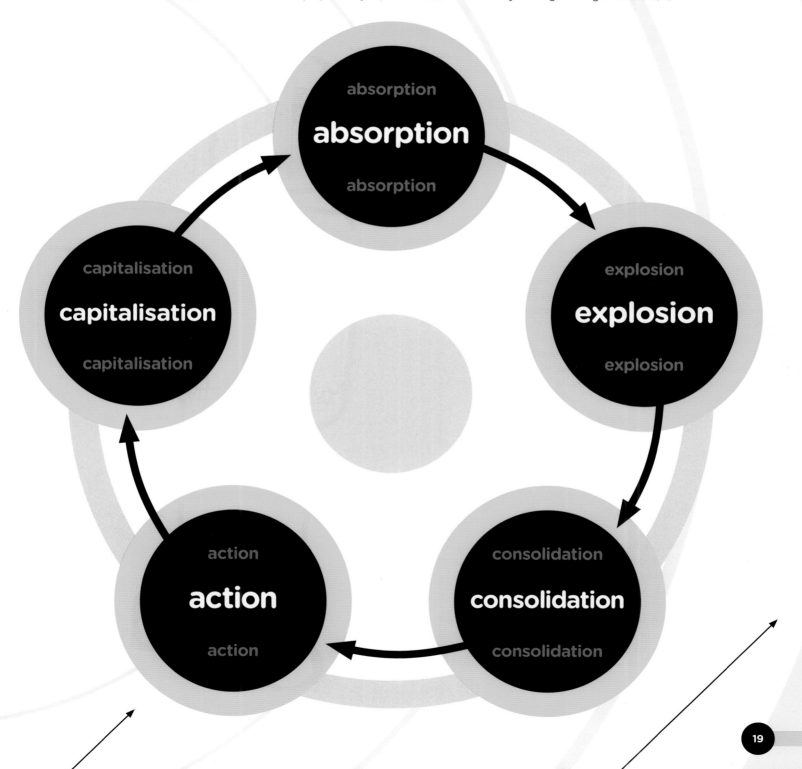

Absorption

We immerse ourselves in the issues, the brand, the products, the culture, the business objectives, the data on target audience and buying patterns, the competition and every other conceivable aspect that could have an influence on a campaign, using primary and secondary research where appropriate. Where possible, we also try the service or buy the product to test the customer experience firsthand. The ultimate aims are:

- To understand and confirm product, pricing and distribution relevance
- To define competitive advantage
- To determine relevant positioning
- To develop a marketing plan
- To develop creative briefs — Absorption
- information providing the background

Explosion

This is where we use the information that we have gathered to create ideas to promote the product/service. The need is for both a communication/media strategy (the means through which we communicate) as well the creative idea itself (what we say and how we say it). 'Explosion' can also be invaluable in the further development of products or services where their relevance has fallen into question during the Absorption phase.

Using our creative briefs as a starting point, we explore every angle, discounting nothing. It is important to use thinking tools and techniques to help stimulate ideas, as one of the best ways to have a great idea is to have lots of ideas!

Consolidation

We take the ideas and give them a reality check against the factors that are critical to the success of the idea; this could be budget, time, brand fit, speed to market, etc. – in fact all of the elements contained in the creative brief. The ideas that survive must be practical and fit for purpose. They must also be arresting, challenging and fresh.

Action

Here we outline how we will put the great ideas into action, using realistic activity planning and scheduling that will move things along. It is, essentially, a process of turning concept into reality.

Capitalisation

Once campaigns have aired, it is time to assess our success. Be it profit, new customers or other measures, we have to ask if our work achieved its objectives so that we can build for the future. Capturing performance data is essential and this data can feed back into the Absorption stage for the next campaign.

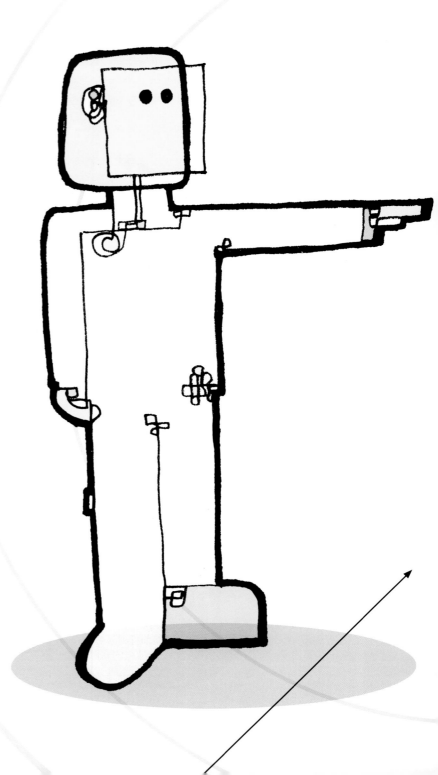

welcome to your new strategy

Absorption

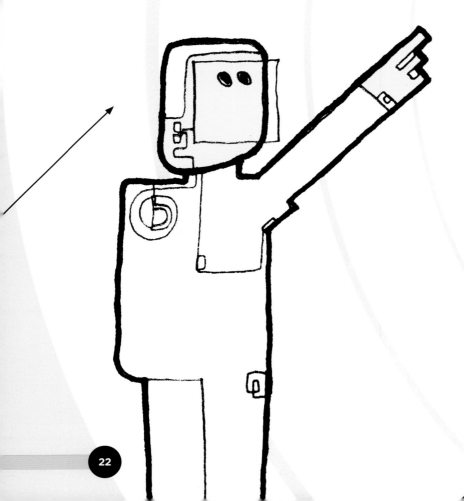

Where are we now?

The aim here is to assess the current situation, define potential and enable a course to be charted between the two. All aspects of a business are examined during this phase, including the audience's need, audience's behaviour, purchasing patterns, competitive environment, pricing structures and product/service delivery. This enables us to confirm the relevance of the current product/service and to identify areas for development.

The outcome of **Absorption** is a Marketing Strategy and a Marketing Plan from which Creative Briefs fall and leading ultimately to a promotional campaign. If the Marketing Plan is already in existence, the Absorption process may raise issues to challenge it or provide additional information that may cause it to be modified.

We are including here a series of exercises as a practical, generic guide to **Absorption.** Every situation is different, of course, so some may be more relevant than others to the task in hand.

Who Do You Think You Are?

The best way to start your strategic activities is to determine how you, the team that you work with, and the business itself operate. Whether you work for a marketing agency, a marketing department, or are marketing your own product, interactions with people are inescapable. By constructing profiles for yourself and those around you, you can make the most of these interactions and more effectively manage, delegate and motivate by pairing people with the right projects and the right team mates.

We know how important it is to have a good understanding of different personalities and how they relate to one another, and so we have found a personality profiling system developed by Dr Susan E. Dellinger — www.psychometricshapes.co.uk — that we can use whenever we take on a new employee or client. It has been invaluable in ensuring that the teams that we assemble are well balanced and fit for purpose, with a good blend of creativity, structure and drive. Once you get to know it, the technique can be easily adapted to profile companies or teams of people. Use the following questionnaire to assess if you and your team have the right personality types to meet the challenges ahead!

Personality Profile

Which of the following do you think you are?

Name: _____

Study each of the following groups of words. Choose the one word in each group that applies to you most often. Once you have chosen the word, mark it with an **✗**. Do not skip any of the word groups.

1. ___ Animated	___ Adventurous	___ Analytical	___ Adaptable
2. ___ Persistent	___ Playful	___ Persuasive	___ Peaceful
3. ___ Submissive	___ Self-sacrificing	___ Sociable	___ Strong-willed
4. ___ Considerate	___ Controlled	___ Competitive	___ Convincing
5. ___ Refreshing	___ Respectful	___ Reserved	___ Resourceful
6. ___ Satisfied	___ Sensitive	___ Self-reliant	___ Spirited
7. ___ Planner	___ Patient	___ Positive	___ Promoter
8. ___ Sure	___ Spontaneous	___ Scheduled	___ Shy
9. ___ Orderly	___ Obliging	___ Outspoken	___ Optimistic
10. ___ Friendly	___ Faithful	___ Funny	___ Forceful
11. ___ Daring	___ Delightful	___ Diplomatic	___ Detailed
12. ___ Cheerful	___ Consistent	___ Cultured	___ Confident
13. ___ Idealistic	___ Independent	___ Inoffensive	___ Inspiring
14. ___ Demonstrative	___ Decisive	___ Dry humour	___ Deep
15. ___ Mediator	___ Musical	___ Mover	___ Mixes easily
16. ___ Thoughtful	___ Tenacious	___ Talker	___ Tolerant
17. ___ Listener	___ Loyal	___ Leader	___ Lively
18. ___ Contended	___ Chief	___ Chart maker	___ Cute
19. ___ Perfectionist	___ Permissive	___ Productive	___ Popular
20. ___ Bouncy	___ Bold	___ Behaved	___ Balanced

Personality Profile Continued

21. ___ Brassy	___ Bossy	___ Bashful	___ Blank
22. ___ Undisciplined	___ Unsympathetic	___ Unenthusiastic	___ Unforgiving
23. ___ Reluctant	___ Resentful	___ Resistant	___ Repetitious
24. ___ Fussy	___ Fearful	___ Forgetful	___ Too frank
25. ___ Impatient	___ Insecure	___ Indecisive	___ Interruptive
26. ___ Unpopular	___ Uninvolved	___ Unpredictable	___ Unaffectionate
27. ___ Headstrong	___ Haphazard	___ Hard to please	___ Hesitant
28. ___ Plain	___ Pessimistic	___ Proud	___ Permissive
29. ___ Angers easily	___ Aimless	___ Argumentative	___ Alienated
30. ___ Naive	___ Negative attitude	___ Nervy	___ Nonchalant
31. ___ Worrier	___ Withdrawn	___ Workaholic	___ Wants credit
32. ___ Too Sensitive	___ Tactless	___ Timid	___ Talkative
33. ___ Doubtful	___ Disorganised	___ Domineering	___ Depressed
34. ___ Inconsistent	___ Introvert	___ Intolerant	___ Indifferent
35. ___ Messy	___ Moody	___ Mumbles	___ Manipulative
36. ___ Slow	___ Stubborn	___ Show-off	___ Sceptical
37. ___ Loner	___ Lord over others	___ Lazy	___ Loud
38. ___ Sluggish	___ Suspicious	___ Short-tempered	___ Scatterbrain
39. ___ Revengeful	___ Restless	___ Reluctant	___ Rash
40. ___ Compromising	___ Critical	___ Crafty	___ Changeable

Personality Profile — Scoring Sheet

Name:

Transfer your X's to the score sheet and add your table

	⚬	▲	◼
1. ___ Animated	___ Adventurous	___ Analytical	___ Adaptable
2. ___ Playful	___ Persuasive	___ Persistent	___ Peaceful
3. ___ Sociable	___ Strong-willed	___ Self-sacrificing	___ Submissive
4. ___ Convincing	___ Competitive	___ Considerate	___ Controlled
5. ___ Refreshing	___ Resourceful	___ Respectful	___ Reserved
6. ___ Spirited	___ Self-reliant	___ Sensitive	___ Satisfied
7. ___ Promoter	___ Positive	___ Planner	___ Patient
8. ___ Spontaneous	___ Sure	___ Scheduled	___ Shy
9. ___ Optimistic	___ Outspoken	___ Orderly	___ Obliging
10. ___ Funny	___ Forceful	___ Faithful	___ Friendly
11. ___ Delightful	___ Daring	___ Detailed	___ Diplomatic
12. ___ Cheerful	___ Confident	___ Cultured	___ Consistent
13. ___ Inspiring	___ Independent	___ Idealistic	___ Inoffensive
14. ___ Demonstrative	___ Decisive	___ Deep	___ Dry humour
15. ___ Mixes easily	___ Mover	___ Musical	___ Mediator
16. ___ Talker	___ Tenacious	___ Thoughtful	___ Tolerant
17. ___ Lively	___ Leader	___ Loyal	___ Listener
18. ___ Cute	___ Chief	___ Chartmaker	___ Contented
19. ___ Popular	___ Productive	___ Perfectionist	___ Permissive
20. ___ Bouncy	___ Bold	___ Behaved	___ Balanced
21. ___ Brassy	___ Bossy	___ Bashful	___ Blank
22. ___ Undisciplined	___ Unsympathetic	___ Unforgiving	___ Unenthusiastic
23. ___ Repetitious	___ Resistant	___ Resentful	___ Reluctant
24. ___ Forgetful	___ Too frank	___ Fussy	___ Fearful
25. ___ Interruptive	___ Impatient	___ Insecure	___ Indecisive
26. ___ Unpredictable	___ Unaffectionate	___ Unpopular	___ Uninvolved
27. ___ Haphazard	___ Headstrong	___ Hard to please	___ Hesitant
28. ___ Permissive	___ Proud	___ Pessimistic	___ Plain
29. ___ Angers easily	___ Argumentative	___ Alienated	___ Aimless
30. ___ Naive	___ Nervy	___ Negative attitude	___ Nonchalant
31. ___ Wants credit	___ Workaholic	___ Withdrawn	___ Worrier
32. ___ Talkative	___ Tactless	___ Too sensitive	___ Timid
33. ___ Disorganised	___ Domineering	___ Depressed	___ Doubtful
34. ___ Inconsistent	___ Intolerant	___ Introvert	___ Indifferent
35. ___ Messy	___ Manipulative	___ Moody	___ Mumbles
36. ___ Show-off	___ Stubborn	___ Sceptical	___ Slow
37. ___ Loud	___ Lord over others	___ Loner	___ Lazy
38. ___ Scatterbrained	___ Short-tempered	___ Suspicious	___ Sluggish
39. ___ Restless	___ Rash	___ Revengeful	___ Reluctant
40. ___ Changeable	___ Crafty	___ Critical	___ Compromising
TOTAL ____	TOTAL ____	TOTAL ____	TOTAL ____

You may have a balanced score, but most people have a dominant shape. Take a look at the profiles on the following pages to see what your shape means.

The Squiggle Profile
A Squiggle is creative, enthusiastic and likes to impress

Strengths
Excellent sense of humour

Can be the life of the party

Tactile

Emotional

Enthusiastic and expressive

Curious

Lives in the present

Quick to change disposition

Always innocent and
sincere at heart

Great ideas

Cannot tell a lie

Weaknesses
Can't remember names

Scares others off with
over enthusiasm

Undisciplined, forgets obligations

Doesn't follow through

Has a loud voice and a loud laugh

Easily distracted and
quick to interrupt

Wastes time and
confuses priorities

Loses confidence easily

Naive

Keeps the office
environment in a frenzy

Hates deadlines

Often late

Priorities
Likes to deal with people

Likes to build relationships

Likes to be liked

Likes to have opportunities

How to Sell Your
Business and Yourself
Be Inspirational

Promote who you have or
are currently working for

Use letters of recommendation
from prominent people

Identify and utilise
mutual contacts

How to Close
Show endorsements by others

Focus on people and opinions

Offer incentive or
opportunity to buy now

Explain how an investment
will improve the client's image

Use compliments

Ask opinions

A Squiggle Client
Will apologise readily

Is not one to hold grudges

Thrives on compliments

Loves spontaneous activities
with lots of people

Is open to big ideas

Is anxious to make the
company feel at home

Is quick to think up new
activities and projects

Is creative and colourful

Has lots of energy
and enthusiasm

Dances to a different beat

Is a risk taker

Lives in the future

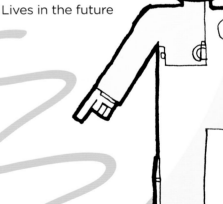

The Circle Profile
A Circle is open, honest and sincere

Strengths
Easy going and relaxed

Warm, likable

Emotionally adjusts

Persistent, well-balanced, patient

Consistent

Quiet but witty

Keeps emotions hidden

The all-purpose person

Is not in a hurry

Can take the good with the bad

Doesn't get upset easily

Weaknesses
Unenthusiastic, indecisive

Avoids responsibility

Selfish, self-righteous

Too compromising but resents being pushed

Sometimes lazy

Dampens enthusiasm

Lacks discipline

Sarcastic and teasing

Priorities
Likes peace and harmony

Likes to be co-operative

Likes to save time

Likes time to adjust to change

How to Sell Your Business and Yourself
Be Supportive

Promote superiority

Present yourself as trouble free

Present image of being trustworthy

Present image of being friendly

Show personal interest in helping the buyer

Ensure that transactions are smooth and steady

How to close
Provide guarantees and assurances to minimise risk

Show product as stable and predictable

Provide support and the personal touch

Utilise the buyer's trust to assert the best time to buy

A Circle client
Is competent and steady

Is peaceful and agreeable

Has administrative abilities

Avoids conflicts

Solves problems

Is strong under pressure

Finds the easiest way

Is a good listener

Has many friends and contacts

Has compassion and concern

Values relationships

The Triangle Profile
A Triangle likes power, and will always endeavor to be in control

Strengths
Dynamic and active

Decision makers

Must correct mistakes

Not easily discouraged

Exudes confidence

Inspiring

Can manage anything

Strong desire for change

Born leader

Usually right

Makes decisions fast

Weaknesses
Little tolerance for mistakes

Can be aggressive and abrasive

Doesn't analyse details

Bored by trivia

Makes rash decisions

Rude or tactless

Demanding

The ends justify the means

Priorities
Likes a challenge

Likes direct answers

Likes to solve problems

Likes getting results

How to Sell Your Business and Yourself
Be Guiding

Describe what you will do to get results

Promote your qualifications and past record

How to close
Be direct, concise and candid

Sell results and facts

Give the buyer options

Provide the buyer with options and then let them be in control

Provide incentives to act now

A Triangle Client
Wants the whole picture

Wants organisation

Wants practical solutions

Wants quick action

Delegates

Insists on production goals

Thrives on opposition

Has little need for friends

Focuses on the task

Excels in emergencies

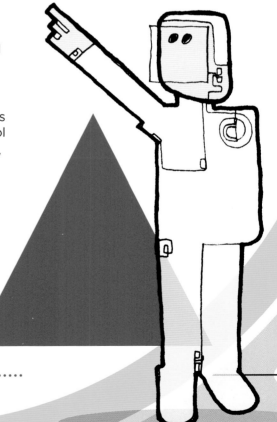

The Box Profile
A Box likes details and systems

Strengths

Deep and thoughtful

Analytical, accurate and precise

Serious and purposeful

Artistic

Appreciative of beauty

Loyal

Self-sacrificing

Idealistic

Weaknesses

Not people orientated

Chooses difficult work

Hesitant to start projects/
double checks everything

Hard to please

Deep need for approval

Sensitive to criticism

Critical of others

Holds back affection

Dislikes those in opposition

Suspicious, unforgiving

Sceptical of compliments

Martyr-prone

Priorities

Likes to be thorough
and accurate

Likes to work in a system

Wants activities to be right

Wants results to be fair

How to Sell Your Business and Yourself

Be Ordered

Show benefits in accurate
factual detail

Be systematic in showing benefits

Show that you can analyse
and solve problems

Demonstrate that you are
well prepared and organised

How to close

Present strong written
evidence and data

Show how product or
service is right for the buyer

Show facts about how
fair the price is

Use facts to persuade the
buyer that the time is right

Involve the buyer in
the purchasing system

A Box Client

Is schedule orientated

Is a detail focused perfectionist

Orderly and organised

Hunts for economical solutions

Likes graphs, charts
figures and lists

Collects data

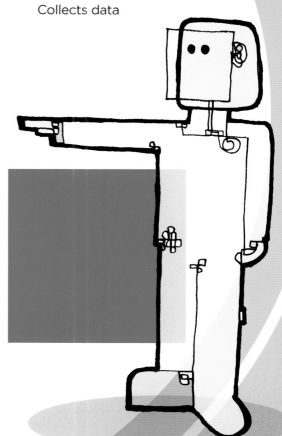

Situational Analysis

Situational Analysis is a process which helps to determine and explain strategic objectives. The aim is to develop an accurate picture of where the company, product or service stands in relation to its environment by collecting and sorting information about the company, its competition and the industry sector that they inhabit.

A detailed situational analysis can be invaluable, but not every strategy requires you to investigate every aspect of the environment in minute detail. The following set of tables and examples should act as a prompt for your own analysis, but the depth in which you explore each aspect is completely dependent on your situation. **Your situation analysis could cover the following:**

- RACI
- Product and Marketing boundaries
- Strategic Thrust
- Customer Segmentation
- External Trends
- TOWS Analysis
- Consider all Stakeholders
- Customer touch points
- Operational Principles and Constraints
- Growth and Return
- Risk

RACI

When considering the composition of your team and those around you it is worth working through **RACI** so that you can identify who occupies the following important roles:

- Who is **Responsible:** The person(s) who is assigned to do the work
- Who is **Accountable:** The person(s) who makes the final decision and has ultimate ownership
- Who is **Consulted:** The person(s) who must be consulted before a decision or action is taken
- Who is **Informed:** The person(s) who must be informed that a decision or action has been taken

Determining who these individuals are, is a crucial step in ensuring that a project proceeds quickly and smoothly as it prevents confusion and buck passing by clarifying the inter-relations element — possibly the weakest link of a process — of a project.

Product and Market Boundaries

As much as we hate boundaries, when it comes to **Absorption** it is worth exercising a modicum of restraint, if only to keep yourself from disappearing down a never-ending rabbit hole of research.

So how do you decide on which markets and which product or service requires the most focus?

You can start by creating a list of the most important characteristics that a successful product/service or market should have. You will find, however, that some are more important than others so to prioritise them, you can attach weightings dependant on the importance of each. Have a look at this example:

Product/Service Characteristics

Characteristic	Weighting
They make financial sense	40%
They are in demand	20%
They will enhance our future reputation	20%
They are hard to copy	10%
They fit with brand	10%

Market Characteristics

Characteristic	Weighting
Growth Markets	50%
The size of the market	20%
Understands what we offer	15%
Creditworthy	15%

Strategic Thrust

At this point you will want to concentrate on priorities and direction. To do this you can make a matrix that takes a business's or product's current position and expands it into the future. In the following example you can see where the current position is, the extension of that position, and a set of entirely new positions.

This example shows the strategic thrust for a business over three years, but it is for you to decide how far you will go based on where the business/product is now and where you want it to be:

Example

Year 1 Priorities
Secure current product and market and begin research into modified products and extended markets.

Year 2 Priorities
Secure current product and market and implement strategy for modified products and extended markets and begin research into new products and new markets.

Year 3 Priorities
Secure current and extended products and markets and implement strategic plans for new products and markets. By identifying the strategic thrust of a business or product you can ensure that any activities from this point onwards serve these future goals.

Direction & Priorities over the next three years		Markets		
		Current	**Extended**	**New**
Products	**Current**	One product in one region of the UK	New UK territories	New Global territories
	Modified	Product Extension New related products	New related products in new UK territories	
	New	New unrelated products		Totally new product in entirely new territory

Customer Segmentation

When dealing with customers, it is important to observe appropriate behaviours depending on the type of customer and the relationship that they have with the business. For example, a customer that a company has had for many years needs to be treated differently to a brand new one. To make this process easier, customer bases should be split into manageable segments by identifying groups of customers that share common buying patterns – how recent, how frequent and how much they spend – or demographics – gender, age, geography, interests or marital status – who should, therefore, react in a similar manner to different marketing activities. An increasingly important opportunity is to segment your customer type by their attitude to a product or service rather than some of the above demographic segmentations. To achieve this you may want to ask why they would buy, what was their need state, or when did they buy?

Here are some of the generic segmentations that you can use:

Customer Value Data
- Current annual value
- Retention rate
- Average purchase value
- Cross selling / up-trading success
- Projected future value
- Average annual returns
- Customer value by segment

Activity & Experience Data
- Purchase frequency
- Average purchase value
- Returns rate by customer
- Queries and complaints

Once the customer database has been segmented, a decision can then be made on the correct behaviours for each of them. The following is a common example:

	Customer Characteristics	Behaviour
Loyal	Open to new thinking Prone to apathy Advocacy	Be proactive Innovate Invest in product excellence
New	Opportunistic Bargain Hunters	Offer core products Offer outsourcing Educate them to the full range of products/services
Dormant	Disloyal Disillusioned	Try to win back Ascertain reason for dormancy

External Trends

External trends are changes that are occurring within an industry that will impact both on what a company can do and how it will do it. These changes can be anything from politics, to economics, or even the weather — it goes without saying that weather conditions and seasonality are critical to our ice-cream manufacturing client.

It is impossible to ignore these trends as they will impact on a business whether you take notice of them or not. Keeping abreast of them can be done by paying close attention to society and the media.

Market information companies like Mintel – Mintel.com — The Future Foundation — Futurefoundation.net — and Keynote – keynote.co.uk. exist to help businesses stay on the wave of the zeitgeist.

Once important trends have been identified, they can be put into a table and assigned scores based on the impact that they can have on a product or business (I), and the urgency with which they need to be monitored (U). This enables them to be prioritised effectively. For example:

Trends	Impact	I	U
Constantly changing zeitgeist	Need to be more proactive or will lose opportunities	9	9
Commoditisation	Differentiation Manage costs Innovation required	9	9
New focus on growth	Growth strategy needed	8	6
New technology	Buying new tech experience can open doors	7	7
Environmentalism	Accreditation needed Losing opportunities	7	7

Make your own notes:

TOWS Analysis (or SWOT)

The most important outcome of the **Absorption** process should be the holistic view and a TOWS — Threats, Opportunity, Weaknesses, Strengths — analysis will urge you to think around the subject in a 360° way. You may know this as SWOT analysis, but we've re-arranged things to end on positive strengths.

Threats	Weaknesses
For Example Think small and are afraid of failure	**For Example** Low priority given to internal needs

Opportunities	Strengths
For Example Exploit emerging technologies	**For Example** Financially sound, good margins and clear targets

Fill this table with your TOWS analysis:

Threats	Weaknesses

Opportunities	Strengths

Stakeholders

It is important to take a step back from your strategy and planning at this point and consider all of the stakeholders. Stakeholders are those people and teams directly impacted by the choices made in a marketing strategy and who need to be either directly involved or considered in the key strategic choices.

Example

Imagine you have been approached to create a new packaging solution for yoghurt. One of the first things you could do is engage with everybody who is involved with the product from the manufacturing process to the consumer. This way you may just stumble across a key issue.

For example when talking to retail staff who stack the yoghurts on to the shelves, you may discover that a large percentage of the current yoghurt pots break while being stacked.

This information can be incorporated into your creative brief and the resulting design ensured that breakages were kept to a minimum. Good marketing is about more than getting a message across and working within budget. In this example by involving stakeholders in the process we have highlighted an important issue that might otherwise have been overlooked.

The table below provides examples of possible stakeholders and the benefits that will be gained by involving them:

Who	Why
Colleagues	Implementation Source of advantage Eyes & Ears
Shareholders	Reason for existence Potential source of funds Senior management involvement
Ultimate Audience	Ultimate purchasers Loyalty to product/brand
Suppliers (inc. Bank)	Service levels Strategic partners Strategic alignment Competitiveness
Communities	Source of employees Partnership Education of workforce

nobody's perfect
— but a team comes close

Customer touch points

This process involves an analysis of all the opportunities to communicate with a customer. This may seem simple but it can be very complex. We have met so many companies who don't fully understand all the communications that they send to their customers. You can understand how some large companies have different departments, even within the marketing department, so it's easy to see how the acquisition team and the retention team, the product guys, the call centre and accounts don't join things up.

You'll notice we included the accounts department in that list. That's because you need to look at **all the communications** not just the obvious ones. Sending an invoice or a remittance advice is a really valuable communication and yet most companies just see it as administration. There is a simple exercise to ensure that:

- You get different stakeholders to map out all the touch points from the beginning of the customer journey right up to the point they stop trading with you. Map it out on a chart like the example opposite.

- After you've set up the chart, put a file together of the examples of the communications for future reference.

- Step back to see if there are any gaps, are there any communications missing? Think about the customer. Are you missing any opportunities?

- Finally go through each touch point and grade it as **RED, AMBER** or **GREEN** to indicate the urgency with which they need to be addressed.

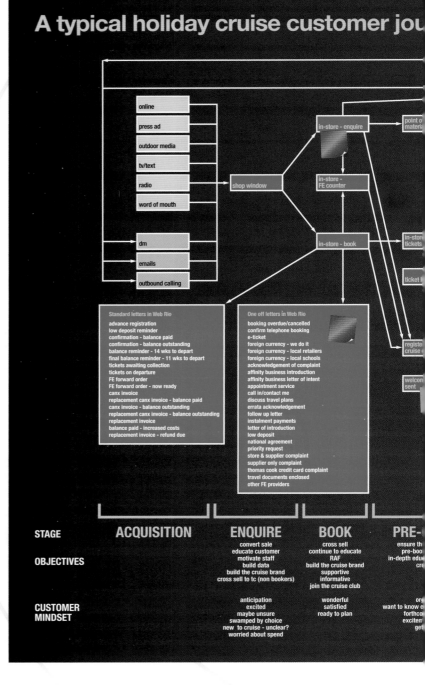

A typical holiday cruise customer jou

| online |
| press ad |
| outdoor media |
| tv/text |
| radio |
| word of mouth |

| dm |
| emails |
| outbound calling |

shop window · in-store - enquire · point o material · in-store - FE counter · in-store - book · in-store tickets · ticket i · register cruise · welcome sent

Standard letters in Web Rio
advance registration
low deposit reminder
confirmation - balance paid
confirmation - balance outstanding
balance reminder - 14 wks to depart
final balance reminder - 11 wks to depart
tickets awaiting collection
tickets on departure
FE forward order
FE forward order - now ready
canx invoice
replacement canx invoice - balance paid
canx invoice - balance outstanding
replacement canx invoice - balance outstanding
replacement invoice
balance paid - increased costs
replacement invoice - refund due

One off letters in Web Rio
booking overdue/cancelled
confirm telephone booking
e-ticket
foreign currency - we do it
foreign currency - local retailers
foreign currency - local schools
acknowledgement of complaint
affinity business introduction
affinity business letter of intent
appointment service
call in/contact me
discuss travel plans
errata acknowledgement
follow up letter
instalment payments
letter of introduction
low deposit
national agreement
priority request
store & supplier complaint
supplier only complaint
thomas cook credit card complaint
travel documents enclosed
other FE providers

STAGE	ACQUISITION	ENQUIRE	BOOK	PRE-
OBJECTIVES	convert sale educate customer motivate staff build data build the cruise brand cross sell to tc (non bookers)	cross sell continue to educate RAF build the cruise brand supportive informative join the cruise club	ensure th pre-boo in-depth edu cre	
CUSTOMER MINDSET	anticipation excited maybe unsure swamped by choice new to cruise - unclear? worried about spend	wonderful satisfied ready to plan	or want to know e forthco excitem get	

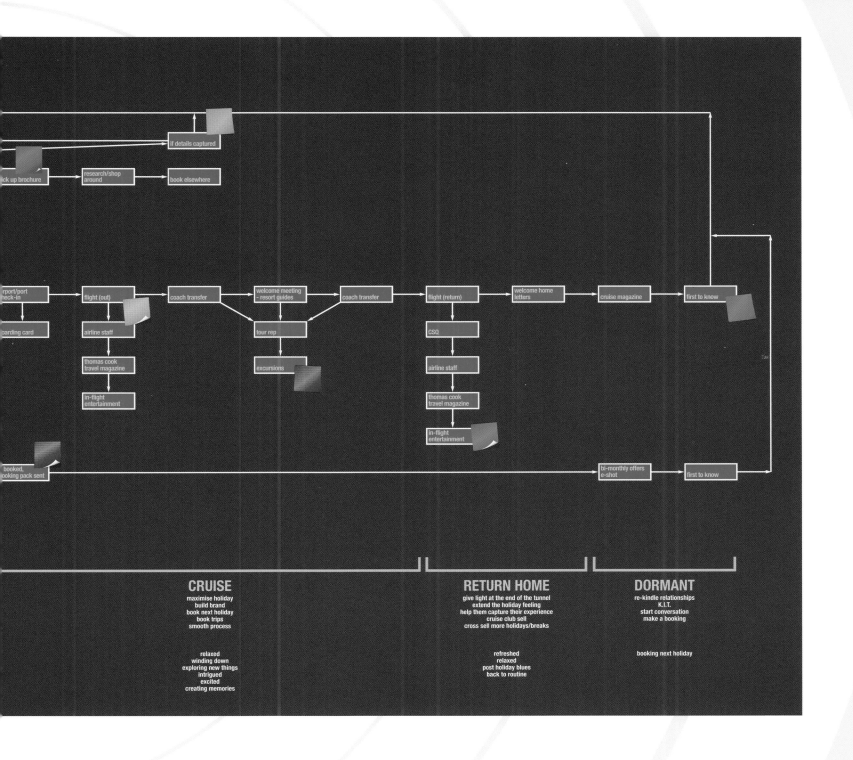

Operating Principles and Constraints

At this point of your situational analysis you need to generate a set of statements that will act as principles/beliefs, which will in turn guide day-to-day actions and decision-making. Having developed the principles, it is important to devise a means of monitoring their implementation. To create your own table, ask yourself what values are important to the business in question and think about how you can show that these values are being followed.

Operating Principle	Evidence
We will be innovative in product/service and process development to meet defined client needs	Investment in product/service development and market knowledge
We will balance the aspirations of all stakeholders through achievement of growth and return expectations	Understand/offer emerging technologies Achieving strategic targets (sustainable growth)
We will always have a clear direction and a formal planning process	Developed and measured strategy, business plan and annual budgets
We will provide personal development for staff in line with business needs	Capability audit and commitment to individual development — training, appraisals, PDPs
We will communicate in an honest manner with all of our stakeholders	Weekly team briefs, developing intranet, internal briefings/debriefings, client presentations.

Fill this table with your own operating principles:

Operating Principle	Evidence

Growth and Return

Remember that all marketing activity is an investment and not a spend, so you should anticipate what sort of return can be expected from a company's investment. What a company measures, and measuring what marketing activity has achieved, are two different exercises. This exercise looks purely at the company, and requires you to decide on what you want to measure. Try to complete the following:

	Last Year	Y1	Y2	Y3
Turnover				
Profit				
R.O.C.E (Return on Captial Employment)				
Share Value				
Cash Generated				
VAPE (Value added per employee)				

Marketing activity can be measured in a different way, and it is really important to decide prior to the marketing activity starting what you are going to measure. We have a phrase that we use, "you treasure what you measure" which means that if you don't measure the effectiveness of something, you will not value it. Don't measure something that is not of value to you as you may be wasting time and resources. Here are some examples of what we measure:

Activity/ Cost	Target Group	Volume	Response	Response %	Orders	AOV*	Total I*	ROI*
Direct Mail 40,000	New	100,000	10,000	10%	7000	10	70,000	30,000

*AOV = Average Order Value
*Total I = Total Income
*ROI = Return On Investment — Total income minus cost of activity

you **treasure** what you **measure**

Risk

Unless your strategy is implemented in a vacuum, there will be various obstacles that will have to be overcome for it to be successful and the best way to approach these obstacles is to pre-empt them during the strategy process.

The following table can be completed to determine the key strategic risks that could present themselves, and the actions that should be taken to minimise the potential threat. For each risk that you can identify, you will need to estimate and apply the Probability of it arising — you can do this as a % — and the Impact — out of 10 — that it would have if it did.

Strategic Risk	%	I	Actions to Protect
Product not available	20%	9	Clarify delivery dates from manufacturer

Thinking about risk can be difficult because you may not know what you don't know! To ascertain the possible risks inherent in a strategy, you can refer to the threats determined by the T.O.W.S. analysis, refer to stakeholders and, finally, ask yourself, 'what is the worst that could happen?'

Make your own notes:

Competitive Advantage

It is impossible for a business to work in a bubble and if it wants to create that vital advantage then it is important to be constantly aware of the industrial and market environment, of which, competition is a huge part. Competition should make a company sharper and better as long as sufficient respect and attention are paid to it; it will also supply the drive to provide customers with what they want.

After compiling a list of the most important competitors there are four questions that you will need to apply to them:

- What are their objectives?
- What are their strategies?
- What are their strengths and weaknesses?
- What is their potential response to your initiatives?

You will then need to delve deeper in to the competition by determining the aspects of each that you want to focus on, and the following are a good start:

- Market total (unit sales, buyers, value) by region and customer type
- Market share (units, buyers and value)
- Competitive shares (units, buyers and value)
- Position in the market (brand leader)
- Share of customer (how much % share do they have)
- Competitor's financial reports
- How do customers rate your company against the competition?

And Breathe...

You have now completed your situational analysis and can reward yourself with a sit down and a cup of tea. With all of this information, you should have a strong, long-lasting, clear foundation on which to develop your marketing strategy and your Marketing Plan.

Marketing Objectives and the Marketing Plan

In the development of marketing objectives, you should make sure that the marketing strategy can be integrated with the company's strategy; ignoring the bigger business picture will lead to lack of resources and engagement.

What resources will you need?

The planning process should clarify the resources required including inventory, personnel, external resources, time and money. The plan should also take into consideration human resource, suppliers, goods, quality of service, funding, anything that is finite within a company. You can refer back to the information that you gathered on Stakeholders to help with this.

TEAM

Marketing objectives will nearly always include volume/financial targets and competitive targets — for example, targeted market share — and they will also, of course, show objectives related to customers like acquisition and retention rates. We use the model **TEAM** to explore objective criteria:

Time Frame
Is the time that has been applied realistic? Is it tight enough.

Explicit
There is no point in being vague in your goals; they have to mean something. There is freedom in a very tight brief as people are clear what their boundaries are.

Achievable
Don't overstretch as this can lead to stakeholder disillusionment. Just as success breeds success, failure breeds failure. Look back to boundaries.

Measurable
Make sure that the vital aspects are measurable, and only the vital ones. Some people measure everything when there is no need, as this will only waste time and resources. Think about your measurements as the dashboard of an airplane cockpit; there may be a lot of dials and flashing lights to look at but there are only a few which need to be constantly checked. Don't, by any means, completely disregard the rest, but don't waste time.

Communication Strategy

A Communication Strategy will define exactly what a campaign will say, to whom, and when, and should be accompanied by a set of defined resources and forecasted results to ensure that it is implemented effectively. The following are the key elements that should be included in a good communication strategy:

- Tactical Communication Objectives
- Audience Selection, Profiling and Segmentation
- Media Selection
- Customer Journey
- Offers
- Creative Positioning and Message
- Fulfilment and Response Management
- Budgeting and Forecasting
- The Contact Plan and Communication
- Action Schedule

Tactical Communication Objectives

This is the stage where you need to show how you intend to meet the corporate and strategic marketing objectives. Ask yourself *"what am I going to achieve with this communications plan?"*

They also allow you to forecast, monitor and evaluate which activity will be most profitable and which segments should be pursued for future activity. Don't start anything without having a firm objective.

Audience Selection, Profiling and Segmentation

This enables you to create a communication plan that is relevant. Assess existing customers first and then use profiling techniques to find prospects with similar profit potential.

Offers

Choosing the right offer is often vital for a successful campaign, and while the specifics will have to vary depending on the project, the goal is always to maximise the perceived value of the offer. For more detail on how to develop the right offer for a campaign, head to the **Offer** section of our **Direct Mail** chapter.

Creative positioning and message

Your overall creative positioning is usually determined by the planning process, so that your uniqueness is clearly defined and the message that you give is relevant to your target audience. This can then be checked with good research.

Fulfilment and response management

This part of a campaign is often neglected but is vital to maximise profits and maintain a good customer relationship. Consideration needs to be given to:

- Order handling
- Payment processing
- Data capture
- Enquiry handling
- Sales conversions
- Complaint handling

Budgeting and forecasting

This is a continuous, cyclical process which will require several attempts before a finalised set of figures can be determined. You will often start with ROI targets and the decision of how you wish to divide the budget between retention and acquisition before forecasting likely responses to campaign activities. If there is a shortfall in customer numbers for the desired ROI, then there will have to be more investment and efforts made in acquisition activities. Plan acquisition efforts in descending order of cost-effectiveness, starting with recommend a friend, and moving towards the individual medium level.

The Contact Plan and Communication Action Schedule

The actual thought processes should have been completed by this stage and all that is left to do is collate everything in an accessible place — a **Contact Plan** — ensuring that it is defined in sufficient detail so that it can be used as a resource going forward.

You can then produce an easy to use chart that shows each action that you need to take, and when you need to take it. This **Communication Action Schedule** chart should be broader in detail than the Contact Plan, covering:

- Target categories — segments
- Media outlines
- Timings
- Briefing dates

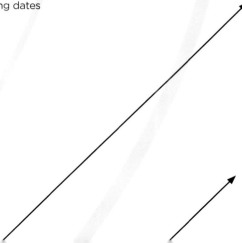

Media Brief

Date:	Owner of brief and contact details:

Client:	Campaign/Product:

Stakeholders—List of people who will be involved in this project.

Client:	Agency:

Campaign/Activity Dates:	ATL Media Budget (excluding production):

1. Background—why are you writing this brief?

2. Campaign objectives/Media objectives:

3. Target audience:

4. Media Hints (any obvious issues that may exclude or require certain media):

5. Evaluation criteria:

6. Additional Considerations—creative message, regionality:

7. Customer take out—what do you want them to think or do?

8. Watch Outs—things to be aware of that may affect media:

9. Timelines:

Media Selection

To best reach the target audience, you will have to decide on the right combination of media. This is one of the most complex areas within a communication strategy as there are a huge number of choices available to the marketer, each with its own relevancies, strengths and weaknesses.

We believe that the most effective way to create waves through marketing is with a cross fertilisation of the different cultures and embedded disciplines which lie deeply within the various media disciplines. It is too easy to look at the different disciplines in isolation, but creating the best waves will require a harmonious combination of media which bolster the effects of one another resulting in a media amalgamation which really brings the campaign to life.

Interactivity and digital sophistication continues to grow as consumers enjoy a richer online experience and there are many surveys in the trade press which explore the public's attitudes to all of the various media choices. Finding the appropriate media is vital to a marketing strategy and we have found that various combinations of direct marketing — direct mail, catalogues, etc. — and online media – websites, email, etc. — can produce surprising results and while there are significant benefits to optimising across digital channels, the big win comes through making online and offline channels work together. Even those consumers confident on the web welcome direct marketing, as demonstrated by the following research from Royal Mail into the preferred media of web users:

Extremely Confident Web Users

11% would prefer to be contacted by Direct Marketing only

55% would prefer to be contacted by a combination of direct marketing and online

Confident Web Users

13% would prefer to be contacted by Direct Marketing only

60% would prefer to be contacted by a combination of direct marketing and online

Less Confident Web Users

19% would prefer to be contacted by Direct Marketing only

64% would prefer to be contacted by a combination of direct marketing and online

It is clear from our experience that people still see a place for a combination of online and offline communications. Have a look at the results of this survey where consumers had to say how much they agreed with the following statement:

"Mail is good at supporting or clarifying the online information I encounter."

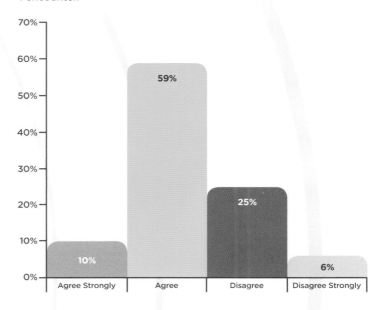

It becomes apparent that the combination of media approach provides two important qualities, clarity and encouragement. The former is important, as it is a difficult task to construct a single piece of marketing that is 100% understandable to 100% of customers and this can often be because certain people are more comfortable and receptive to certain media; an issue easily solved by providing multiple media. As for the latter, the combination of online and offline encourage action by adding to the consumer's awareness of the campaign message and acting as a prompt to purchase, without adding to the fatigue that comes with repetition; variety is the spice of marketing. So, if the consumer reacts positively to a combination of online and offline media because of clarity and encouragement, then selecting media which naturally provide optimum levels of those two qualities for a campaign will likely lead to the best responses. It's just common sense really!

Most of the remaining chapters in this book examine each of the major media used in direct response marketing including digital marketing, and from that you should be able to determine the right media mix for **Making Waves.**

The Customer Journey

Once you have decided on a campaign's media, you need to consider when and where each media should be used along the customer journey through Acquisition, Development and Retention. Here's an example:

Acquisition

Generating prospects Enquirer conversion process Previous enquirer	Cold Acquisition — when approaching customers for the first time email is considered inappropriate Spam is a growing problem 60% have started ignoring email Consumers consider mail and DRTV more appropriate Email does have an important role to play in the acquisition process — particularly around follow-up activity e.g converting enquirers

Development

Welcome phase Second purchase Getting to know you Up/X-sell models	Online is perfect for confirmations e.g., that an order has been received or is being processed Mail is also valuable to consumers at this stage in the journey for thanking and welcoming, encouraging future business Getting to know customers is key — including their channel preference Surveys can be conducted via mail and/or email

Retention

Staying in touch Managing problems	Mail is up to 8 times more likely than email to make customers feel valued, although it does cost more A segmented approach — not only based on channel preference but also profitability and potential — to customer communication is appropriate Arguably, both email and mail should be used to handle complaints Email provides an opportunity to confirm receipt/explain the complaints handling process without delay Mail is perhaps more appropriate for more important/sensitive messaging

Contingency Planning

As we mentioned in our **Making Waves** chapter, there are a number of things that can disrupt a strategy and create 'Bad Waves' and it is important to establish contingencies for these as part of the strategy process. To make sure that you are following a preparation, rather than reaction, approach all you need to do is work through each stage of the campaign and ask:

'What could go wrong?'

'What if responses are too low?'

'What if they are too high?'

'What if you run out of stock?'

By simply identifying the possible problems that you could face, you are already in a good state of preparedness even before you determine how you would tackle them. Be thorough, but don't get carried away, and start constructing doomsday scenarios that will never happen; as always, common sense should rule. A final point on contingencies is that people rarely consider what they will do if their marketing is too successful and the responses generated by the communications become unmanageable, so always remember to prepare for success as well as difficulties.

if you can't solve a **problem,** it's probably because you are playing by the **rules!**

Explosion

The **Explosion** phase is usually everyone's favourite. You get to stretch your mind, be creative and come up with the next big thing. But the big ideas can't begin to be formed until robust creative briefs have been developed to fulfill the Marketing Plan.

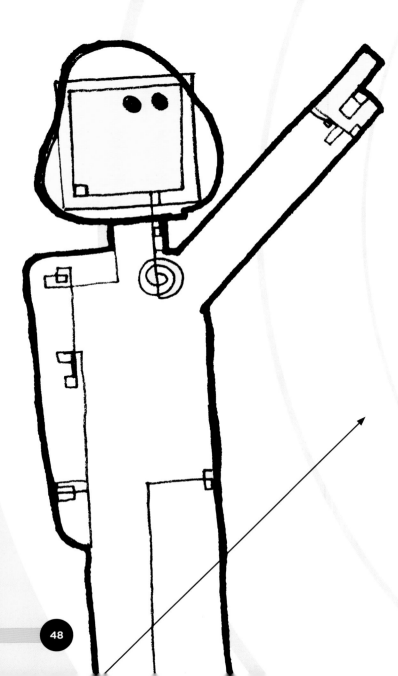

Brief Encounter

The importance of the quality of a brief cannot be overestimated – **'garbage in' will result in 'garbage out'.** The brief is the document against which all creative output will be measured further down the line. 'Does it meet the brief?' is the telling question, which should always be raised during any creative review or presentation.

The key to good briefing is the **KiSS** effect — Keep it Short and Simple. Clearly, it is imperative to include all the background information for the teams who will work on the brief but the detail should be confined to appendices. Crystallising the important facts with precise and unambiguous communication will ensure clarity of thinking and guide a creative team.

During the brief writing process, there are aspects which can become strained or difficult — notably the proposition.

It is vital that all of the great work that has been put into creating a strategy is correctly interpreted and results in a great creative marketing campaign that captures the imagination of the target audience. When difficulties are experienced in arriving at an agreed creative execution it is nearly always true that the problems stem from a failure to define and agree the brief.

You are no doubt familiar with **Michelangelo's frescoes** on the ceiling of the Sistine Chapel, one of the greatest works of art of all time. Imagine the briefs he might have been given for this work by his client Pope Julius II:

"Please paint the ceiling"

There is no doubt that this is what Michelangelo was being asked to do but this brief gives him no hint as to what the solution to the request might be. It leaves all of the decisions and thinking to the artist but provides him with few parameters in which to work. The outcome will, therefore, probably bear little resemblance to the Pope's wishes.

"Please paint the ceiling using red green and yellow paint"

This brief is even worse as it not only doesn't tell him what to paint, but it also gives him a number of restrictions without justification which will inevitably prove irksome and which will distract him from his main task.

"We have got terrible problems with damp and cracks in the ceiling and we would be ever so grateful if you could just cover it up for us"
This is the worst of them all as it still does not tell him what to do, and it gives him irrelevant and depressing information which implies that no one is interested in what he paints because it will not be long before the ceiling falls in anyway.

"Please paint the biblical scenes on the ceiling incorporating some or all of the following: God, Adam, Cupids, Devils and Saints"
This one is better, as they are beginning to give Michelangelo a steer as, although they have not given him the full picture yet, he can at least determine the important elements of the project. This is the sort of brief that most of us have been given; it contains everything the creatives need to know but it does not take the next vital step towards an idea. Towards a solution.

"Please paint our ceiling, for the greatest glory of God and as an inspiration and lesson to his people".
This is probably much closer to the brief which Michelangelo was actually given. Now that he knows what to do and is inspired by the importance of the project, he can devote his attention to executing the detail of the brief in the best way he knows.

To summarise, people cannot produce great ideas without the best possible knowledge and understanding of what they are trying to achieve.

The Creative Brief

Here are our headings that should be addressed for the perfect, comprehensive creative brief:

Background
Give a quick summary of the project history. Stick to short salient points — detailed information should be confined to appendices.

Objectives
These are the objectives for the campaign. What do we want to achieve? Some may be strategic, eg 'to create awareness' others may be quantifiable, eg 'to deliver a sales increase of 20% during the campaign period'. The following are unacceptable objectives that we see all the time:

'To sell more' — who doesn't?

'To produce a brochure' — this is a creative requirement NOT an objective.

Target audience
Name them in short, precise terms. Full profiles should be placed in appendices.

Proposition
The single thing that differentiates the product/service/company from the competition.

Supporting evidence
Those things which make the Proposition true.

Desired response
What do you want the audience to say? This is often expressed as the volte-face of the proposition. For example:

Proposition: Massive discounts available in August

Supporting evidence: Products will be discounted by at least 15% during August.

Desired response: "I must buy these products in August — I'll get a really good deal".

Creative strategy
This is the 'way in' to the creative solution and often comes out of audience research and the resultant planning. For example, 'launch the product using the strength and credibility of the organisation from which it comes'; 'use advocacy since the product has a good reputation with those who buy it'; 'use humour since research has shown that this audience will respond best if this type of category is presented in a humourous way'. Do NOT provide creative solutions — just direction on what will deliver the best response.

Creative requirements
List the campaign requirements — TV commercial, Press ad, Direct Mail, Website, etc.

Legal/creative constraints
In the case of broadcast media, be precise on duration of the spot. Where printed material is concerned, list the number of colours and maximum finished size. Refer here to corporate guidelines, the legal constraints of what it is possible to say, and the addition of terms and conditions.

Budget
Production budgets will constrain creative output so make sure they are known in advance. Don't try to hide the overall budget as there's no point wasting everyone's time by coming up with ideas which can't be done within the budget. Be precise.

Timing
Produce a timeline, including projected times for creative reviews, presentations and delivery.

Creating those big ideas.

It can often be difficult getting the creative process moving and we believe that the usual idea generation practice of brainstorming sessions really aren't fit for purpose.

We hate brainstorms... we hate the word, we hate the process, we hate the way they are run and we don't think they produce the best ideas. Brainstorms are banned.

A wide range of studies show that brainstorming is actually detrimental to ideation because of the occurrence of **Cognitive Blocking, Enforced Turn Taking, Piggy-Backing** and **Self-Censorship.** Cognitive blocking happens when you have an idea, but forget it as you listen to somebody else, while having to take turns steals concentration away from ideation as you have to pay attention to social clues so that you know when it's appropriate to take your turn. Piggy-backing is the practice of riding on the wave of other people's creativity and, finally, self-censorship occurs when people repress their ideas in the face of possible embarrassment in front of the group.

Despite being a very inefficient means of forming ideas, group brainstorming continues to take place, probably because it is more fun and easy creating ideas as a group than as individuals. Groups are also good for the ideation process as they provide a crucible in which the thoughts of individuals can be combined to create something greater than the sum of its parts. This turning of thought lead into idea gold is very valuable, but brainstorming's flaws heavily outweigh its benefits. To remedy this, **outside the box** decided that we needed idea creation exercises that had all of the fun and idea alchemy that is achieved with group ideation, without the drawbacks of the traditional brain storming session. The following are a series of these exercises that can be followed to expand your thinking and help to generate new and creative ideas.

brain storming does not work!

Exercise One — Morphological Matrix

Overview

This method is simple: break down a product or service into its component parts, consider these parts separately and then recombine them to find new solutions. It is a process of deconstruction and then reconstruction. On an idea per second basis, no other technique can beat the **Morphological Matrix.**

How to Apply it

The key to the Matrix is understanding the difference between attributes and items: An attribute is a component part of a problem, so if the question is coming up with ideas for a surprise party, an attribute might be the Theme, Location or Music so, for example, two items that may fit into the Location attribute are "In a boat" or "In the garden".

- Consider a goal or a problem; this is best described as either a How question or a Statement. For example "how can we charge more money for what we do?", or "To generate ideas to improve team working".

- Discuss the attributes for your objective.

- Select the best attributes — 3 or 4 are best for the first go — with the best meaning the most interesting or just those that make best sense given your objective.

- Discuss items within each attribute. Work through one attribute at a time. Write each of these items on Post-its and line them up under each attribute.

- Select the combinations that you particularly like.

Example

Our objective is to hold a surprise party. We selected some of the best ideas for attributes. In this instance we chose:

1. Theme   2. Location   3. Music

Once these attributes had been selected, we came up with a list of items under each attribute.

Theme	Location	Music
Wild West	Boat	Jazz band
London Underground	Rooftop terrace	Pianist
Film star	By a pool	Karaoke
1960's	At home	DJ
Black tie	In a shop window	Gospel choir

We then chose the best combinations randomly — or you can pick combinations that seem to fit. A good tip is to make sure that the items that you place under each attribute have a mixture of safe ideas and outrageous/unusual ideas. To achieve this, try to focus on the task in hand. For example, when you are thinking about locations, just think about all of the types of locations that there are in the world; don't think about a party, just locations. We chose this party theme:

a Wild West party in a shop window with a gospel choir!

Make your own notes:

Exercise Two — Random Words

Overview

This exercise aims to generate fresh, new ideas by linking random words with your innovation or objective. By taking a step away from rational thinking and the limits that you place on your thoughts, you are able to open your mind to a whole new level of creativity. This forces you to think differently.

How to Apply It

- Firstly, choose a topic that you need to create ideas for.

- Make a list of random words, chosen at random from books, newspapers, etc. then number them.

- Pick a number. Use the word that is next to that number on the list of random words — *by selecting a word in this way, it prevents you from sub-consciously picking a word that is relevant to your goal.*

- Take the word and write down some of the things that this word means to you. For example, if the word was "pretty" — what does "pretty" mean to you? — It may mean delicate or small or pink!

- Then use these words to help stimulate — by association — links between the random word and your topic and write them on the flip chart.

When all of the ideas are exhausted, pick another word and start again.

Example

We are going to create new ideas for Ice Cream.

1. We picked number 12.

2. The word number 12 is **War**

3. War means explosions, fire, blood, hurt, etc.

4. We thought of every way that we could link **War** to **Ice Cream**

Our ideas

- The packaging could be camouflaged

- The cone could be hand grenade shaped

- The texture could be an explosion of different tastes

- The sauce could look like blood

- It could have a sparkler sticking out of the top

- The flavour could explode as you bite into the ice cream

Make your own notes:

Exercise Three — Brain Writing

Overview

This method is simple, and in thirty minutes can produce loads of ideas. This technique really works well if there are people in your team who are being overpowered by other team members as it allows the quieter, more thoughtful people to get their ideas across.

How to Apply It

- Identify the topic for which you need to generate ideas.

- Everyone sits in a circle, and each writes down three ideas — *we generally find that if people are invited to a meeting to generate ideas they prefer to be told in advance what the topic is. Also we find that they will normally have some ideas that they come to the meeting with so it is worth getting those ideas from them first, otherwise they may get frustrated.*

- Participants then pass their ideas on to the next person in the circle.

- This person considers the original ideas, adds value to them and/or develops new ones, writing these beneath the ideas offered by the previous person.

- The process is repeated until every person has contributed to every other person's original thoughts.

- When you have gone all around the table, put all of the ideas in the centre of the table and discuss them as a team to see which you feel are the best ideas, and see if you can develop them even further.

Example

Let's suppose then that our objective is to come up with a new ice cream product. My ideas that are written on my paper could be:

1. **A taste of the seaside** — because I associate ice cream with the seaside

2. **A masculine ice cream** — something that appeals to men

3. **An ice cream that doesn't melt**

This is then passed to the person on my right who adds:

1. **"A taste of the seaside"**
   It could have shell shapes in the ice cream; the packaging could be designed to look like a deck chair; it could have a pinch of salt.

2. **"A masculine ice cream — something that appeals to men."**
   It could be football shaped; you could get top football teams to endorse it and you could sell them at football grounds.

3. **"An ice cream that doesn't melt."**
   The packaging could be like a thermos flask so that it keeps it cool; it could be an ice cream that has already melted — like yoghurt.

Then this is passed to the next person to add value and so on, until you go all around the table. The results are then discussed as a team.

Make your own notes:

Exercise Four — Brand Senses

Overview

Tapping into the world of neuroscience, we have developed a technique for teams to literally **come to their senses.** Olfactory and other sensory cues are hard wired into our brains' limbic system, the seat of emotion which, once triggered, stimulate vivid recollections. This technique encourages the use of all the senses of Sight, Smell, Touch, Sound and Taste and enables you to move your thinking into fresh areas. This expands current ideas about brands by asking questions like, "What does your brand **Smell** like?"

This will give you new insights, unique words and fresh ideas which you can use in your marketing.

How to Apply It

- Start with a work surface full of stimulating things which will arouse all of your senses
- Work through each of the senses
- Start with Sound and ask the team, "What does the brand Sound like?"
- Use the stimulus to help you
- Capture the sounds on a flip chart
- Don't forget to ask **Why** a specific sound has been chosen
- Repeat the exercise with all of the senses

Example

We took this technique to **Arup,** the largest engineering company in the world and, after splitting them into teams, asked each team, "What does your brand Sound like?"

We gave them a work surface full of things that make a noise, like iPods, bubblewrap, party blowers and at first the teams produced the usual answers:

A phone ringing

People talking

Keyboards

Radio

However, after a little coaching and exploration of the materials — for example, they tasted fizzy sweets and looked at sparklers — the team started to describe sounds that represented the brand rather than what an office sounds like. Words like:

Rhythm, Pulse, Electric, Crackle, Fizzes and Still

We then moved onto the other senses, of Sight, Taste, Smell and Feel. **Arup** can now be described as **"A company that Fizzes with intelligence!"**

Make your own notes:

Exercise Five —Jugaad

Overview

Jugaad is the Indian tradition of working around a problem with limited resources. The best example is, fittingly, from India itself where the most common usage of the word Jugaad is in reference to a form of transport normally comprised of a diesel engine fitted to a simple wooden cart. So, the Jugaad approach is not to innovate through addition, but rather through reduction; the goal is to move away from complexity and reduce something to its purest, most functional form.

Antoine De Saint-Exupery said it best when he stated that, "perfection is achieved, not when there is nothing more to add, but when there is nothing left to take away."

So what would you do if, instead of having to find the next big addition to a product/service, you had to take an aspect of it away? It would force you to rethink your proposition and you would find that it is often the elements of a product or service that have always been there that get in the way of fresh thinking.

How to Apply It

- Begin by discussing the vital component parts of a product/service — consider what is offered to the customer and how the product or service is delivered.

- Write the key elements down in a list.

- Choose the one that you think may be the most fundamental component part. It is important that you just choose one element and ensure that it is clear and not woolly.

- Now imagine that the element is removed; for example, if a business has a direct sales force, imagine that they do not have a direct sales force. How would you get their product/service to market then?

- Pose the deletion to the team as a question and consider creatively how to manage a new way around the deletion and still ensure commercial viability. Keep the unmet needs of customers and prospects in mind as you do so.

Example

If you were running a restaurant you may consider that the vital component parts to this business model were:

- Having a venue
- Food
- Having a good chef
- Having Waiters
- Tables
- Chairs
- Music
- Toilets
- Selling Wine

We chose the aspect that we thought was most critical to a restaurant: **Food**. We then had to ask ourselves, **"How can a restaurant that does not make food, make money?"** After a discussion about how to make this novel new model work commercially we came up with the following business suggestion: **"People can bring their own food to the restaurant and rent a table. They will pay for the services of a wine waiter and not having to do the dishes"**

Make your own notes:

Exercise Six — 20/20 Vision

Overview

The 20/20 vision approach moves participants into the future by looking at the past and then building a proposition for focus.

How to Apply It

- Start 20 years in the past and move forward one decade at a time

- Look at social, economical, technological, political and cultural trends

- Move thinking 20 years into the future to get some distance from today

- With the feel of the future defined, focus on a specific area of great change

- Discuss ideas for products/services

- Keep focus on the future and don't let people drift back into present

- Consider the customers of the future and what their unmet needs might be

- If possible try to relate ideas to current technology, markets, etc.

- Summarise the top few ideas to present back and prompt discussion

Could you create an advertisement for a product/service that will be coming to market in 20 years time?

Example

Coke Burn

In this example we have focussed on the future trend of obesity and created a product that moves from Zero calories to a product that actually burns 500 calories with every can consumed. The innovative packaging emphasises the proposition.

Make your own notes:

the best way to have a great idea is to have **lots of ideas**

Consolidation

The **Consolidation** phase involves taking the ideas that have been generated in the **Explosion** process and choosing the best. This can be as difficult as generating the idea itself since choosing the idea to move forward with, to invest in, involves an element of risk. How can you be sure that the idea you just dismissed wouldn't have made you a millionare?

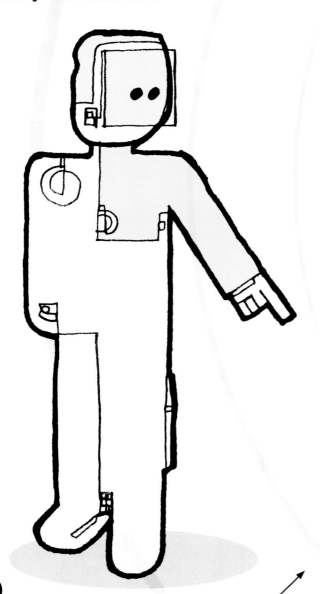

Unfortunately, it is not always the case that a single idea stands out from the rest, making it difficult to decide on the best one to take forward. To make these scenarios easier, we like to take our ideas and look at them in a different way by visualising and empiricising them so that the hierarchy of idea quality and practicality becomes clearer. The two systems that we use for this are **Matrices** and **Critical Success Factor Tables.** They may not have the sexiest names but will produce conclusive results, which, when combined with common sense and instinct, can add a vital element to the decision making process. Normally we use these methods to filter ideas before they go into a research phase.

Before you begin either of the processes there are a few preparations to make:

- Know the brief and keep it with you throughout Consolidation.

- Focus on the key elements of the brief such as:
  Target audience
  Objectives
  Proposition

- Train yourself to react as a consumer.

- Remove all preconceptions from your thinking — we know that this is hard to do but keeping an open mind will lead to better results.

- Ideas are like little siblings, they need nurturing, and they need attention and a little love. Avoid killing little ideas too soon!

Matrixes

Creating a **Matrix** is the quickest and simplest way to clarify where all of the ideas sit in relation to one another. Firstly, number all of your ideas, and then decide on two important features that make for a successful campaign — for instance, cost of production and originality. It is important to get the right axes so make sure that you think this through by referring back to the brief and thinking about the objectives. These can then be applied to an axis as in the diagram below.

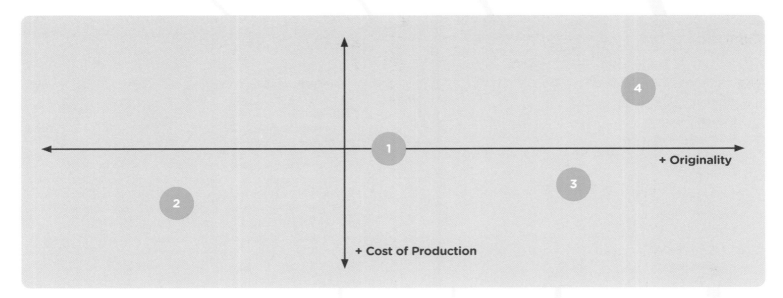

Each idea is then placed on the matrix depending on how it performs against the axes, with the best — in this case, Idea 3 — being the one that scores highly on originality while having a relatively low cost of production. This is best achieved by using stakeholders to debate and help you decide. The beauty of this method is that it forces you to concede to the fact that the best idea is that which strikes a balance of quality over a range of factors rather than just being exceptional in one. This is demonstrated by Idea 4 in our example, as it scores best on originality, but does not perform well enough on the cost axis. And that's it, simple but very effective!

what does **success** mean to you?

Critical Success Factors

The **Critical Success Factor Table** is more complex than a matrix, but will result in each idea receiving an incredibly useful numerical score. This is achieved by focusing on the fundamentals of a business and attaching a weighting to each based on its importance.

The first step requires you to decide on the critical factors that will make an idea successful. This is best performed with stakeholders, an array of individuals who understand different elements of the business and can therefore provide a holistic range of perspectives. For instance, if we were creating a new ice cream for an existing brand, the critical success factors could be:

- Unique
- Magical Element
- Cost of Manufacture
- Scalable
- Fun
- Easy to sell
- Easy to share
- Brand Fit
- Family/Sharing
- Interactive/Fun

This list addresses the consumer experience, the brand and the manufacturing process, but is a bit long for our needs – it is best to keep the list to between four and six factors – so our next process is to prune it down to a more suitable size. This can be achieved by simply discarding the least important factors from the list, or the factors can be combined if they cross over with one another. We chose to combine 'Family Appeal' with 'Easy to Share' as families are likely to appreciate an ice cream that can be shared. After condensing our list it looked like this:

- Family/Sharing
- Interactive/Fun
- Scale
- Brand Fit
- Unique/Magical
- Cost of Manufacture

After compiling a manageable set of factors, the next stage calls on the group to apply a weighting to each from a common pool of 100%. Once again, everybody in the group should be included in the decision, with the final weightings settled on through discussion, debate, voting and compromise. If an individual feels that any weighting should be changed then they can make their case and try to persuade others to support that change. Facts, research and experience should be cited until the weightings are as close to objective as possible; the more consensus that occurs, the better the results.

Blank Critical Success Form

In our example we decided that, for our ice creams, the 'Family/Sharing' aspect was paramount and so attributed it with a full 25% of the weighting. This was closely followed by 'Unique/Magical' and 'Scale' as the ice cream had to be original enough to stand out in the market and have a big enough scope to make as much money as possible. With our weightings decided we made the following table:

Critical Success Factor	Weighting	Idea A	Weighted Score	Idea B	Weighted Score	Idea C	Weighted Score	Idea D	Weighted Score	Idea E	Weighted Score	Idea F	Weighted Score
Family/Sharing	25												
Interactive/Fun	15												
Scale	20												
Brand Fit	15												
Unique/Magical	20												
Cost of Manufacture	5												
Totals	**100**												

To complete the table, the final stage involves scoring each idea on how it performs against each factor. This should, once again, be a discussion allowing for debate and deliberation until a score out of ten has been decided for every idea. Now that the hard part is over, the final score can be determined by multiplying an idea's scores with the corresponding weighting and then adding them together.

Critical Success Factor	Weighting	Idea A	Weighted Score	Idea B	Weighted Score	Idea C	Weighted Score	Idea D	Weighted Score	Idea E	Weighted Score	Idea F	Weighted Score
Family/Sharing	25	8	200	5	125	7	175	9	225	8	200	8	200
Interactive/Fun	15	5	75	8	120	9	135	7	105	7	105	9	135
Scale	20	4	80	2	40	5	100	2	40	5	100	4	80
Brand Fit	15	9	135	4	60	4	60	9	135	7	105	4	60
Unique/Magical	20	7	140	8	160	8	160	5	100	9	180	4	80
Cost of Manufacture	5	7	35	9	45	4	20	8	40	4	20	7	35
Totals	**100**		**665**		**550**		**650**		**645**		**710**		**590**

In our example, Idea E won through its strength in the 'Family' and 'Unique' factors. With these results we would be reassured, going forward, that we were pursuing the best ice cream concept, though it is obviously wise to apply some common sense to the decision and not just follow these results blindly. Now that a decision has been made, and an idea picked it is time to make the next step and turn the concept into action.

This model not only works for ideas, but can also be applied to most of the decisions that a business needs to make; deciding on market positioning, for example. And, finally, don't just discard the ideas that weren't chosen as they may be useful in the future; the ones that scored highly on originality but lost out on the weakness of their practicalities, may become far more viable as production costs fall.

Action

Now that the first three stages **Absorption, Explosion** and **Consolidation** have been completed it is time to turn all of your attention to **Action,** to formulate the best way to communicate your ideas. This is the stage where you will become focused and specialised, shedding any superfluous elements and concentrating on a single direction.

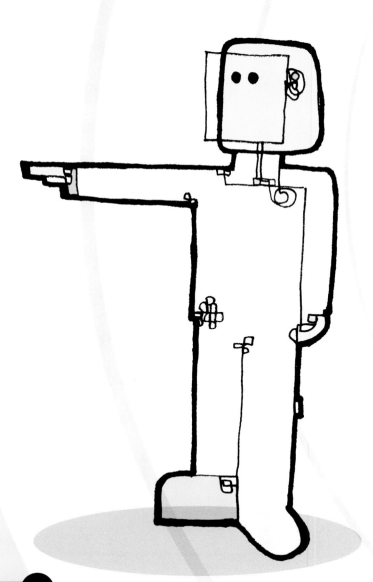

It is impossible to action any campaign without a fully developed schedule, budget and brief. Your **Contact Plan** (see the **Absorption** section) now becomes the bible from which detailed implementation can take place. There will be elements that you and your team can fulfill yourselves, but much will depend on suppliers and other external factors. Make sure that you allocate time to select external partners who are of the right calibre and with whom you will establish an empathetic working relationship.

See it, feel it, touch it

Visualising the future using the following simple technique can be very helpful. The overall task can then be broken down into manageable segments, with notes on what actions need to be performed in each segment. You can even use this method to develop ways to bring the end of the project forward.

1. Begin by imagining a timeline of the future.

2. Visualise the end of the project and place it in time on the line.

3. Divide the line into days, weeks or months and keep the image in your mind of the completed project.

4. Visualise the end of each day, week or monthly segment with its tasks completed and consider what has to be done in each segment in order to complete the project; as you do so you can start to note some of these actions.

5. Now, imagine pulling the end image closer, condensing the timeline and consider the implications of this action and note any changes that would need to be made.

6. Imagine that you can see the project completed; that the product has been designed, manufactured and sold into the market. See it sitting on the shelves of the store with lots of customers clamouring to buy it. See the spreadsheet with the profit line looking great.

7. Imagine the job has been done and then all you have to do is do it!

As an alternative twist, you can use pieces of paper to represent the timeline. Place the papers on the floor, with each one representing a time period and the final piece of paper representing the completed project. You can write down the critical tasks that need to take place in order to move the project to completion on the papers which can then be experimented with, moving some closer together, or removing some entirely, to help the discussion of the implications of moving the end goal closer.

Creating ideas is great, but turning them into action and bringing them to life is just as important. Having an impressive communications strategy, pitch and brief is the key to making sure that an idea is realised, as an average idea actioned well has a much better chance than a great idea actioned poorly.

It's worth investing in some software that will outline all the stages of the project and can be updated as timescales and budgets move around. Keeping control of all the aspects of the project is vital to its success.

Data Action Plan

Essentially, a business's remit is to continually improve the ratio of profit to investment from marketing and it is only through continual testing and refinements that this will be achieved. Without data skills and a good solid database for information, it is difficult to produce effective marketing.

At **outside the box** we take a three phase approach to our data management – for information on data collection, refer to our **Direct Mail** chapter — firstly, addressing the **Basics,** before **Enhancing** the data, and finally looking for data **Innovation.**

Basics

Your goal should be to utilise and develop your data function so that you can create sophisticated **Customer** Relationship Management — **CRM** — and customer acquisition programmes that deliver real **Return On Investment — ROI.** You cannot do this if you do not have the basics right. The Basics process is one of essential data cleansing and standardisation that will help provide a solid foundation for moving forwards. It should include some or all of the following:

Cleansing the data
You can clean up and standardise address details by comparing them to the **Postcode Address File** — the biggest and most up to date address resource — and identifying and rectifying poor quality contact name data. This ensure that your data is up to date.

Validating
You can carry out name and address validation against the current electoral rolls. Telephone validation can also be carried out at this stage, identifying live and disconnected numbers.

Deduping
This is a process of cleaning up the data by finding duplications within the data and removing them.

Suppression
You can identify and suppress gone-aways — those individuals who either no longer exist, or have removed themselves from mailing lists — by checking against the **Bereavement Register** and screening against the **Mailing Preference Service** and **Telephone Preference Service.** It is essential that this activity is carried out on a regular basis to maintain the integrity and legality of data files.

At this stage, you can enhance the data by adding some or all of the following profiling information to current data:
- Gender
- Age
- Marital status
- Length of residency
- Personal income
- Geo-demographics

You can also look at historical customer information, which is often referred to as **RFM — Recency, Frequency, and Monetary Value:**
> **Recency** — how recently did the customer buy?
> **Frequency** — how often have they bought?
> **Monetary Value** — how much did they spend?

You should also look to add:
- The type of product purchased.
- If a customer has responded to an incentive.
- Which communication channel a customer has responded by.

Innovation in Data
Once you have carried out the previous phases and are adding to this information on a regular basis, you have the framework to be much more sophisticated with data usage. The first step is to consider the segmentations that were defined earlier in **Absorption** and make sure that they are applied to all of the data. The aim is to create 'pictures' of these customer groups based on a combination of the following factors:

- **Who they are**
- **What they do**
- **What they buy**
- **How they buy**
- **When they buy**

Accurate profiling will help you to find the most profitable customers and find more like them, utilising what you know about offers and timing to bolster results. It will also help in finding the best media options to test.

Solid customer information will also help you to fully inform the CRM strategy and this is essential to ensure that you are hitting the right individuals, with the right message and offer, and via the most appropriate communication channel. **RFM** analysis can then be utilised to identify when to hit them, how often and what it is worth spending on them based on their profitability.

Affinity partnerships

With accurate profiling information, you can seek out likeminded, non-competing brands, with customers that have similar characteristics to form **Affinity Partnerships.** You can essentially piggy back their mailings and explore the opportunity for list swaps, both of which are very cost effective mechanisms. You can seek out brands with customers that have similar purchasing attitudes. For example, late bookers may also have pay as you go phones, underlining their attitude to spend and risk; or early bookers may be on fixed mortgage deals. The data will help you greatly with this. You should use all data information to provide regular reports so that you can continue to learn and add innovative thinking over time. Given the level of activity required to carry out effective data management and manipulation, companies generally need to decide whether to develop the necessary skills in house or to outsource.

Response prediction and analysis

It is critical that you apply your experience and knowledge with regards to likely response and conversion rates. However, as there are multiple factors which affect these numbers, we use a predictive modeling tool to consider the scenarios and variables. Use these scenarios before you start the project because you need to make sure that the economics of the project work.

This data management process should be continual, with each phase being revisited on a regular basis so that data is always up to date. This may seem to be a considerable task but data is such a fundamental element of marketing that the application of sufficient time and resources is vital. As a bonus, you can always use the data as an income stream, as large volumes of clean and insightful data are always in demand in the marketing world and can create additional revenue that can be used to fund new marketing initiatives.

Getting the Plan Approved

A vital stage in actioning a campaign is to get it approved. Whether you work within an agency or you are 'selling-in' internally, all the elements from Strategy to Planning, Creative to Activity Planning will prove both the logic and quality underpinning the thinking and the ability to execute the campaign on brief, on budget and on time.

We have developed a 13 point check-list to help you succeed in getting approval.

1. Lay the groundwork

When it comes to pitching your plan, most of the selling happens before the actual pitch. To make sure that you have as much of an advantage going into a pitch as possible, there are a number of measures that you can take:

- Send something to the people that you are presenting to as a reminder of the approaching pitch. Be creative and make sure that it is relevant.
- Visit their blog and write something interesting.
- Contact them through their social network.
- Perform a search on the company for any interesting facts that you can mention in the pitch
- Make sure that any actions that you take catch their attention. There is no point taking these steps if nobody knows about them.

2. Big picture

Most projects that you will be pitching for will come with a brief, but it is always worth looking at a wider scope of possibilities than the brief demands. You can use all of the information that you have gathered in the **Absorption** process to create new ideas that will expand on the brief and demonstrate your ability and enthusiasm to go the extra mile.

3. Know the people you are presenting to

Not everyone hears the same presentation. A finance director looks at things very differently to a bank manager, so it is always worth determining who you will be pitching to and adjusting the tone and content appropriately.

4. How will you present?
Will you be informal and light-hearted or formal and serious? This decision should be based both on the content of the project that you are pitching for and the individuals that you are pitching to. It is a good idea to rehearse the pitch with someone that knows nothing about the job as it is easy to get too close to the project, and a fresh perspective will often help to perfect the presentation or at least add some polish to it. How you present is often more important than what you present.

5. Quick sell
You should start with what is often called an Elevator Pitch, which is essentially a one-minute condensed explanation of the pitch. Tell them the cost, why it will sell, how it will sell, who it will sell to, the expected responses and ROI before initiating the main presentation.

6. See it their way
People have a tendency to concentrate too much on their own feelings and not what the client is going to gain from the project. This can be combated through a keen sense of empathy and the knowledge that most of the individuals that you will pitch to will be mostly interested in a good return on their marketing investment, so be sure to mention that.

7. Props
PowerPoint presentations are all well and good, but their virtual nature will invoke a sense of detachment in the client. When possible, this should be compensated for with real life props; something that the client can get their hands on.

8. Create excitement
It is always worth including a 'ta da!' moment in the presentation; something that will generate an air of excitement around the project. This can simply be the unveiling of a new deal, an idea, an offer, or you can create an entirely original 'wow' moment with balloons and pyrotechnics thrown in for good measure.

9. Strength in numbers
Delivering a pitch solo can be a lonely business so it is always worth having two or three team members who can jump in when needed, particularly when it comes to answering questions. Choose team members who can bring a good balance to proceedings and compensate for any perceived weaknesses that you might have. If you're young, for example, bringing in some 'grey hair' can add to your credibility.

10. It's all about you
People buy from people, so mention a few things about yourself that will encourage the client to warm to you. Don't spend too much time on yourself – it's not a Miss World pageant – but a quick mention of who you are and why you are so excited about the project can really get the client onside.

11. Honesty = Best Policy
Never try and wing it with a prospect; it is likely that they've heard it all before. Instead, do your homework, and if nobody in your team knows the answer to a question, then admit it, apologise and promise that finding out will be your next priority, before professionally moving on.

12. Have you answered the brief?
Make sure that you are always demonstrating that you have addressed the brief; call back to it regularly throughout the pitch. It is only after the client has been assured that you have considered and delivered what they wanted, that you can add value to the brief or offer alternatives.

13. What will you leave behind?
One day after the presentation the people that you have pitched to will likely have forgotten 98% of what you have said, so it is important to leave a few things behind to remind them. These can be print outs, idea boards, a digital book of the presentation, or anything else that you feel can jog their memory, both of the information that you presented and the style with which you did it.

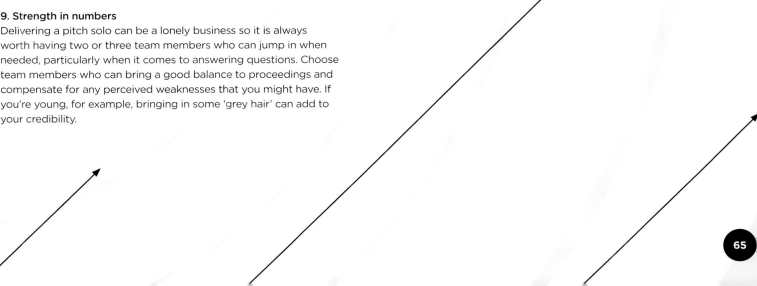

Capitalisation

Capitalisation is all about measuring the effectiveness of the campaign and feeding this information back into Absorption for the next wave of campaigns.

Throughout the duration of a campaign, opportunities to collate data will present themselves and this data can be used to assess just how successful the campaign is. Ascertaining the success of a campaign will set the platform for successive campaigns to reach targets and provide good returns. This is easily the shortest stage in **Strategy,** but it is vital for future campaigns.

The first step in the **Capitalisation** phase is to go back to the objectives determined in your strategy, and turn them into targets. A phrase that we often use for this is, "I will know if this campaign has been successful when..." so what is it that will make it successful? It is not, however, just about measuring success, it's about measuring all relevant aspects of performance. It is just as important to measure things even if they don't meet the targets/objectives as this will allow you to learn from it for next time. There is no such thing as failure, only feedback.

If an objective was successful, you need to determine why and, similarly, if it was anything less than successful you should be asking what could have been done differently. Testing, tracking and research of the relevant qualitative and quantitative factors of a campaign will all inform future planning and decision-making. A full report containing, well categorised and concise findings will be invaluable next time around.

It is not enough to simply collect the data; you will need to interpret it to see if there is anything to learn for the next campaign. To do this you need to reflect on the data available and one way to achieve this is by applying the question 'so what?' to each piece of the captured data. For example, "47% of people did not open the email"... so what? What does this mean? What are the implications? These are the reflections that are required.

Do not, however, become inflicted by what we call **Analysis Paralysis,** where you become overly concerned with analysis, to the detriment of the rest of the campaign. Over-analysis leads to a mass of useless data which not only wastes time to create, but also swamps the useful information, making it much harder to find. To ensure that you don't become bogged down in analysis, you must identify the valuable information that warrants further examination, such as the different sales metrics, changes in perception and response by different demographics. And finally, don't waste time and effort measuring anything unless you are going to invest time and effort analysing the results.

reflect on what you've learnt and don't forget to **apply it** going forward

brand building

Good brands live in the hearts and the minds of consumers

We have paid special attention to the strategy of building a brand because we believe that integrity is more sustainable than novelty. Brands may start life in planning documents but ultimately they rest in the minds and hearts of people. During an economic downturn or recession, brands that invest ahead of the competition do better during the slowdown and recover much more quickly on the upturn. Brand building acts as an overarching discipline, bridging the natural lifecycle of any customer from acquisition through to dormancy and is, therefore, an important part of a marketer's role.

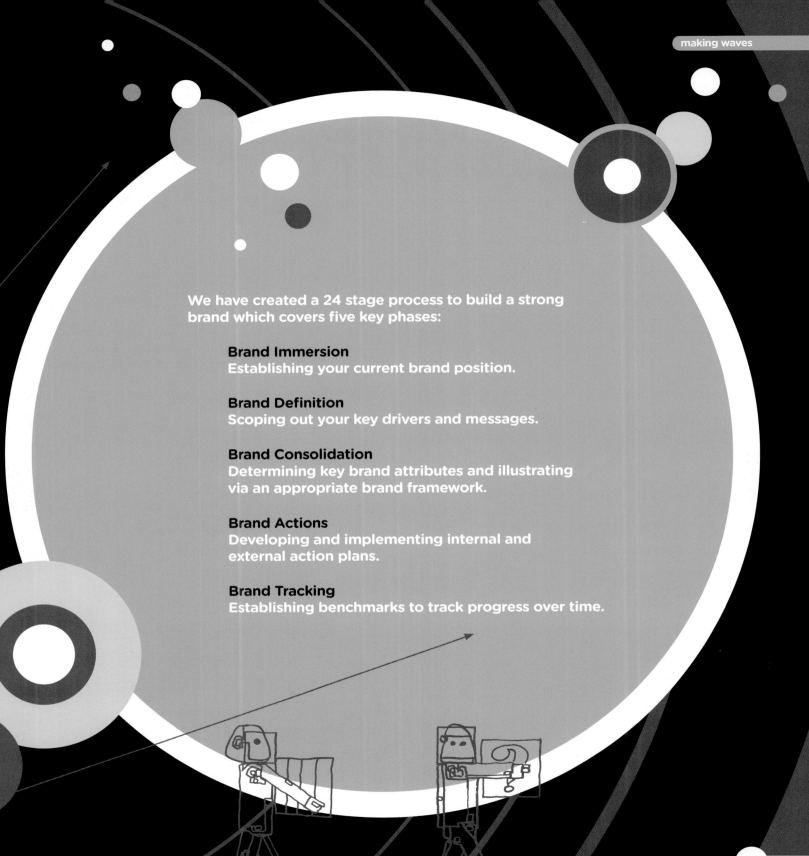

We have created a 24 stage process to build a strong brand which covers five key phases:

Brand Immersion
Establishing your current brand position.

Brand Definition
Scoping out your key drivers and messages.

Brand Consolidation
Determining key brand attributes and illustrating via an appropriate brand framework.

Brand Actions
Developing and implementing internal and external action plans.

Brand Tracking
Establishing benchmarks to track progress over time.

Brand Immersion

Objective — To establish the current brand position.

Methodology — Carried out via workshops with key stakeholders, desk research and customer research, most of which should have been covered in Absorption.

Benefits — Collates all of the background information necessary to develop a coherent and relevant brand strategy.

1. **Brand strategy** — understand/develop brand vision — Where is the brand going? How does it fit with the corporate strategy? What are the BIG goals and objectives?

2. **Brand context** — understand how the brand sits amongst sister/parent brands — map out the product range, look at the regulatory environment/macro-economic environment and understand the positioning relative to major competitors.

3. **Brand needs analysis** — understand customer needs and how the brand attempts to meet them.

Brand Definition

Objective — To scope out key messages and drivers.

Methodology — Uses our Brand Pyramid tool to determine key strategic areas.

Benefits — Defines the entire framework upon which to build relevant brand activity, covering all essential areas and obtaining input and buy-in from all relevant stakeholders.

Brand Pyramids provide key tools for fully digesting and understanding the brand portfolio and for implementing relevant and successful marketing solutions. You can populate the Brand Pyramid in a collaborative way involving all major stakeholders.

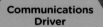

12. The overriding message we wish to portray about the brand — **Communications Driver**

11. Shorthand distillation of the brand's reason to exist — **Key Proposition**

10. Factual features, attributes and properties that help underpin the proposition — **Brand Truths**

9. Human characteristics guiding tone, feel and style — **Brand Personality**

8. Key emotional reasons for buying the brand — **Emotional Benefits**

7. Key functional reasons for buying the brand — **Functional Benefits**

6. How the brand improves the everyday life of the consumer — **Core Insight**

5. Define what market you are in — **Market Definition**

4. Who we are selling to — **Target Audience**

Brand Consolidation

Objective — To agree key brand attributes and illustrate it via the most appropriate brand framework.

Methodology — Use tools such as the Brand Pyramid or Brand Onion to bring all key areas together and act as a focus for the next stage.

Benefits — Clarifies the pivotal point against which all brand activity is developed and measured.

13. Example Brand Onion

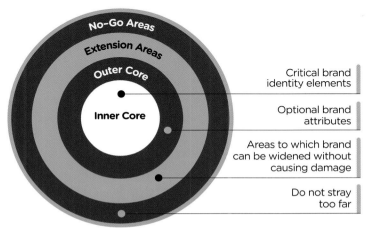

14. You can then develop brand insights by illustrating the core brand attributes and target audiences through use of imagery.

15. And also consider the wider brand remit by looking at the brand in all of its applications.

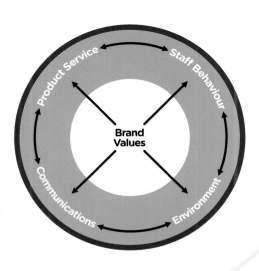

Brand Actions

Objective — To agree and implement an action plan to put the brand into practice.

Methodology — Develop a creative strategy for your marketing communications.

Benefits — A creative style is developed and set in stone which can then be briefed into all relevant stakeholders and controlled centrally.

16. **Develop graphic interpretation** — creative styling to support the brand.

17. **Develop brand guidelines** — production of directional document to ensure the consistency and integrity of the brand, resulting in clear and simple brand messages values and perceptions. This should include pyramids, logo usage, fonts, colours, tone of voice, icons, photography, do's and don'ts.

18. **Brief all relevant stakeholders** — agencies, staff, suppliers, etc.

19. **Develop marketing materials** — use the other chapters within this book to determine the best use of the media available.

20. **Establish brand efficiencies** — maximise economies of scale.

21. **Establish controls** — put measures in place to make sure that the brand is managed effectively over time.

Brand Tracking

Objective — Put in place benchmarks to track progress over time.

Methodology — Determine the most appropriate tools and implement the action plan.

Benefits — Provides a basis to see how the impact of the brand changes positively over time against set objectives.

22. **Benchmark research** — Track brand impact, emotion and loyalty amongst customers.

23. **Exploit marketing communications** for maximum impact and Return on Investment.

24. Continue to **manage the brand** over time.

direct mail

An indispensible part of your marketing mix

Direct mail is an indispensible medium in direct marketing. By utilising a database of existing and potential customers, as well as mailing lists available to be purchased from brokers, the customers who are most likely to be responsive to promotions can be directly targeted, and the use of direct-response mechanisms allows for easy and accurate measurements of the success of each campaign.

This also makes direct mail highly conducive to testing as just about every aspect of a direct mail campaign can be tweaked, tested and optimised in order to produce increasingly higher returns on marketing spend.

In addition, direct mail affords greater freedom in how to construct creative work. Whereas print advertising is restricted to a two-dimensional, small-sized advertisement, often in black and white and is subject to the editorial restrictions of the publication, in direct mail there is an enhanced allowance for independence to experiment with different ideas, resulting in the only possible constraints being budget and imagination.

For these reasons, direct mail has steadily grown more popular as a marketing medium which means that it is increasingly becoming more of a challenge to create direct mail packages that stand out amongst the other post that comes through a recipient's door. Furthermore, while an organised and well thought out direct mail campaign can be very cost effective, if approached badly it can become very expensive. A poor campaign could, therefore, not only fail to bring in high returns, but could potentially lose a lot of money. This chapter will provide you with some useful advice to aid you in getting the most out of direct mail campaigns, including developing a database, producing effective design, creating and also renting mailing lists.

Databases and Mailing Lists

The most crucial element of a direct mail campaign is the quality of the database. It does not matter how effective the design and copy of a mailing might be, if it is sent to the wrong people it will not be successful. On the other hand, if a business has access to a high-quality database, then even a poorly executed mailing can bring in good returns. Most businesses will have two separate databases: one for **Customer Relationship Management – CRM –** and one for **Transaction History.** The CRM database will hold information on existing and potential customers according to geography, age, buying behaviour, and other such factors, which allows you to promote a business in a much more personalised and targeted way. The transaction history database is fairly self-explanatory as it will simply be a collection of data on the **Recency, Frequency** and **Monetary value – RFM –** of customers' purchases with a business. This form of database is important in differentiating customers in terms of their value to the business, so that more time and energy can be devoted to contacting the people who are most likely to respond to promotions and spend more when they do so. It will also lead to a decrease in the wasting of resources on unresponsive and low-value contacts. The effective use of both of these databases in tandem will aid in indentifying what has been sent to a customer, when, and with what success rate and this knowledge will produce a highly targeted campaign which should, consequently, reduce costs and maximise returns.

Mailing lists can also be rented to supplement a business's own database. These lists can be highly specific and targeted to particular criteria such as geographical location, age, or past buying behaviour, and they therefore enable the types of people who are most likely to be interested in an offer to be contacted. It is also possible to **Cross-Match** a database against external mailing lists if the current database has incomplete data on an individual. For instance, if a database has the name and email address of prospective customers, but not their home address, then the database can be cross-matched with an external list to populate the missing addresses, leading to a more complete and useful database.

Developing a Database

It is relatively simple to set up a database using a software package such as **Microsoft Access** or **Oracle Database 11g**, while larger, more complex businesses can take the more expensive route of commissioning customised database software that exactly suit their requirements.

There are a number of different ways to procure customer information to add to a database. If a business posts any products, then it will already have a legitimate method of collating customer information as names and addresses are obviously fundamental to the posting process. To supplement this data, the order form can also request additional information, such as their age, income and what type of house they live in. If this method is unavailable – as is the case with new companies, for instance – it is necessary to be more creative in acquiring information about customers. It is a good idea to use every appropriate opportunity to request people's names, addresses, dates of birth and other such information; sales teams, receptionists, complaints departments, retail outlets and anyone else coming into contact with customers should be told to find opportunities to record contact information. If guarantees are offered for any products then this can also be a valuable source for data.

If you are seeking to contact businesses rather than individuals, then you will be able to find a large amount of information regarding them online. As well as their contact details, you should include data about their revenue, how many people they employ, what type of products they sell, what type of people or businesses they sell to, and any other potentially relevant information that you can find. You should also try to capture the names of key individuals within companies; try to find out who the decision makers are within the appropriate departments so that you can target them directly.

You can also use incentives to persuade people to provide you with detailed information about existing and potential customers. You can produce a detailed questionnaire in the form of a door to door leaflet, a webpage or an insert in a magazine, newspaper, or product

customers consider
direct mail
appropriate for cold
acqusition activity

mail is up to 8 times more likely than email to make customers feel valued

Supplementing the Data File

In addition to developing a database, there are a variety of other ways to procure contact details. If a company already has a substantial database then it can be used to effectively trade for other contacts with another establishment in what is referred to as an **Affinity Partnership**. These partnerships usually happen between likeminded companies with similar target audiences but non-competing products – a ski holiday provider and a winter sports store, for example – and have the benefit of being virtually free.

Hint

Another tact to easily acquire further contacts is to use **Sponsored Questions**. This is the practice whereby a company pays for the inclusion of pertinent questions within a survey – a ubiquitous one being 'when is your insurance renewal'.

delivery and offer people incentives such as discounts or free samples in exchange for completing the questionnaire in full. You can also encourage existing customers to provide you with the contact details of some of their friends and offer incentives for doing so, that will be received once their friends have made a purchase.

Once you have started to collect information about customers, you should continue to update it whenever a new interaction takes place. So, if possible, you should be keeping a comprehensive record of the purchasing activities – how often they buy, what they buy, how much they spend, and so on – of every customer. In addition, you should keep track of how often each customer has been contacted with mailings, telephone calls, emails, or any other form of communication and record any occasion when they have made a purchase as a result of one of these promotions. This information will be extremely useful in helping you to identify the most profitable customers and those who are likely to be most receptive to direct marketing efforts.

Finally, all marketers should be conscious of the legal quagmire that is **Data Protection**. The use of personal data is a delicate and complicated process which can lead to serious problems if dealt with incorrectly. The chief issues to be aware of are disclaimers and opportunities to opt in or out, so always have these in mind when organising mailings. Unfortunately, we cannot hope to cover all of the legal detail in this book, and if we did it would likely be out of date by the end of the year, so for detailed, up-to-the-minute information and advice, we would refer you to the **Direct Marketing Association – DMA** – which can be found at **www.dma.org.uk.** or at **www.makingwaves.co.uk**

As mentioned above, you can also choose to purchase a mailing list. There are two main types of lists available for purchase: **Direct Response Lists** and **Compiled Lists**. Direct response lists are comprised of people or businesses who have responded to a direct marketing promotion in the past, whether from a mailing, a print advertisement, or another medium. It is possible to purchase direct response lists specific to the type of response that you are looking for; for example, there are lists of people who have purchased a product, subscribed to a publication, donated to a charity, or recommended a friend. Past behaviour is one of the most reliable indicators of future behaviour, so it is more likely that a person will respond to a promotion if they have responded to something similar in the past. direct response lists can, therefore, be extremely useful in a direct mail campaign.

Compiled lists are made up of details of people or businesses taken from a mixture of public and private resources such as directories and phone books. There are various different types of compiled list available according to the particular type of segmentation that you are looking for with the most common lists focusing on a specific geographical area, demographic – gender, age, profession, etc. – or a combination of such factors; you could request a list of women aged over 35 living in London, for example. It is also possible to purchase compiled lists containing more detailed information about the lifestyle of the featured individuals discovered from surveys or questionnaires. This could include information on their hobbies, sporting activities, newspaper readership and other factors. For business-to-business marketing, it is common to request lists of businesses belonging to a particular field as well as other criteria, including the location, job titles and size of the businesses.

Renting a Mailing List

When purchasing a mailing list, you are advised to go through a list broker. List brokers are experts on the complicated process of sourcing the most appropriate list for any particular needs and budget, and they will handle the administrative side of renting the list. Enlisting a broker will also provide cover for any of the data protection legalities mentioned above, making them indispensable for a business's peace of mind.

Brokers tend to be paid by the sellers of the list rather than the buyers, so their services will be free – or it will at least seem as such, as the charge is likely to have been integrated with the price of the list. You should bear in mind however, that the broker is ultimately working for the seller, so it will fall to you to ask tough questions to make sure that you are purchasing a high-quality list.

. . . .

You might want to start with these:

How exactly did the contacts respond to previous marketing campaigns - did they make a purchase or simply make an inquiry? It is important to know exactly how the contacts on the list have responded to promotions in the past as not all responses are of the same value. Obviously, someone who has responded by making a purchase is much more valuable than someone who has responded by agreeing to try a test sample of a product without proceeding to complete a purchase.

How recently did the contacts last respond to a direct marketing promotion? This is useful to know because even if a person has been a frequent and valuable purchaser in the past, if it has been a long period of time since their last such purchase then this could indicate that there has been some change in their circumstances or that their contact details are no longer correct. More recent purchasers are much more valuable.

How often have the contacts responded to direct marketing promotions? Frequency of response is very important in determining the quality of a list. If people have been shown to consistently respond to promotions in the past, it makes it more likely they will respond to a similar promotion in the future.

How much did the contacts spend when responding to previous direct marketing promotions? This is useful because it helps you to estimate the value of a list's contacts, and is also indicative of whether they are likely to buy a product; if the average purchase from a list is just £5 it is unlikely to produce good returns for a company selling products for £200.

When was the list last checked for out-of-date details? Lists can start to age very quickly as people move house and this can have a detrimental effect on the profitability of your direct mail campaigns. If 20% of a company's mailings are being sent to the wrong addresses, their campaign will fail to produce good returns regardless of the quality of their creative work. A good list will be **Cleaned** regularly – i.e. checked for out-of-date details and updated appropriately – and will have a **Deliverability Rate** of 95% or better.

How many companies have tested the list, and how many of those subsequently proceeded to rent the list after the test? Of course, if the list has proved to be successful for similar companies, then this suggests that it is likely to produce a high number of responses for your campaign. If a lot of different companies have tested the list and then gone on to rent it in its entirety, then this suggests that their results were positive, and if the same companies have chosen to rent the list multiple times, then this suggests that it has succeeded in bringing in good returns. However, you should be aware that if the list has been used too many times then it may start to suffer mailing fatigue as the same people are unlikely to continue making purchases over and over again.

. . . .

If you pay attention to the issues highlighted above, then you should be able to identify good quality lists that will give your direct mail campaign the best possible chance of succeeding. Nevertheless, you should produce a test mailing of around 5000 units before agreeing to rent the whole list just to make sure that the list produces the expected results.

Creating the Direct Mail Package

When constructing a mailing package – as with any other direct marketing medium – personalisation is key. Marketing is about giving people what they want, when they want it and so the more personalised, and therefore, relevant a mailing is, the higher the ROI generally becomes. The data held on each customer should, therefore, be used to maximum effect, resulting in a package that reflects customer preferences, interests, status and transaction history in every facet. This may sound expensive, but clever use of lasering – where pertinent information is added after the primary printing phase – can be very cost effective.

On the more expensive, yet far more exciting, side of personalisation media is **Digital Printing**. This allows for the most profoundly personalised mailings, where recipient's names are, for example, written in the sand, sea or sky of their potential holiday destination. Once again, although this is an expensive option, presenting mailing recipients with a package that speaks to them specifically about their own needs in as much, relevant, detail as possible is likely to provide far greater returns.

To – literally – add an extra dimension to mailings, 3D items, that jump out or stand up when the mailing is opened and sensory inclusions such as sounds – a la those exciting/annoying talking birthday cards – textures, scents and taste can be included, leading to a much more memorable mailing package and consequently boosting response. However, although there are edible papers and inks out there, we would suggest that recipients' taste buds should be amused by a product sample rather than the mailing itself.

Traditionally, the direct mail package consisted of a letter, a brochure and the envelope that contained them. Direct mail is, however, much more sophisticated and varied now, coming in multiple permutations that are chosen depending on the stage of the CRM journey and customer value. For example, a low-cost, high volume one piece mailer is ideal for sending to a large volume of current customers who are low spending or low margin. It is generally a good idea to take advantage of this wide range of mailing options and create a variety of mailings that can be employed for every type of customer at every stage of their CRM journey.

We have included sections that address each of the traditional elements of a mailing, but we would stress that the format of a mailing campaign can be as varied and original as the product and medium allows and that you should pursue and test every option available, within reason.

The Outer

A mailing will not be very successful unless people actually open it, and there are several techniques that can be utilised to encourage people to do this. First of all, the outer does not have to be a traditional envelope – hence why we have named this section 'outer' rather than 'envelope' – but can, instead, be the entire mailing in of itself, either as a 'postcard' style mailing or another form of one piece mailer; a piece of card folded in two with the address on the outside and marketing copy on the inside, for instance. People generally receive large amounts of direct mail and, often, their natural instinct will be to throw it away. In our experience, between 45% to 65% of direct mailings go unopened depending on relevance and attractiveness so it is paramount, therefore, that they are given a positive reason to take the time to open – or even look at – the outer, so you need a design that makes an almost instantaneous impact.

One way to generate interest is to reveal little about the mailing's contents; if the outer is left largely blank, then the recipient will be unsure as to whether it is a marketing communication and this may encourage them to open it to check whether it is important – which, as a properly targeted piece of mailing, it should be. Furthermore, this can be a good tactic when working with business to business marketing, where the **Gatekeepers** of a company – receptionists, secretaries, personal assistants – are likely to vet mailings before passing them on to the actual addressee. If a mailing is too overt in its marketing agenda, it may not make it past these individuals, while one that looks official and important has a much better chance of breaking through. This option also has the advantage of being cheap to produce, which is always a bonus.

At the other extreme, a bright, bold design can be used, employing vivid colours and attention-grabbing imagery in order to make the outer as appealing and obvious as possible, and then supplement this design with some **Teaser Copy** that encourages the recipient to open the outer.

There are various levels of compromise available between these two extremes; you could choose to have an outer with no teaser copy but with interesting imagery, or conversely you could use teaser copy on an otherwise plain white envelope. If you are choosing to include imagery, then don't forget about the back of the outer as there is no way to know how it is going to land on someone's desk or floor and, if you want to be sure that it will be the most noticeable piece of direct mail in all situations, then you should aim to make the back of the mailing just as eye-catching as the front.

It is also worth considering whether brand identity should be displayed on the outer. If so, then this is usually done in the top left-hand corner and can be especially useful if a brand is one that recipients are likely to know and trust. Other options to experiment with include different sizes of outer – very big or very small mailings may catch the recipients' attention – using different methods of printing the recipients' names and addresses – printing straight onto the outer or using a window through to the letter or even using multiple windows – or you could try to come up with something more unique and outlandish such as using plastic rather than paper, or printing the envelope upside-down or back-to-front. There are no concrete rules; it is really a matter of knowing what options are available, deducing the type of design that would most appeal to a particular demographic, and then continuing to test alternatives in order to maximise returns.

The Letter

For most people, the letter will be the first aspect of a mailing that they read and it offers an ideal platform for convincing recipients to respond to an offer. The type of letter will differ greatly according to brand, customer demographic, and aim of the campaign – whether a business wants to encourage existing customers to increase the value or frequency of their purchases, or convince people who have never heard of a company to buy something from them for the first time. A direct mail letter from a financial services company is likely to adopt a very different style to a fitness club or a children's toy store, so it is essential that, before any writing takes place, the target customer is identified so that the design and copy can be consistently appropriate. There are, however, various elements of a letter that are applicable in the vast majority of cases.

Headline

Direct mail letters often include a headline. This presents a chance to mention the core benefit to the recipient at the outset, so that their attention and interest is caught, and an understanding of the context of the subsequent copy is imparted, immediately upon viewing the page. The headline should concisely explain the key benefit available to the recipient and, if possible, address them personally by name – subheadings can also be included to provide additional information.

Hint

An alternative to headings and subheadings is to use two or three short bullet-points at the top of the page to summarise the basic message of the letter.

Salutation

The salutation should be as highly personalised as possible; the standard 'Dear Sir/Madam' should be avoided at all costs. Depending on brand and demographic, the salutation could be relatively informal – a fairly minor alteration such as the use of 'Hi John' rather than 'Dear John' can have a significant effect on the tone of the letter. If the information in a database doesn't allow for such personalisation then there should always be a default salutation that can be used instead. For instance, a friendly – and unisex – alternative such as 'Dear neighbour', or 'Dear music fan' could be employed when a name and gender is unavailable.

Opening

After the salutation, the first one or two sentences of the main copy should seek to make an immediate, attention grabbing, impact on the reader, by explaining some of the main benefits in greater detail than was possible in the headline. Try to start a sentence that immediately brings the focus onto the reader; so rather than talking about the company – 'We take pride in providing...' or 'I wanted to let you know about a great offer...' – it is far more effective to immediately address the benefits of the product or service to the recipient – 'Your drive home could become so much easier if...' or 'You could save hundreds of pounds today if...'. An interesting and engaging way to begin the letter is to ask the recipient a question, such as 'Do you want to get the most out of your bank account?'. This takes personalisation further by establishing a discourse with the recipient which is all important in marketing; the recipient may well not have thought about their bank account satisfaction.

Writing Style

In most cases, it is best to use short words, short sentences, and short paragraphs. Unless you know that you are marketing exclusively to a well-educated demographic, you should not assume the recipients' reading level, and should therefore try to use simple language that will be understood by the vast majority of people, and remove any superfluous words or phrases to make sentences concise, punchy, and easy to read; think **The Sun** rather than **The Times**.

Short paragraphs are also recommended as a recipient will be unlikely to read a letter if they are confronted with large blocks of text. You should, instead, break up the copy into small paragraphs and perhaps also include multiple headings, notes in the margin, and bold or italic formatted text within the body copy to signpost the content of each paragraph to the reader in order to aid skim-reading. Ideally, a reader should be able to know the key points of a message with only a quick glance at the letter. However, while you should aim to use short words, sentences, and paragraphs, the letter itself does not need to be short. People will take the time to read a long letter if they feel that it is relevant to them and is written in a compelling and accessible way.

As mentioned above, a letter should be written with the recipient – and not the business – as its main concern. At all times the offer, and what it will do for the recipient, should be highlighted; how it will make them feel, how it can make their life easier or more enjoyable, how much money they will save, and so on. Most people would much rather read about the benefits that a company will be able to provide to them, than the company itself. A useful way to check that the reader is the focus of the letter, is to count the number of times that the words 'you' or 'your' are used, compared to personal pronouns such as 'I', 'we', and 'our'; there should be many more instances of the former than the latter. That is not to say that marketing literature should not include mention of a company's credentials or charity work, but this should always be presented as a benefit to the customer – 'by buying our product you are helping conservation efforts in Borneo.'

Hint
Each campaign can have more than one letter. If a company's database has been segmented effectively, then the literature should reflect this by being targeted individually for each segment that it is sent to.

Presentation

To make a letter as easy to read as possible, make sure that the text used is large enough, and maintain a consistent typeface throughout the letter so as not to confuse readers. Also, text should not be set over a coloured background that will negatively impact on legibility. On the subject of coloured backgrounds, it is also worth noting that

by far, most customers prefer to be contacted by a combination of post and online

it is very hard to laser onto yellow so any segments of marketing literature that are going to be personalised should preferably avoid pictures of sun, daffodils, ducklings and the like.

A rule that **outside the box** likes to live by is that letters should look like letters. Through testing, we have found that letters with a traditional format – serif fonts, spaced paragraphs, writing on the back of the page, a date, salutation and P.S. – outperform other formats so, as long as it fits into the campaign, we would suggest following this tact. Other presentational devices such as bullet-points, asterisks and numbering can also be used to help people skim-read a letter.

Postscript

The postscript — P.S. — is an important section of the letter that can be used to reiterate a key message, add an additional call-to-action, or remind the reader of any time-constraints applicable to the offer. Despite being at the bottom of the page, the postscript is one of the most read sections of a direct mail letter — we ran a **Direct Holidays** mailing with a P.S. versus no P.S. and the P.S. got the higher result — so it is a good idea to include a P.S. and to make sure that the space is used well.

P.S.

The P.S. shouldn't be anything new; it should be a reiteration of the most important element of the letter.

The Brochure

Certain mailings will include a brochure and this can serve various purposes. It can be used to provide more detailed technical information that would be inappropriate on the letter; it can develop and expand upon facts and figures already mentioned in the letter, including the potential benefits to the recipient and testimonials from previous clients; and it can contain attractive imagery or photography to demonstrate the product on offer, to help the recipient visualise how it might be used and how it might benefit them personally.

To entice a recipient to read a brochure, there needs to be a reason for them to do so, and this is usually achieved by producing an eye-catching and compelling front – and preferably back – cover. It is often a good idea to include a reference to the main benefit on the cover as this is usually what will be of most interest to the recipient. This should be supported by more subtle techniques to entice the recipient, such as particularly attractive graphics with a short invitation for the recipient to read more about the offer. The brochure should be as visually appealing and engaging as possible.

If the letter has successfully sparked the recipient's interest they should now be wanting to see more of the product, and the brochure should therefore use photography, illustrations and other imagery to highlight the benefits of the product. Charts, graphs, and tables should be used to make your other data and information more accessible and visually stimulating.

While the brochure can, and usually should, be used for more detailed and technical information, just as in your letter, the copy should be divided into small sections, and be written in simple language with short sentences, headings, subheadings, bold and italic formatting, bullet-points, and different coloured text to make it easy to read. It should also be peppered with call-to-actions so as to never miss an opportunity to remind the reader that now is the time to buy and that the buying procedure is an incredibly easy and stress-free process.

Although the content of a brochure can differ greatly according to the type of product, your budget, whether you are selling to existing or potential customers, and other factors, the average brochure will include:

- A section dedicated to testimonials, positive reviews and awards

- A small section offering details about the company highlighting expertise, experience, and history of success

- A thorough look at the product, including its history and all of its uses and applications and the many benefits that it can provide the user, as well as favourable comparisons to other similar products currently available from competitors

- A more in-depth look at the offer available to the recipient, explaining in greater detail the price, payment options, deadlines, contact details, repeating the call-to-action and explaining step-by-step all of the different ways that the recipient can respond to take up the offer, and perhaps also including an additional response mechanism within the brochure itself

- A very important aspect of the brochure is to produce it in such a way so as to maximise its retainability. A key measure to achieve this is to ensure that the brochure can stand alone without the supplementary literature that accompanied it so that the recipient is not required to save everything from the mailing if they wish to make an order in the future. A brochure should, therefore, be constructed with terms and conditions, all contact details and order forms within its pages.

Hint
Another great way to extend a brochure's life-span with the recipient is to include discount vouchers that are only valid over certain time periods – for example, '25% off product A 1st Jan – 28th Feb' and then '2-4-1 on product range B 1st Mar – 31st Apr.' This makes the brochure far more useful over a period of time and, consequently, much more retainable.

Other Elements of the Mailing Package
As we have already mentioned, there are no concrete rules on what should be included and it is advisable to experiment with offers, gimmicks and unusual ideas that will help catch the recipient's attention while demonstrating the strengths of the product, service, or brand.

The Offer
It isn't enough to simply tell recipients about products or services, they need to feel as though they have a good reason or incentive to respond. A common tact is to provide a discount, and there are many different ways of expressing this – '10% off', '3 for the price of 2', 'free delivery' – which, generally, amount to the same benefit to the consumer, but which can bring in very different returns. The aim is to heighten perceived value so, for example, offering a free child place can often give the appearance of being worth far more than the cash equivalent.

Hint
An offer doesn't have to be a discount, it can simply be added value. There are even opportunities to utilise offers that don't cost anything, such as flight operators offering priority boarding.

Other types of offer include free gifts for making a purchase, entry into prize draws, free accessories for the product being purchased, favourable credit options, or, when selling a product that requires a subscription, it can be beneficial to offer a free or discounted trial period. Another option is to contact existing customers and offer incentives for them to recommend a friend to make a purchase. There are a number of different ways to approach this, but generally, a small reward is proffered for the provision of a friend's contact details and a greater reward if that friend proceeds to make a purchase. The friend can also be rewarded for taking part to further incentivise this scheme. It is also usually a good idea to include a money-back guarantee as part of the offer in order to further reassure potential buyers, and a sense of urgency can be instilled by setting a time limit or by suggesting that stocks are limited and that products are being sold on a first-come-first-served basis.

Hint

Brochures are not the only part of a direct mail package that can stand alone. It is also a good idea to provide a voucher to accompany any offer, which can be retained even if the rest of the package is disposed of. Any such vouchers must, therefore, have a prominent call to action, be easy to remove if attached to any other literature, and have any instructions and details pertinent to the offer, printed on them.

Testimonials

People are wary of a salesperson in any context, and direct mail is no exception. No matter how convincing the explanation of the benefits of a product or service, consumers – the cynical creatures that they are – are likely to remain sceptical about the validity of the claims made by marketing materials. Endorsements and testimonials can be an effective way of negating some of this scepticism, as people will always pay more attention to their peers' opinions than to advertising copy, however persuasive it may be. Testimonials from satisfied customers can be included throughout a letter to reassure readers and reinforce the statements throughout the sales literature. When marketing to businesses, where a list of past and present clients with

a particular emphasis on well-known brands is the best approach. It is also worth mentioning any awards or positive reviews that the company has received from independent sources, as well as any online polls or surveys that portray it in a favourable light.

Call to Action

A strong call to action can be crucial in encouraging recipients to take up an offer. Even if the mailing has caught the reader's attention, persuaded them to read the letter in full, and inspired a genuine interest in the offer, if that recipient then puts the literature to one side rather than immediately proceeding to respond, then there's a good chance that they may never get round to doing so. They should, therefore, be specifically asked to take action straight away, and be given an explanation as to the simple, straightforward steps that they need to take in order to take advantage of the offer. Give customers a reason to respond sooner rather than later – there could be a time limit on the offer or limited stocks, or you could simply remind them that the sooner they take up the offer the sooner they can be enjoying all the wonderful benefits available – or risk losing their business entirely.

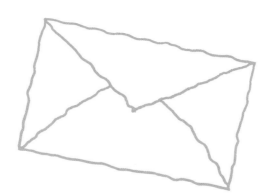

CROSS MEDIA

Irritation

The primary obstacle to overcome with direct mail is to make it stand out from the copious other mailings that drop through the letterbox with it and a great way to do this is through subconscious irritation and disruption. Although irritating a recipient is rarely a good thing, there are certain shapes and patterns that can subliminally bother us as human beings and make us take notice. You see, the brain likes order; it likes straight lines, symmetry and uniform angles and any disturbance of that is more likely to draw the recipient's attention.

This approach can also be used to some degree across other media, though it's not quite as easy to produce an 'L' shaped email as it is an 'L' shaped mailer. You could, though, use asymmetrical patterns or come up with other, more creative, ways of causing a bit of visual disruption. By providing the recipient with the means to solve the disruption, you can also encourage them to take certain actions as, for example, you can perforate the asymmetrical portion of a mailing so that it can be removed and you can turn that section into the response mechanism. You could also place links on the odd things out in emails and web pages, which correct themselves when the cursor is placed over them.

direct mail case study

one piece mailer outer

Imagine what your mailer will look like amongst all of the recipient's other post. You have two seconds to make an impact. The best ways to do this are through a striking shape, message or imagery.

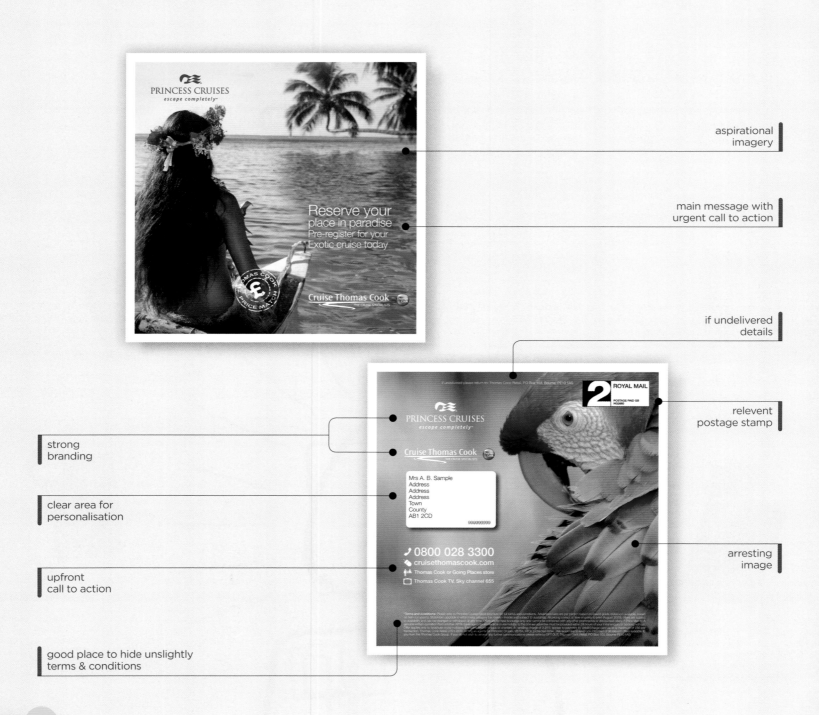

aspirational imagery

main message with urgent call to action

if undelivered details

relevent postage stamp

strong branding

clear area for personalisation

upfront call to action

arresting image

good place to hide unslightly terms & conditions

direct mail letter pack

A letter is the main point of contact in a mail pack and needs to sum up the entire campaign and put the reader in the right frame of mind through copy and visual cues.

relevant imagery to add impact and aspiration

impactful, action-focused main headline

for smiles all round. Book early!

Dear Mrs Sample,

We know you and your family like to book early and this year it really pays. Your family is one of the first to get our bigger and better, **full Summer Sun 2010 brochure** - loaded with the best and most popular spots for family fun! Now you can beat the rush to book, so you can grab the holiday that floats your boat (or lilo) and get a deal to really make your family smile too - that's the direct effect.

More exciting resorts, more family fun...

When we say our brochure is 'bigger and better', we mean it! We've loads of **exciting, great value resorts** for you and the family everywhere from Spain to Egypt. Our **14 Aquamania resorts** are cool for fun pools and wicked waterslides, and don't forget Egypt resorts come with our unique **"sunshine guarantee"** (now doesn't that sound great after last year's wash-out summer?). Plus there's also 31 kid's club properties to give you some well-deserved rest!

Grab your FREE kids holidays and 3 FREE nights

You heard right...they're limited and going fast! Book before 31 January 2010 and say goodbye to pestering - you can splash out on the holiday you want and splash the cash on ice cream treats. (Save enough for your evening cocktails too!). Plus you can also save the equivalent of **'3 FREE nights'** on selected 14 night holiday prices. But hurry, when they're gone, they're gone!

£50 off all holidays

Thinking about escaping with the family later in the year? If you book your Summer 2010 holiday by 31 January 2010 we'll also give you £50 per booking off any holiday departing from 1 November 2010 - 30 April 2011.

No extras to pay!

As usual with Direct Holidays, unlike with some travel companies, there's no nasty hidden extras - your meals, transfers, rep service in resort, flights from £90 and 20kg luggage (an extra 5kg over most operators!) - plus, a really useful extra 10kg for the under 2s are all included.

You won't pay more for your holiday either with our **lowest price guarantee** plus your money is 100% ATOL protected. And with our low deposit what are you waiting for? Book early and get smiles all round!

Happy holidays
The Direct Holidays Team

P.S We've also included our brand **new 'Hotspots' supplement** - full of your hottest family favourites and our best recommendations for summer 2010. Take a look - the family fun starts here!

subheads help direct the flow and bring out key messages

overcome risk barriers

From the moment we arrived to the moment we left, it was outstanding. Staff were brilliant and kid's entertainment was second to none.

Helen Paterson, Aberdeenshire

customer testimonial adds more credibility

good use of P.S to give further details

All inclusives are huge this year! Eat and drink as much as you like without reaching for your wallet! There's nearly 300 to choose from!!

handwritten notes draw the eye in and add a more personal touch

the BIG PICTURE

NEW! Get real honest reviews of your holiday before you book at **thebigpicturedirect.co.uk**

cross-sell other services

Browse or book at directholidays.co.uk or call 0844 800 75 76

strong call to action

terms & conditions demoted to base

personalisation

Exceptional and unusual personalisation sparks a recipient's interest and adds value and relevance to the mailer. The longer you have someone's attention, the more likely they are to buy from you, and personalisation is a great way to achieve that.

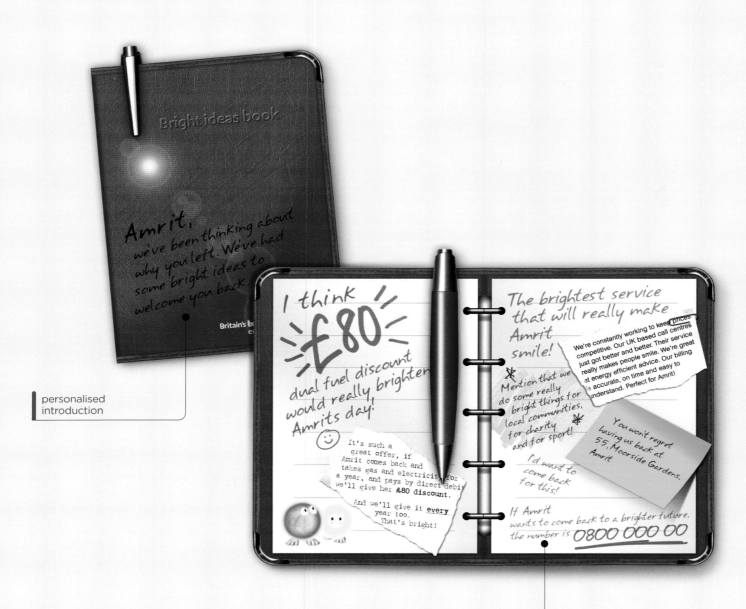

personalised
introduction

very personalised benefit-led
messaging to create real
doormat appeal

personalisation

Personalisation can be expensive, but the opportunities for originality that it offers are almost limitless. Use it well and you'll see great returns.

full colour personalisation
creates a very intergrated
aesthetic feel

customer's
address details

personal feel
to messaging
with chatty
tone of voice

clever use of customer's street name
gives a real sense of individuality

As well as a showcase
for your products,
catalogues persuade
customers to purchase

catalogues

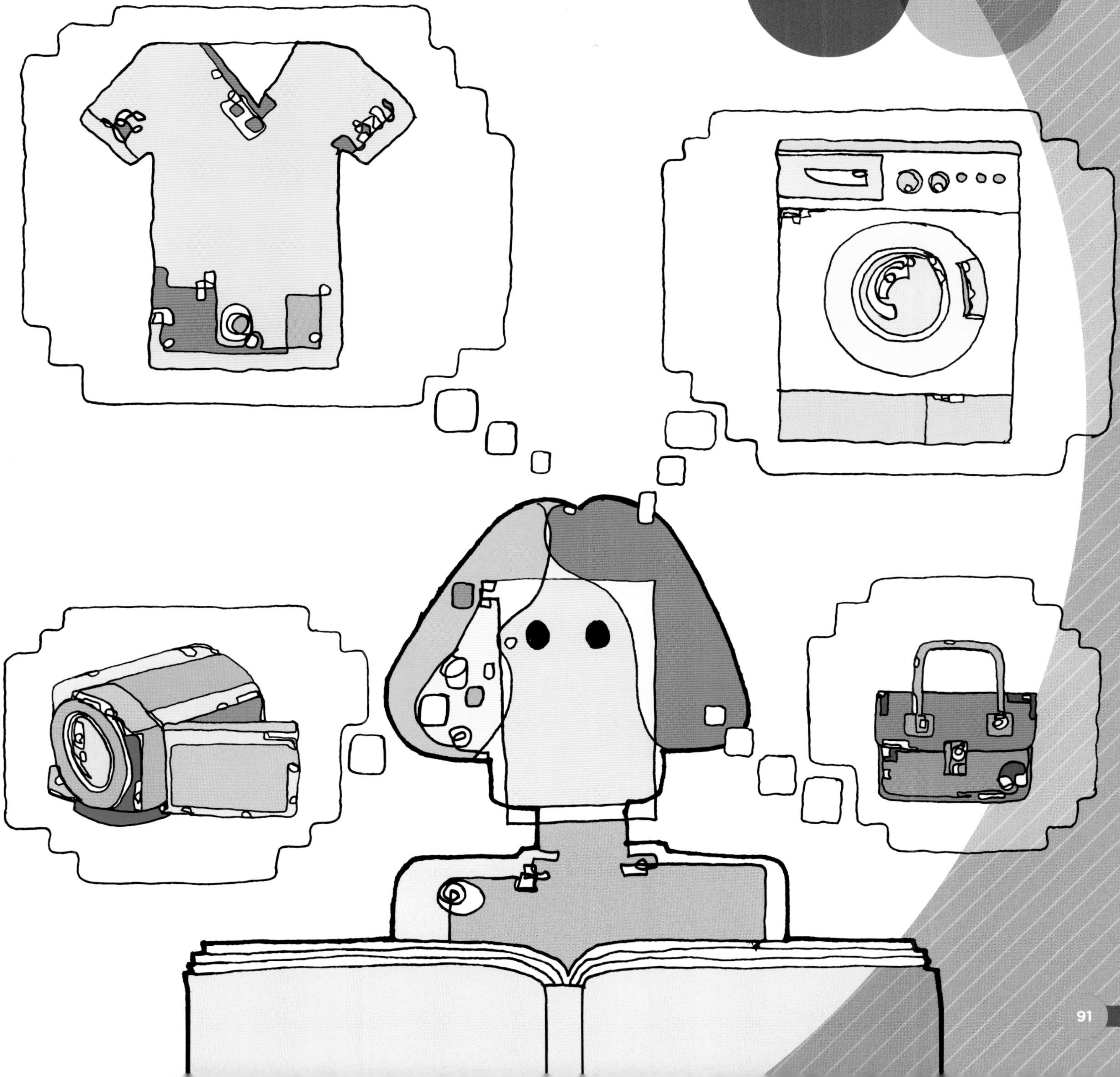

Back in the Golden Age of Print Marketing/ The Dark Ages, before the internet, catalogues were hugely important to direct marketers as they were the only means by which customers could browse through a range of products and make a purchase from the comfort of their own home. As well as simply showcasing products, catalogues also enabled retailers to persuade readers to make a purchase through the use of sales copy and imagery to demonstrate how the products might be used and how they could benefit the reader.

Needless to say, with the proliferation of e-commerce, the unique selling point that catalogues used to have has somewhat diminished, and websites can now offer customers a wider choice of products and can use a range of media, including video and audio, to demonstrate them. However, catalogues are still very important in direct marketing; they simply play a different role and must now be integrated into a broader direct marketing strategy that incorporates a range of offline and online media. A catalogue on its own is increasingly unlikely to be sufficient in producing enough sales to keep a business profitable, but it can be a highly valuable supplement to other marketing activities and can be very effective in bringing in new customers and persuading previous customers to make additional purchases.

Catalogues can also provide the tangible element to a campaign that certain customers will really appreciate. They may, for example, browse a catalogue to find the products that they want and then go online to order from the website. Never underestimate the value of an actual, physical item that customers can hold in their hands; look at how books continue to be the favoured medium for literature despite technology's encroachment into the field.

Before moving onto the body of this chapter we would like to stress that there is one word that you should be constantly returning to when creating a catalogue, and that is **Clarity**. It is extremely important that with all of the beautiful visuals and persuasive copy, readers are still able to identify product sizes, product colour options, prices and so on, with ease.

Customer Acquisition

The long-term success of a catalogue rests upon its ability to generate repeat customers. In time, it will be these customers who will provide the regular, substantial sales revenue that will make for a successful catalogue. However, when producing a new catalogue there will, of course, be no previous customers and, therefore,

convincing people to make their first purchase is the priority Presuming that the initial purchase was a pleasant experience, once a customer has bought from a catalogue, they are far more likely to use it again in the future.

There are several different ways of securing customers. If a company is already generating sales from other media – online, retail outlet, etc. – then they should have, hopefully, developed a database containing the details of people who have bought from them in the past. Although these people have never actually purchased from the catalogue before, the fact that they have bought something from the company shows that they have some interest in what the business sells and it is, therefore, likely that a relatively high proportion of them would consider purchasing something from the catalogue. These customers can also be asked to recommend friends who may be interested in receiving the catalogue, and rewards can be offered if the friend goes on to make a purchase.

We have assembled a quick list of some of some of the alternative methods of collecting data to get you thinking:

Place a Sticker on Every Piece of Packaging with a unique serial number stating that 'someone has won a prize so go online, register your details and see if it is you; even if you don't win, you will still get a voucher for 10% off your next order.'

Leaflets at Point of Sale stating, 'register your details and every month a winner will be drawn at random to win new products' or 'register your details and get 10% off your next purchase.'

Place an offer on Till Receipts to push people online for a special discount off products in that specific store or enter the till receipt number, and the products purchased, online to win a prize. This tact can also be utilised online with confirmation of sale emails or the invoices that accompany products bought online.

Place copy across all marketing literature urging customers to **Register for Regular Email Updates** of new products and offers so that you are always ahead of the game.

Time Sensitive Vouchers for different product ranges can be advertised for download online with customers having to enter their details to claim.

Prize Draw Boxes in-store or online where customers can fill in details to win a prize.

Another source of contacts is rented mailing lists. Mailing lists contain the details of people who have responded to direct marketing promotions in the past – the subject of databases and mailing lists is dealt with in more detail in the **Direct Mail** chapter – and it is possible to find lists focusing on people who have made purchases from comparable catalogues, who are, consequently, more likely to buy

something from the catalogue that you are producing; perhaps even more likely than the people from the website or store databases. These contacts are, therefore, hugely valuable and, although lists such as these can be quite expensive, are often the only way to contact large numbers of people likely to be interested in making a purchase making them indispensible for most new catalogues.

As mentioned above, few businesses rely entirely on catalogues for sales and, as such, will have other avenues which can be exploited for the further distribution of catalogues. For instance, free copies of a catalogue should be made available for people to pick up in-store, and likewise, any affiliated website, email campaign, publications or direct mail should inform visitors about the catalogue and enable them to request a copy. Mobile phones are also a great request vehicle for any catalogue marketer as customers can be urged to text their details to a number to have a catalogue sent out to them.

Finally, although the initial purchase is important, it is the second that indicates repeat custom and just as much effort should, therefore, be applied to generating the second purchase as attaining the first. Once a customer has been captured by the methods above, follow up emails/mailings should be employed in order to urge them to open the catalogue again.

Positioning

In order for a catalogue to be successful it should fill an otherwise neglected space in the marketplace. If a catalogue only does what other, more well-established, catalogues are doing, it is unlikely to attract enough customers to be a success, as people would rather maintain a relationship with a company that they have dealt with previously and whom they know they can trust. If you are going to lure them away you need to create a catalogue that takes a unique approach, and there are a number of different ways to do so.

The most obvious way to do this is to sell different products than those being offered by anyone else by concentrating on niche or specialist areas that are currently being neglected by the main catalogues within the industry. Even if the products in a catalogue are similar to those available elsewhere, all of the positive differences in the product and benefits of the service should be heavily emphasised and compared to the short-comings of the competitors. Failure to do this can result in a situation where the catalogue succeeds in catching people's attention, building their interest and persuading them to want to make a purchase, only for them to go and buy a similar product from a different vendor that they have dealt with before and trust more. By highlighting the uniqueness and superiority of a catalogue's products you leave the customer with nowhere else to go to make their purchase.

Another way to differentiate a catalogue from the competition is through discounts and offers. Of course, if the prices in a catalogue are significantly lower than its competitors' then this will be a good selling point, but this is not an option for most businesses. Instead, you could look at what special offers, payment options, and other inducements you could include that would be affordable and which are not currently available from any of the main competitors. Offering a discount on people's first purchase from the catalogue can be a good idea; this individual sale isn't likely to make a significant profit, but once they have bought something and see that the service provided is swift, efficient and reliable and that the product lives up to their expectations, they will be more likely to become a frequent purchaser. This tact can be very effective in bringing in new customers but it is just as easy to lose them again if the service fails to meet expectations.

There are a range of other incentives that you can offer to customers, and you will have to research what competitors are doing in order to indentify a way to make your offering a little different. This might include favourable payment options, free accessories to go with the products being purchased, and so on.

Hint

Here are a few additional offer ideas that can make all the difference:

Prize Draws are self-explanatory, and can be treated with scepticism by customers, but if one company has a free prize draw with a purchase and a competitor doesn't then why wouldn't a customer favour the former.

Order Builders such as money off any order over a specific amount or 'get your 5th product free' work really well to increase the value of a customer once they have already decided to make a purchase.

A **Money Off Next Order** offer is a great way to bring customers back after their first purchase.

Affinity Deals where companies team up to provide offers that include one another's products – for instance, an airline might offer a discount on a stay at a specific hotel chain that they have partnered up with – provide relevant and timely customer targets.

Once the competitor research is completed, it is also worth doing plenty of consumer research and testing to ensure that any gaps found are actually worth stepping into. Testing of positioning equates to live customer research and should be used at every opportunity to ensure that the company's direction is a reflection of consumer expectation and need – for more detail on this topic, look to our **Testing** chapter.

Another option is to highlight the quality of the service provided. Fast delivery times, a means for customers to track the progress of their orders and the ability to place orders via a number of different media – by web or phone – are all fairly standard and should be included and emphasised in a catalogue campaign. The trick is to be better, stronger, and faster than the opposition and make sure that every customer is made aware of where the company shines.

As well as the product and the offer, the catalogue can also be set apart from the competition in terms of branding and the presentation of the catalogue itself. This is obviously a less significant selling-point than offering a lower price or superior product, but people's perception of a brand can make a significant impact on their buying choices. If you can design a catalogue in such a way that it portrays a company as being more innovative, sophisticated, trendy and/or fun than the competition, then this can make customers more inclined to purchase from that catalogue even if the actual offer is no better than that of the competition – refer to our **Brand** chapter to find out how to do this.

Organisation

A well-organised catalogue will enable people to quickly and easily find specific products that they are looking for and will group different products effectively so that similar or complementary products are positioned close to one another. Firstly, a clear contents section – usually placed on the right-hand side of the first spread – is fundamental as it is the initial step in most readers' search processes. You will usually want to divide the catalogue into different sections, each focusing on a different category with each category colour-coded to make navigation as simple as possible. Although the division of products is dependent on the product range, it is important to put the products into groups in such a way that if a person is interested in buying one item, other relevant items that could also appeal are in close proximity. This is a standard and logical way to order the catalogue that will make items easier to find whilst also encouraging customers to consider additional purchases by presenting them with related products. It is near impossible, however, to place every related product next to, or even near, one another. The answer to this, is to use **Cross-Sell Messaging**, where the location of related products are clearly signposted to remind people that if they are buying a TV from the electronics section, that they might also want to buy the stand for it from the furniture section. The images of products can also be used to pair items so, for example, the images for both the TV and the stand would include each of the other products, with the TV and stand looking so good together that customers looking at the TV cannot help but follow your directions to the furniture section and vice versa.

Hint
Although obvious, it is worth mentioning that, throughout this whole process, you must always be aware of the most popular products in a catalogue and grant them the most prominent spots throughout. This is referred to as Hero Positioning and is very important for the marketing of products that are very popular and/or will make the most money.

Grouping Products

There are different ways of grouping products. If a catalogue is, for example, selling furniture, you could choose to group all of the different types of furniture together into separate sections – chairs, tables, beds, sofas, etc. This provides a very easy process, both for compiling the catalogue and for the customer's search if he or she knows the specific product that they are looking for. Alternatively, you could group them according to what type of room they would be appropriate for; for example adult bedroom, children's bedroom, dining room, etc. This option would probably be more helpful to customers though it would possibly create problems regarding products that would be appropriate for more than one section which may require you to list some items more than once in different sections. As with the popular products, you should aim to put the most popular sections of the catalogue in prominent places; i.e. towards the front.

Design

In our first year of trading, one of our clients was an upmarket French fashion magazine called **Le Club** which wanted to make inroads into the UK. In a seemingly logical step, they decided to emulate the design of one of the most popular catalogues trading at the time: the **Avon** catalogue. The problem was that, although the products and offers were great, the Avon format provided customers with the wrong visual cues for an exclusive, expensive fashion range, making it difficult for them to understand and buy in to the brand. As such, the catalogue severely underperformed.

The lesson here is that design plays a huge role in marketing and that throughout every feature of a catalogue, it is imperative to stay on brand and not give in to the temptation to imitate other successful brands. Every aspect should reflect the brand's ideals, vision and personality – for more detail, see the **Brand** chapter – so that all marketing literature come together to present a cohesive and unmistakable brand persona, for customers to relate with. One of the features where this is most evident is in the choice of colour scheme. It should be consistent with the colours used elsewhere such as on the brand's website or direct mail correspondence, so that people will immediately associate the catalogue with that brand. However, this focus on brand should not be at the detriment of the appearance and legibility of the catalogue. For instance, you should always make sure that you use a light-coloured background behind product photographs so that they stand out as much as possible and grab the attention of the reader.

Coffee Table Value

Magazines have a readership of many more than the original purchaser as they are often left lying around the house – probably on the coffee table – where they can be picked up and read by others. To instil catalogues with some of this Coffee Table Value, lifestyle elements such as hints and tips, more editorials and attractive photography should be included so that the catalogue becomes more suitable as a decoration and more eye-catching for the non-purchasers. The inclusion of celebrities in a catalogue will also make them far more like a magazine and imbue it with added coffee table value.

Front Cover

Generally speaking, people are often pleased to receive a catalogue in the post and are likely to, at least, glance through it in search of bargains. Furthermore, some people will have specifically asked to receive one. As such, it is less of a challenge to pique people's interest with a catalogue than is the case with other media such as direct mail. Nevertheless, a catalogue that has an attractive, eye-catching cover, that encourages recipients to explore further into the catalogue, is likely to out-perform those that appear dull or technical. As well as including photography or other imagery that is attractive and catches the attention of the reader, the primary objective of the cover should be to explain clearly and unambiguously what type of products are featured inside. This is especially important for new catalogues that people won't be familiar with. You could include a short sentence summarising the general type of products in the catalogue – for example, 'Sportswear for all the family' – and you could supplement this with a list of some of the most popular items available.

I keep **catalogues** on my table for weeks and **weeks**

Sometimes, purely stating the products for sale will not be sufficient; people need a reason to open the catalogue and to provide this, you need to bring their attention to one or more of the main benefits that it provides, such as superior customer service, special discounts or exclusive products. As well as encouraging people to open the catalogue and explore what's inside, the cover could, and usually should, feature a selection of popular products. Experience tells us that a product will receive many times more sales if it is included on the cover of the catalogue so you should certainly consider using this valuable space for a small number of products – perhaps only two or three – that are likely to be of most interest to customers and which are particularly profitable. This also serves the purpose of effectively demonstrating the type of products that the rest of the catalogue is likely to contain.

Hint

Many catalogue front covers include a picture of a person, or group of people, thoroughly enjoying its products, or looking rather fetching because of them. When doing this, it is usually best to make sure that the eyes are all facing the camera to entice the reader.

The front cover is also the place where you can commence efforts to call the reader to action. Clear CTAs should be interspersed in prominent positions throughout the catalogue, and you should start by placing one on the front cover so that pertinent information can be found with ease. It is easy to forget about such small details when putting together a beautiful, eye-catching cover, but features such as the season and date should always be found somewhere on the cover. Another good idea is to put a **Banner** around the cover. This is likely to draw the reader's eye and bring their attention to an exciting new product, a special discount, or some other key benefit associated with the catalogue.

Gloss

The Banner is a small piece of card that wraps around the catalogue and contains a message.

Page Layout

An attractive design that complements brand image and enables products to be presented in a compelling and easy-to-follow manner will have a significant positive impact on the success of a catalogue, and one of the key design factors to consider is the page layout. The chief concern to consider is the inevitable trade-off between trying to include as many products as possible while, at the same time, giving enough space to each product to allow for sufficient imagery and copy to explain and demonstrate the product; we call this the **Sell and Tell Equilibrium**. At the same time, you will want to vary the amount of space dedicated to a product dependent on its popularity and profitability; it can also be a good idea to give pride of place to new products

Products can be displayed in a standardised grid format in which, for example, each page features a set number of items with a small photograph of each, together with a few bullet-points explaining its key details. This has the advantage of being easy for the reader to follow and understand, though it can often look quite dull and technical and often doesn't leave sufficient room for any truly persuasive sales copy. As an alternative, you could use a more relaxed layout with greater variety in how products are presented. So, for example, you could have a number of pages featuring a lot of different products, while dedicating a whole page, or even a double-spread to a particularly important item. You could also have several different products featured in a single photograph rather than having regimented rows of small individual photographs. This free-form layout allows for greater flexibility and makes it easier to drive more focus to particular products. It can also aid in breaking up the pace of a catalogue so that the reader does not become fatigued by repetitive layouts. However, if it is not executed effectively, these unregimented layouts can sometimes make it more difficult for readers to find what they are looking for. Whichever way you decide to approach layout, we cannot stress enough how important it is to always remember to continue to place call-to-actions throughout.

Imagery

After the layout, the imagery is probably the most important design feature of a catalogue. Images allow you to show-off products in the best possible light and, if necessary, demonstrate how the products are used. One of the main concerns that people often have about buying from catalogues is that they are detached from the physical object; unable to see or touch an item in the same way they could if they were to browse in a shop. For this reason, you need to provide imagery of a sufficiently high quality, that people feel that they know almost exactly how the real product will look and feel once they receive it. Consequently, it is almost always best to use photography rather than illustrations except, perhaps, for demonstrating how a product is used. However, there is a difference between showing how to use a product and showing a product being used. The latter is definitely a subject for photography and is a potent marketing technique for crossing the divide that exists between the reader and the actual product rather than a glossy picture of it. This is best demonstrated by clothing catalogues where a photo of a dress sported by an attractive model is bound to look much more appealing than one of the dress by itself.

There may be certain instances where no imagery is necessary; for example, if you are selling copper wire to construction firms, you may only need to include the specifications of the different types of wire available, making photographs superfluous and an unnecessary extra cost which would serve only to take up space that could be used for something more useful. With most briefs, a company will supply a selection of imagery guidelines with which to conform. This is usually in order to make sure that the integrity of the brand is maintained and will, therefore, include directives concerning the use of a brand logo or colour palette. For example, when working with **Boots, outside the box** was presented with a simple sentence, 'We are the Nation's chemist', which we had to make sure that our campaign corresponded with. Based on the words 'nation' and 'chemist' we concluded that the imagery would have to be clean, prescriptive and inclusive.

Here are a few generic imagery guidelines that it is always worth taking into account when adding imagery to a catalogue:

- Don't crop off heads
- Show entire products
- Highlight key features and benefits
- Intersperse with lifestyle imagery
- Bring the product to life and enhance it
- Make it aspirational
- Include close-ups
- Maintain colour accuracy as it is essential for certain products such as make-up and clothing.

Other Design Features

The typography should be carefully selected so that it is attractive, easy-to-read and in-keeping with brand personality. Text should usually be organised in columns with a reasonable width as any that are too wide are likely to make it difficult for the reader to keep their place on the page. A justified text alignment will make a page appear tidier and more symmetrical and will give it a sleek and professional impression.

The size of the text is also important. If it is too small, people will be less inclined to read it and it may be completely incomprehensible for those with poor eyesight. At the same time, if the text is smaller, you will be able to include more sales copy in the catalogue, thereby providing more opportunity to persuade people to make a purchase. Other text based elements of a page, such as section headers, page numbers, pricing and product codes should also be bold and clear, leaving the reader with no chance to mistake a **5** for a **6** or a **6** for an **8**, for example.

Hint
Remember that prices should always be presented with any related discounts so that customers don't have to make connections between offers and the products that they apply to or apply any mathematical effort to ascertain the post-discount price.

Although space is often at a premium when putting a catalogue together, there will be instances where the layout produces areas of unwanted emptiness. In these cases you can use **Space Fillers** to occupy the void, making a page look better and providing the reader with valuable information and sales copy.

Here are a few examples of space fillers to get you started:

- Testimonials
- Returns Policy
- Call-to-actions
- Reminder of Offers
- Hints and Tips
- Usage and Ideas
- Cross-Sell Copy
- Key Benefits
- Key Product Features
- Warranties and Guarantees

An effective catalogue should be distinctive, and there are a number of design techniques that can be employed to introduce an individual character to a catalogue. If possible, you could include product samples, allowing the readers to test the quality of the product before making a purchase. This can have another positive effect, in that the product sample can serve to remind a potential customer of the catalogue and company from its position in the home. The fact that the catalogue contains something three-dimensional, will also make it more interesting and more likely to demand attention. Another classic technique is to include a last-minute special offer, usually an insert placed inside the catalogue containing details of an extra discount or incentive if the reader acts immediately.

Copy

The purpose of a catalogue is to sell products, and the copy is an important tool in persuading them to do so. Despite this rather obvious fact, many catalogues continue to provide only the details of the product, while making little or no effort to highlight the benefits to the customer or to explicitly encourage them to make a purchase. This may be fine for somebody who knows that they need a specific item and knows that they definitely want to buy it from a specific catalogue. However, if a catalogue is going to appeal to the as yet unconvinced, the positive features of the company and its products need to be explained. Needless to say, the product specifications still need to be included and the copy for each item should never be too long so as to bore the customer or occupy too much space but, nevertheless, by adding some concise, relevant and compelling copy for some, or all, products, you can see a dramatic increase in sales.

In addition, the aforementioned detachment between customer and product – where a customer has to rely on pictures rather than the item itself – is not only an issue that has to be considered when approaching imagery, but should also be addressed by good copy, explaining how a product feels, sounds, smells or tastes, appropriately; 'our range of chocolates have an intense, dark flavour, with a fantastically smooth mouth-feel', for example.

With regards to tone of voice, it should be conversational rather than dry and technical while, at the same time, avoiding any long-winded, superfluous descriptions. The aim should be for short and snappy sentences explaining, in simple language, all of the advantageous elements of each product and the direct positive impact that it is likely to have on the customer's life.

While highlighting all of the great things about the products, you should try to make sure that your copy retains credibility. If your sales rhetoric is over-hyped or over-egged, then readers are going to assume - perhaps correctly - that any offers are too good to be true and that you must be, at best, exaggerating or, at worst, lying to them. Your copy should, of course, never contain any false claims about any product and, although you can omit some of the negatives about certain products, you should always ensure that the claims that you make about the benefits of offers are entirely truthful as exaggeration can deter savvy customers from purchasing and can lead to legal difficulties.

Given that customers clearly value sincerity, demonstrating this characteristic is paramount to a successful catalogue campaign. A great way to do this is to give reasons that explain how the company is able to make great offers. Stating that a particular item is overstocked and, therefore, able to have a particularly generous discount applied to it, provides the basis for an offer and, in doing so, reassures customers that the offer is not too good to be true; this is part of the reason why closing down sales tend to do so well.

The dedication of certain sections of a catalogue to articles that are not directly focused on convincing the reader to make a sale can also make an impact. For example, if you are writing copy for a business-to-business catalogue you could include a selection of pages that offer advice on common problems relating to the industry, or if the catalogue sells fun products such as toys or games you could include an occasional joke, puzzle, or funny story. In fact, a sense of humour and fun can find its place in most catalogues in order to make them more interesting, enjoyable to read, and coffee table friendly; remember the more time customers spend reading a catalogue the more likely they are to ultimately make a purchase.

A letter from one of the senior figures of the company, positioned towards the front of the catalogue – perhaps on the inside cover – makes for an engaging start to a reader's experience. This can be used to introduce the catalogue and is an ideal space for the explanation of some of its positive aspects, while addressing possible concerns that a reader might have. This should contain an explanation of the types of products featured in the catalogue and the key reasons for the reader to place an order, as well as providing basic information on the placing of orders, the returning of goods, and so on.

Hint
In the body of the catalogue, headers should, of course, be used for the name of each product, and given that the headers are likely to attract the most attention from the reader, they may also be used to state a key benefit — for example, 'The new, fastest-ever computer'.

In addition to the sales copy, catalogues should also contain all of the necessary details regarding terms and conditions, rules regarding returns, all of the different payment and credit options, the full details of any special offers or incentives, and any guarantees or warranties available. A clear explanation of how quickly the customer can expect to receive their items and how they will be delivered – first class, special delivery, etc. Much of this information is inevitably dry and unexciting, but if a company has any particularly favourable policies regarding any of the above topics, this provides an opportunity for these to be emphasised. For example, if they can ensure faster or cheaper delivery than their competitors then you should highlight these elements as evidence of superior customer service, and explain the relevant benefits to the consumer – 'thanks to our unique next-day delivery service you can start enjoying your new xxx tomorrow!' In addition, it is always worth stating that customers can return any products that they are not satisfied with for a full refund. This service is a legal obligation, so it may as well be used as a selling point.

Order Form

The order form should not be a bland after-thought. It should include every technique learned from direct marketing and stand by itself as a piece of marketing literature. This means making sure that the form is attractive, involves plenty of call-to-actions and contains all terms and conditions.

Very often customers want to look through the catalogue...

...but then buy online or instore

Ease of use is an important factor when it comes to ordering. A purchase is often an impulsive action and any obstacles or difficulties present in the ordering process allows time for the customer to rethink their decision; even if only a small percentage of customers decide to abandon their purchase, that is still revenue that has been needlessly lost. The only time that a customer should pause while ordering is when they see your ingeniously placed advert for a product that should be added to their order. To make the process a more stream-lined experience, the customer details – Name, Customer Number, Address, Telephone and Email – should be prepopulated if possible. It is also worth including an example order, so that customers can be left in no doubt about how to fill out the form.

The form also needs to make it easy for the order to be processed so be sure to include all of the following so that a customer's purchase speeds through the system and is in their hands as quickly as possible:

- Item Code
- Description
- Size
- Colour
- Quantity
- Unit Price
- Total Price

Another feature that can make things easy for the customer, is perforating the form so that it can be detached from the catalogue without much trouble and without making other pages fall out. It is a sign of a sub-par catalogue when an order form must be either ripped or cut out, causing the page to which it is attached to come loose.

Hint
It is a good idea to make the order form out of a good quality material so that it is easily distinguishable from the rest of the catalogue, and is durable enough to survive outside of it.

The order form is a great opportunity to garner more sales and one way of doing this is to place a selection of hero products on the form – or in the catalogue near the form – as a last-ditch prompt for customers to snap something up at the last minute; we stole this idea from the terribly tempting chocolates that they put at checkouts in supermarkets. Details of any special offers should also be built into the form in case a customer has missed all mentions of them in the catalogue proper. Time sensitive vouchers are often a profitable inclusion near the order form. Date them throughout the length of the catalogue's lifespan, covering different product ranges and ideally tailored to any customer

segmentation being utilised; this can help with increasing product penetration as well as profitability and frequency levels. Not only can you use the order form to gain more sales, but it is also a good idea to utilise it to glean extra customer information that might be useful in the future, with a few well placed questions, but remember to keep it straightforward and painless.

Finally, people often use an order form to log details of an order with no intention to post it, so put the other order options – website and phone – on the form. It may seem like a waste to have a beautifully produced order form used as a glorified post-it note, but postal orders tend to cost a lot more than the online or telephone counterparts, so it is an excellent practice to promote.

Have you followed all of our order form guidelines? Well now it's time to replicate the form a number of times so that each catalogue has multiple copies, as a catalogue will usually have a wider shelf life than the initial order.

Downloadable and Online Catalogues

At the beginning of this chapter, we claimed that the power of the catalogue lies in its tangibility; that an online campaign can be bolstered by a physical piece of literature that can be casually flicked through without turning on a computer. While this is definitely the case, a catalogue's charm has been shown to extend beyond being able to actually touch it. The proof: online and downloadable catalogues.

Catalogues can usually be downloaded as pdf. files to be viewed on applications such as **Adobe Reader**, while certain software makes things even simpler for the reader by allowing brochures and catalogues to be placed on a website and viewed in its own window. These online catalogues can be flicked through in a very natural way, by using a touch screen or the mouse to click and drag a page corner to turn to the next page.

Having an online catalogue option is a great way to widen the scope of a customer's experience and present the company as contemporary and tech savvy. They also cost a fraction of the print and postage of an actual catalogue, making them a very smart inclusion in a business's campaign.

Direct TV

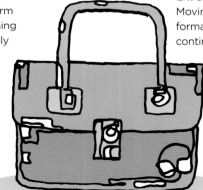

Moving even further away from the traditional paper format of the catalogue, brings us to a media, which continues to make large profits and spread into more markets and, as such, manages to resist, and in many cases, completely buck the trend for non-web cataloguing having to take a secondary, supporting role in marketing: **Direct TV**. Direct TV — **DRTV** — also known as **Home Shopping**, has many of the characteristics of a catalogue, such as displaying a large number of products segmented into categories, and not requiring the customer to leave the house, and is best illustrated by channels such as **QVC** or **bid TV**. DRTV is, essentially, a live presentation of products, usually broadcast on specialised television channels.

Now it may appear that we are moving away from our remit at this point as we are a direct marketing agency, specialising in focused, targeted marketing, and this book is supposed to follow suit, denouncing the broadcast and extolling the narrowcast, yet we are including a televisual, broadcast medium. However, with digital TV, the large number of channels available to the consumer has allowed DRTV to become a self selecting medium where the only audience accessing its content are those for whom it is relevant and who are, therefore, likely to make a purchase; in essence, the consumer chooses to accept the marketing, making it just as direct a medium as websites.

The key to Direct TV's efficacy is that each product is displayed, demonstrated and sold by a human being. Not only are the public far more receptive to buying from a real person, but the presenters of these programmes are usually highly charismatic personalities who viewers can quickly learn to trust. In short, people sell better than paper, so the ability to put faces and personalities next to products can provide a huge boost to sales.
Another of Direct TV's strengths is the high level of immediacy that broadcasting live allows. Offers can be promoted as literally last minute rather than the days, weeks or months that other direct marketing demands. Offers can also be presented as limited with a live counter to demonstrate just how few opportunities there are left to buy. All of this immediacy leads to one of the most valuable assets in the marketing world: **Urgency**. Urgency encourages the customer to make their purchase quickly, rather than checking competitor prices or postponing it only to forget their intentions to buy. By combining the urgency and trust that Direct TV breeds, marketers can find themselves in the possession of a powerfully persuasive medium.

There is, of course, a certain amount of stigma attached to selling products through Direct TV, mostly due to the caricaturish representation of 'The Bored Housewife', as their only audience. Whether this stigma has been fairly earned or not, the medium is taking great strides into new markets, while retaining the sizeable 'housewife' market. Direct TV is, in fact, something of a misnomer as television is not the only viable platform; it can also have an online presence through live streaming video. Companies such as **Thomas Cook** and **JML** may have established their own channels on the TV, but there is just as much opportunity to create a successful online channel at a fraction of the cost. There are a large number of brands for whom the traditional format and reputation of DRTV doesn't fit and these brands are unlikely to consider investing in the medium but we believe that with a bit of retooling and a focus on consumer behaviour, DRTV can be appropriated for almost any business with a catalogue of products.

There is nothing stopping DRTV from becoming as natural a buying platform for the masses as e-commerce websites.

DIY DRTV

As DRTV is, essentially, a catalogue in a live video format, many of the fundamentals for creating a successful catalogue also apply. For instance, there needs to be a good balance of 'Tell and Sell'; plenty of prominent call-to-actions; and products need to be categorised and ordered in a logical way, with associated products clearly linked and the best and most profitable products placed in the best positions.

Once these basics have been dealt with, you will need to consider the specifics of the DRTV medium. The first major consideration with DRTV is positioning; whether you will simply use one of the existing channels to sell the product, or start an entirely new channel on the TV or online. Utilising an established channel removes a large amount of the hassle inherent in setting up a new one and there are a good range of channels to choose from. The downside of this approach, however, is the lack of control that you will have on how a product is presented and the amount of time that can be dedicated to it. This is, by far, the safer route, but it seriously limits your freedom to be creative and utilise the medium in an original way. Creating a new channel will allow you to tailor the format and the content so that, if the target audience are trendy 25-35 year olds, everything about the channel – style, presenter, time of broadcast – is optimised to appeal to that demographic. The most logical place for most brands/companies to establish a DRTV presence is online through a streaming service which can then be linked to or embedded on the brand/company's website. Users of the website can then see the products that they are browsing on the site, demonstrated live, with great last minute offers that they can take advantage of.

> ### Hint
> An interesting aspect of DRTV that you should look to take advantage of is the tendency for its viewers to watch it while doing something else. If you can manage to perform a balancing act of creating content which is inoffensive enough to not be too distracting, while being able to catch the multitaskers' attentions at the right time, then you could find that people stay tuned into the channel for remarkable lengths of time.

The most important considerations for a new DRTV channel are, as described above, to broadcast live and have a good presenter and crew. Deals are perceived as far better when presented dynamically in real time and, although streaming or broadcasting live comes with an obvious series of issues, the benefits more than compensate for them. In fact, if you get a good presenter who can think on their feet and has plenty of charisma and a crew who can quickly and calmly deal with any technical difficulties, then most of the live issues should no longer pose a problem.

CROSS MEDIA

Eye Tracking and Hot Spots

When the average person looks at a page their eyes are automatically drawn to certain elements and will move between them in a predictable pattern. Marketers often apply this knowledge to their catalogue page layouts in order to highlight specific products and encourage specific behaviour from the customer. Although this is predominantly employed in print media, it can be just as useful for any medium that is in any way visual.

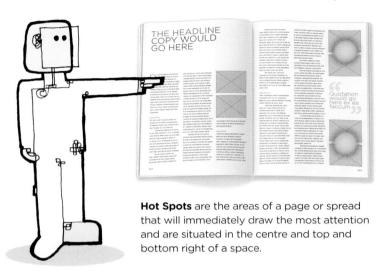

Hot Spots are the areas of a page or spread that will immediately draw the most attention and are situated in the centre and top and bottom right of a space.

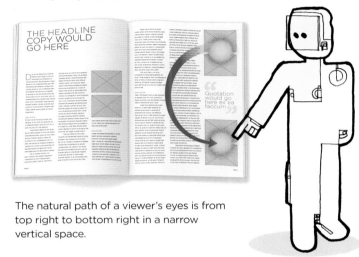

The natural path of a viewer's eyes is from top right to bottom right in a narrow vertical space.

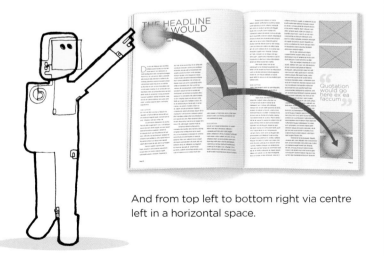

And from top left to bottom right via centre left in a horizontal space.

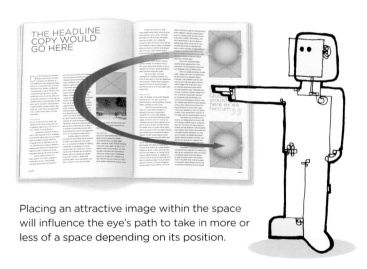

Placing an attractive image within the space will influence the eye's path to take in more or less of a space depending on its position.

Whether you are making a website, email, mailer, presentation, or even a video, strategic positioning can have a great impact on what is seen and what goes unnoticed so use it to your advantage.

section intro & product spreads

A catalogue's strength lies in its physicality — in the fact that it can be picked up and flicked through — so make it bold and interesting to really engage with the reader.

strong, eyes to camera image
use of key product in range

clear
pagination

quotes from fans
add personality

contents by section
is very useful

clear section
labelling

good use of
hero product

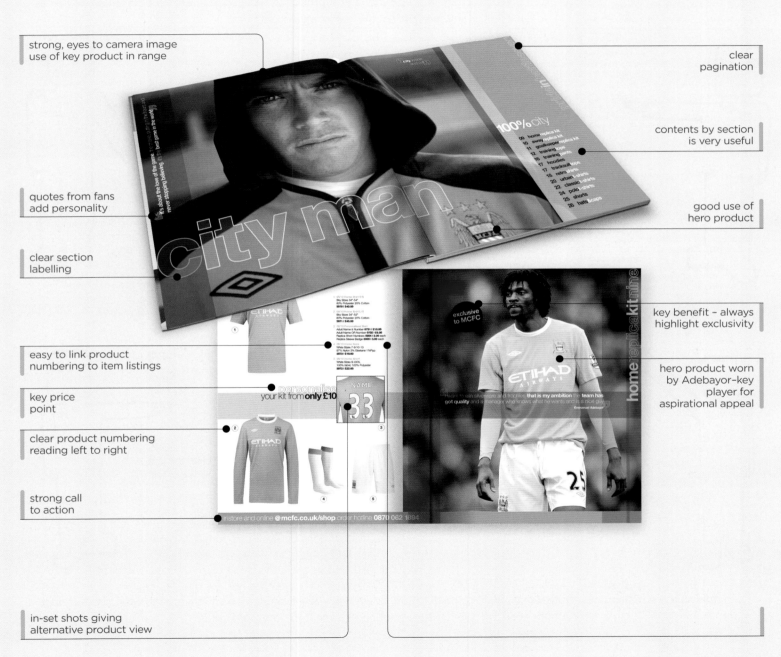

easy to link product
numbering to item listings

key benefit – always
highlight exclusivity

key price
point

hero product worn
by Adebayor–key
player for
aspirational appeal

clear product numbering
reading left to right

strong call
to action

in-set shots giving
alternative product view

all key ordering
information included

order form

The importance of the order form cannot be stressed enough. Make it simple, clear and don't forget to mention offers, discounts and any products that the customer may have forgotten they wanted to take advantage of.

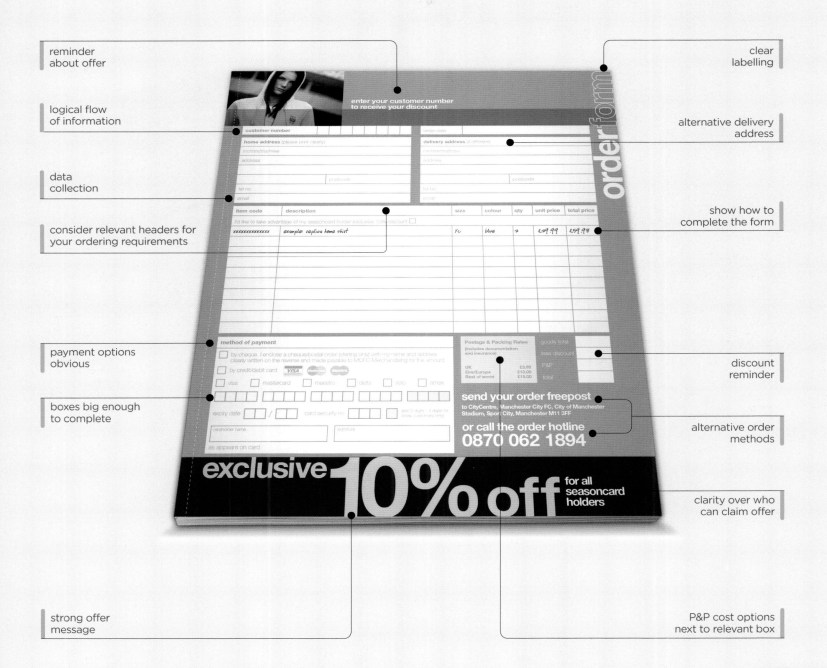

reminder
about offer

logical flow
of information

data
collection

consider relevant headers for
your ordering requirements

payment options
obvious

boxes big enough
to complete

strong offer
message

clear
labelling

alternative delivery
address

show how to
complete the form

discount
reminder

alternative order
methods

clarity over who
can claim offer

P&P cost options
next to relevant box

innovative brochure

To instil a catalogue with coffee table value, you need great imagery and interesting copy. A lot of people keep catalogues, and you want yours to be in pride of place, in full view, on the coffee table.

balanced with
strong benefits

quirky copy

fun imagery but
aspirational and
reminiscent of holidays

magazine feel

testimonials for credibility

strong welcome message sets the scene

key differentiator

clear navigation

aspirational images

"Welcome to our new Hotspots brochure, our collection of YOUR favourite hotels**"**

We had the greatest holiday you could have, but then again we always go with direct holidays and always have a fab time!
Mrs. Sherwood, Kent.

"As Arnie the terminator once said... – We'll be back!" – Mr. Williams, Staffordshire.

"This holiday was amazing, I'd go back in a heartbeat"

NO hidden extras

With Direct Holidays you'll get everything you expect from a holiday included as standard unlike some other Tour Operators...

✓ in-flight meals
✓ an extra 5kg luggage allowance
✓ transfers in resort
✓ dedicated rep service

and we even include 10kgs for little ones under 2

...all this for a low Deposit! †

† Not available on late bookings

Your sizzling hot favourites and top Summer Scorchers

£100 Off every booking **GUARANTEED***

OR

FREE KIDS holidays*

PLUS

✓ **3 FREE Nights** on selected 14 night holidays**

✓ ...and to top it all off we'll also give you **£50 OFF** your next holiday with us departing 1st November 2010 – 30 April 2011

*Please see pages 42-43 for Terms and Conditions.
** At selected properties. Please see pages 42-43 for full Terms and Conditions

Visit our new-look website at www.direct-holidays.co.uk

Find out more about your favourite hotels and apartments in our fantastic new brochures

Find your perfect holiday hotspot

Kenya	6
Maldives	6
Caribbean	7-12
Florida & Las Vegas	12-13
Balearics	13-16
Mainland Spain	17-19
Canaries	19-24
Algarve	24-25
Bulgaria	25
Tunisia	26
Egypt	27-28
Cyprus	29-30
Greece	31-37
Turkey	38-41

DIRECT HOLIDAYS

directholidays.co.uk

happy holidays with no hidden extras **– that's the direct effect!**

benefits summary

interesting asides

show calls to action graphically

cross-sell messaging

strong offers

email marketing

One of the most widely used applications on the web

Email is an ideal medium for direct marketing and can be used, to some extent, by almost all businesses. The advantages of email marketing are clear and substantial: Email is increasingly widespread; is one of the most widely used applications on the internet; the costs of producing and distributing email are considerably lower than print media; personalisation is comparatively easy; and email has a faster production lead time and an instantaneous response mechanism which facilitates impulsive responses. In addition, measuring and testing the effectiveness of an email campaign is quick and easy, allowing for improvements to be made to increase the quantity and quality of respondents. For these reasons email marketing can be very lucrative. However, there are many common mistakes in email marketing and an unsophisticated campaign will, at best, be ignored and, at worst, alienate customers and damage brand.

While there are, of course, many principles that can be appropriated from traditional marketing methods, you should be aware that email is a distinct medium with its own particular rules. The design of an email has to account for preview planes and download times; factors that don't have to be considered when designing a direct mail campaign. Similarly, you can't simply apply the principles of web design to email marketing as, for example, making someone click a link on an email is very different from trying to persuade someone to buy something once they have visited the website.

Capturing email addresses

The first stage in creating an email marketing campaign is to compile a list of email addresses. This can often be a slow process, yet there are some simple and effective techniques that can be used to help in the development of a permission-based email list with large numbers of high quality contacts. Keep in mind that customers are likely to be receiving large numbers of emails every day and will be reluctant to sign-up to yet another email list. You should, therefore, explain clearly the benefits of subscribing to the email and consider offering an immediate incentive to encourage them to do so.

Website

The most common place to gather email addresses is through a website and there are a variety of means that you can utilise, either individually or combined, to effectively capture addresses.

Data Capture Boxes

The advantage of **Data Capture Boxes** is that they allow users to enter their details without having to transfer through to a different page. This encourages impulsive decisions to sign-up. They commonly comprise a single box asking for an email address, but you may want to include several different boxes asking for additional information that will allow for greater personalisation of emails.

Buttons

Buttons are graphic representations of links that take users to a separate sign-up form. They come in a variety of different shapes – and you may want to experiment with some creative graphics – but often they will take the form of a simple text-box in the sidebar, allowing users to access the link at any time and on any page of a website. The advantage of buttons over data capture boxes is that they can link to a more detailed form, allowing you to capture more information.

Text links

Text Links are small sections of text linked to a separate form, allowing the option of subscribing within the context of other information. This is a useful tool for highlighting the benefits to the user of signing up to the email list; while talking about any particular aspect of a company, you can highlight the fact that the user will have access to more information/offers relating to that aspect by signing up to the email list, and then include an appropriate text link.

Check boxes

When customers are engaging or transacting online, you can make it compulsory for them to provide an email address in order to complete the purchase. In this case you should include a **Check Box** allowing them to indicate whether they wish to be contacted by the company in the future.

Other Online Opportunities

While websites are usually the main vehicle for capturing email addresses, you should make use of any other contact with potential or existing customers to encourage them to subscribe. Online advertising, third-party websites, online directories, and email signatures can all be used for sign-up links. It is also a good idea to allow – and urge – recipients to share emails with friends, and this is easily achieved through the inclusion of a link button that will take them to a landing page with a form for them to add friends' email addresses to. Make sure that you provide a good reason for the recipient to do this, either through an incentive, or by having content that people cannot help but share.

Offline Alternatives

Traditional marketing methods can also be used to help build an email list. It may be productive to include the sign-up information on business cards, direct mail, and any other print or broadcast advertising in which the company is engaged – never miss an opportunity to encourage subscriptions.

Permissions

Data capture legislation is a sensitive business and you can get in a lot of trouble if emails are sent to individuals who have not given permission for their email addresses to be used. The following is **outside the box's** e-marketing policy that we require our clients to agree to before we can send emails for them. If you follow these then you should stay on the right side of data capture laws.

· ·

What kind of email addresses are OK to send to with outside the box? To send emails to anyone using **outside the box**, you must have **clearly obtained their permission.** This could be done through:

- An email newsletter **subscribe form** on your website.

- An opt-in checkbox on a form. This checkbox must not be checked by default, the person completing the form **must willingly select** the checkbox to indicate they want to hear from you.

- If someone **completes an offline form** like a survey or enters a competition, you can only contact them if it was explained to them that they would be contacted by email AND they ticked a box indicating they would like to be contacted.

- Customers who have purchased from you **within the last 2 years.**

- If someone **gives you their business card** and you have explained to them that you will be in touch by email, you can contact them. If they dropped their business card in a fishbowl at a trade show, there must be a sign indicating they will be contacted by email.

· ·

Basically, you can only ever email anyone who has clearly given you permission to email them specifically about the subject you're contacting them about.

Less is **more**

What kind of email addresses ARE NOT OK to send to with outside the box? Anything outside the examples above doesn't equal permission in our eyes, but here are some examples to make sure that we are crystal clear. By using **outside the box**, you agree not to import or send to any email address which:

● You **do not have explicit, provable permission** to contact in relation to the topic of the email that you are sending.

● You bought, loaned, rented or in any way acquired **from a third party,** no matter what they claim about quality or permission. You need to obtain permission yourself.

● You **haven't contacted via email in the last 2 years.** Permission doesn't age well and these people may have either changed email address or won't remember giving their permission in the first place.

● You **scraped or copy and pasted** from the web. Just because people publish their email address doesn't mean that they want to hear from you.

Sure, some of these people might have given you their email address, but what's missing is your permission to email them commercial messages. Sending promotional emails to any of these people won't be effective and will more than likely see your email marked as spam by many of your recipients.

Email Content
The Sender
If subscribers are going to open emails, they have to recognise and trust who is sending it, and for this reason, the sender name and address is very important. You should use a sender name that will be easily recognisable to the subscriber and keep this sender name consistent. For this reason, it is usually best to simply use the brand name rather than the name of any individuals. Of course, this doesn't prevent you from using the names of people from the company within the email itself to add a personal touch.

The Subject and Snippet Text
Subscribers are busy people and they receive *a lot* of emails. If you want yours to be opened and read, you need to have a subject line which manages to be both informative and compelling. You should inform them of the product or service being offered and the benefits that they stand to receive – discounts, free gifts, and the like. Including the recipient's name can be effective in getting their attention, and you may also want to include a reference to the brand.

You should also be aware that some email clients, such as **Gmail**, include a **Snippet** from the beginning of the email next to the subject line. At the very least, you should ensure that the text in the snippet complements rather than detracts from the content in the subject line.

Writing Style
Subscribers want to digest the key information as quickly as possible, so copy should be simple, scanable, and to the point. Try writing out the entirety of what you want to say in the email, and then shorten it as much as possible by removing any superfluous or melodramatic language and by making use of lists and bullet points.

Hint
An informal tone of voice is usually acceptable in email marketing as long as it corresponds with brand personality, so don't worry about split infinitives and other grammatical dogma, especially if it aids in making the email more succinct. If opting for an informal style, make sure that it is replicated across the whole email; for example, instead of using links labelled **Read More** or **Visit Our Website**, try **Check it Out** or **Dive In.**

Less is more
As well as avoiding using too many words, you should also avoid using too many different messages in any one email. Each email should have just one primary topic or objective, whether that is to sell a particular product or to welcome a new customer. It is a common mistake to attempt too many things at once, but an email which is too cluttered is likely to be less successful than one with

an uncomplicated and focused message. If you do want to convey additional messages within the same email, you must ensure that the layout is simple to understand and that the different sections of the email are clearly signposted and delineated.

More Than Just Sales

Emails can be about more than simply promoting products and pushing subscribers to make purchases; they can be used to develop brand and strengthen relationships with subscribers. You may occasionally want to send an email to subscribers which is entirely designed for their entertainment with no effort to sell them anything; try sending something funny or silly, with jokes, cartoons, and videos. Making emails unpredictable and entertaining in this way can help create a more favourable brand view and encourages subscribers to open emails more often.

User-Generated Content

User-generated content can be used to great effect in emails. Testimonials and ratings provided by website visitors can be included to help to persuade subscribers of the quality of services and products so that it is one of their peers, rather than a salesman, who is championing a product.

Another way of utilising user-generated content in emails is to create a dialogue with email subscribers. You could include a survey or quiz in every e-newsletter that's sent out, creating a more interactive experience for the reader and providing you with valuable information about subscribers.

Social Media Synergy

Emails should have a means by which recipients can choose to follow the company through a variety of social media. This can take the form of a footer with buttons linking to the relevant pages of a variety of social media such as **Facebook**, **Twitter**, and so on. It should also be supplemented by a short section of copy explaining that the recipient can follow the company, and the reasons/benefits of doing so as well as an example of the content that they would be party to – the most recent Twitter feed, for example.

Be Mysterious

Human curiosity should not be underestimated and one possible marketing technique that takes advantage of our innate inquisitiveness is the use of deliberately cryptic emails. You could distribute an email consisting of a single sentence or even just one word, or perhaps just a collection of imagery or graphics. If you make the content unusual and interesting, then subscribers will want to see what is going on and many will click through to the website to see what it is – the **Andrew Peace** photo competition in the case study section of this chapter is a great example. This is, however, a risky strategy as the prevalence of email fraud and viruses has made people wary about clicking on a link that they are unsure

about and there are also those who will not have time to read vague or ambiguous emails. Such emails may, therefore, fail to grab the attention of some of those people who would have been interested in the offer if you had clearly explained what it was. The obvious way to offset this risk is to run such an emailing campaign in parallel with a more traditional one.

Hint
If following the mysterious route, making an email of exceptional quality will go some way to allaying any fears that the email has despicable goals.

Email Design and Layout

Scanable Layout

Subscribers are unlikely to carefully read through every bit of information in an email. Instead they will scan for the key information and the layout should allow them to do this as quickly and easily as possible. The reader should be able to understand the core message of an email – what is being offered, who is offering it, and how they can take the offer up – within seconds. To this end, it is crucial that you avoid using large blocks of text and that you break up the copy. To achieve this, use multiple headlines and bullet-points, as well as lines, borders and boxes to divide the email into different sections. The most important components of the message will, in most cases, be the details of the offer and the call-to-action, and you can use **Visual Anchors** to draw the reader's eye to these and to any other important information.

Gloss
Visual Anchors can include different typefaces, sizes, colours, or images such as arrows or buttons.

Pre-header Text

Pre-header text is, as you may have guessed, text which goes above the header of an email. Most of the time the pre-header text is used for a link, allowing subscribers to view the email as a web page in order to enable them to safely view any blocked images or graphics. There are, however, a number of other functional items that can be included in the pre-header text:

- Unsubscribe link
- Forward to a Friend link
- Edit Preferences link
- Permission information
- Mobile Version link
- A Whitelist request — to add you to the recipient's address book

Header

The header will usually include the company logo, or at least some reference to the brand, as well as a navigation bar linking to the different sections of the website. Any headers that you use in emails should be similar in style, if not exactly the same, as the headers used on the website in order for emails to be consistent with brand identity.

Footer

The footer of the email can be used for additional links to different sections of the website, viral links – options to forward the email to a friend, or share the email on a social network – or options to subscribe or unsubscribe. You may also want to include a link to the privacy policy.

Images

Most subscribers block images in their primary inbox by default. While this shouldn't deter you from using images altogether, you need to be aware of the challenges that this poses. As such, you need to make sure that all emails include text that is capable of effectively communicating its message in the absence of supporting imagery, whilst also using **Alt Text**. Email recipients also need to be given a way to click through to the website, so ensure that this action is not dependent on imagery. Alternatively, you can provide links in the pre-header text to enable the recipient to choose to view the email as a web page.

Gloss

Alt Text is placed in an email during the coding process and is used to replace blocked images with copy. It can also enhance accessibility by providing the screen reader programs used by the blind or partially sighted with a description of the picture.

People are attracted to pictures first but this can detract from the efficacy of the email if it has nothing to do with the email's message. Often people will put imagery onto an email simply because they want it to look pretty. Imagery attracts more attention than copy, so use images wisely, think about the message you want to get across and then consider if the image you are using is helping or hindering your communication.

Videos

Videos can be effective in making emails more entertaining, informative and distinctive. You can choose to embed videos in the email itself or you can link to videos on the website. If you choose to embed videos, you should remember that subscribers usually spend only a few seconds scanning an email and you should, therefore, present videos in a clearly recognisable video player format if you want them to be played.

You should also be aware that there may be technological obstacles to viewing videos in email. While most email clients that consumers will be using – **Hotmail**, **Gmail**, etc. – will be fine, many of the email clients used by business – such as **Microsoft Outlook** – are not necessarily enabled for viewing videos.

Colour

Colour schemes should be consistent and simple as too many different colours can make emails appear cluttered, less attractive and more difficult to scan quickly. Ideally, you should choose one dominant colour and one or two secondary colours. Make sure that the colours used complement one another; navy blue text on a bright red background will not be attractive or easy to read.

Position

As aforementioned, you need to ensure that email recipients can see the main details of the email almost instantaneously and they will be unable to do this if they have to scroll down the page to find important information. You should, therefore, try to include all of the crucial elements of the email – the brand, the offer, the call to action – towards the top. A normal preview pane will be approximately 500 pixels wide and 350 pixels tall, so you should try to include all of the most salient information in this area.

Email Opportunities

Most of the emails that companies send are likely to be regular newsletters and notifications of special offers and new products. However, there are a lot of other great opportunities to contact subscribers in order to strengthen the relationship and encourage them to make a purchase.

Welcome Emails

Welcome emails can generate some of the highest open rates and they can set the tone for future emails. They can therefore have a significant impact on the future success of email marketing campaigns. As well as serving as a thank you for subscribing, a welcome email is a good opportunity to make clear, in greater detail, what subscribers can expect from emails in the future. It can also be a good idea to use welcome emails to request that subscribers **Whitelist** the sender address in order to ensure that future emails arrive in their inbox without having images blocked or being treated as spam.

Abandonment Emails

Frequently, when customers place items in their online shopping cart or basket, they do not go on to complete the purchase. There could be any number of reasons for this – they may have intended to go back and purchase the item later but forgotten about it, or they may be using the basket as a wish list with no firm intention of completing the purchase – but whatever the reason, it is a good idea to send

How can you make your email contact more relevant?... ...and more responsive?

Browsing Activity Emails

If you track the pages that subscribers are viewing, you will be able to send personalised emails based on the particular products or services that each individual has viewed, informing them of any relevant special offers that arise, as well as recommending similar products that might interest them. However, there is a danger that customers might not appreciate their activity being closely monitored, so some tactful measures should be implemented so that the emails are always viewed as helpful rather than intrusive. If possible try to get feedback on how subscribers regard these emails.

Win-Back Emails

If a previous customer has not been active for a certain amount of time try sending them a **We Miss You!** email to persuade them to return. You can also provide an exclusive incentive to encourage them to come back.

Hint

Customer inactivity can sometimes be linked to buying cycles, as customers will have times of the week, month or year that they are likely to buy specific products. Timing the win-back email to coincide with these times is a good idea, but don't neglect the customer in between. You can maintain brand awareness in the interim by informing the customer of news or by sending them one of the aforementioned entertainment driven emails.

them an email reminding them that they have items waiting in their basket. This could be done after a given period of time, or when the stocks of the particular products in their basket are running low so as to warn them that they should buy quickly before the product sells out. You could also think about including an incentive for the customer to complete the purchase, though there is a danger that this could lead to savvy customers deliberately abandoning baskets in order to receive incentives.

Reactivation Emails

Another opportunity for email contact is when a customer reactivates their lapsed account. Simply sending them an email thanking them for coming back and informing them of recent changes and new products and services can be useful in strengthening the relationship with the customer and increasing sales.

Transaction Confirmation Emails

Once a visitor to a site has made a purchase, the aim is to make that person revisit and an effective way of doing this is to send them a confirmation email which is highly personalised and attractive, and which includes recommendations and special incentives to encourage repeat purchases. You should, however, ensure that any promotional copy is to the side or below the confirmation copy so as not to confuse or frustrate the receiver.

You could also send recent purchasers a follow-up email, asking for reviews of the product and its delivery. You could then ask those who provide positive reviews to send referrals to friends.

Special Occasion Emails

Birthdays, anniversaries, Christmas, Valentine's Day; there are a lot of special occasions that you can use as an excuse to contact subscribers. At a given time before the event, send them an email reminder with relevant product suggestions and incentives, including copy and imagery specific to the recipient.

This is easy to do on generic holidays such as Christmas, Mother's Day or Valentine's Day, but for birthdays it is a little trickier as a date of birth has to be appropriated from somewhere – possibly during website registration. Remember that emails sent to somebody before their birthday should be aimed at providing ideas for gifts that can be bought *for* rather than *by* the recipient and should, therefore, be almost entirely focused on the benefits of the product or service and how it will enrich the life of the birthday boy or girl.

For anniversaries and other people's birthdays, you have to be a bit more creative. One option is to provide the customer with an online calendar that they can input special dates into so that an email is sent to them to remind them of the impending occasion. The email will then be tailored to the event, offering ideas and discounts on great presents for dads, for example, if the customer's father's birthday is approaching.

Re-stock emails

If you can determine the average consumption period for products, then you can send customers an email at the time when they are likely to need to replenish their stocks. If a product usually needs replacing after three months, send them an email after three months with incentives for a repeat purchase or recommendations for alternative products.

But don't get carried away

While it is productive to contact subscribers regularly, you don't want to annoy them by pestering them too often. It is very important to get the overall frequency of emails right, otherwise there could be a lot of unsubscribe requests. A potential problem in large organisations is that there are different teams or departments wanting to email the same subscribers all at the same time. One way of avoiding this is to assign someone with responsibility for managing the frequency of emails who can decide which emails should get priority and whether the different messages can be compiled into a smaller number of emails.

Email Service Providers

Investing money in a good **Email Service Provider – ESP** – can be a good idea as they can help with the administrative, technological and creative challenges involved in an email marketing campaign.

Delivery rates should increase as most ESPs are approved by internet service providers as a legitimate email delivery service and they usually offer easy methods to authenticate emails. Most ESPs also provide clients with comprehensive tracking of their emails which will help to keep track of Key Performance Indicators. This information can be used to help create a segmented list so that the individuals who would find the message most relevant are targeted. ESPs will manage subscribes and unsubscribes which will be a big time saver especially if it is a large subscriber list. Also, ESPs will usually offer HTML templates that can be adapted and used for campaigns, allowing emails to be personalised easily so that they include the subscriber's name, past purchase history and other information directly into the message.

CROSS MEDIA

The Quick Message

Emails have one big advantage over other direct marketing media and that is speed.
Email is all about speed: speed of delivery; speed of response; speed of disposal; and it is
this last point that drives a lot of the design, copy and format decisions of emails as recipients of
an email can dispose of it with a couple of clicks and don't even have to open it to decide to do so. It is,
therefore, imperative that emails can deliver a message quickly and with sufficient impact.

In a world that continues to move ever faster, the speed at which you can convey your marketing message
becomes increasingly more important and we believe that although other media are not traditionally as disposable
as emails, the public's desire for messages to be quick to grasp and understand continues to grow, making email
techniques ever more applicable to the rest of the direct marketing world. *The following are the most effective
email techniques that can be used to speed up message comprehension:*

Bullet Points

- Simple, but effective
- Bullet points break up text for the reader
- Make it easy for them to scan
- And pick out the most important aspects of a message.

Big Text

The size of text is another easy way to signpost **critical points,** so offers, call-to-actions and hero-products
should be differentiated through **bigger,** more **prominent** text.

Shapes

A great way to quickly draw attention to specific points is through the shapes that they make or are
positioned on. For instance, most people will look at a vertical shape before a horizontal shape, so placing
important copy or images in narrow, vertical borders will go some way towards highlighting them
to the reader. Other attention grabbing shape facts include:

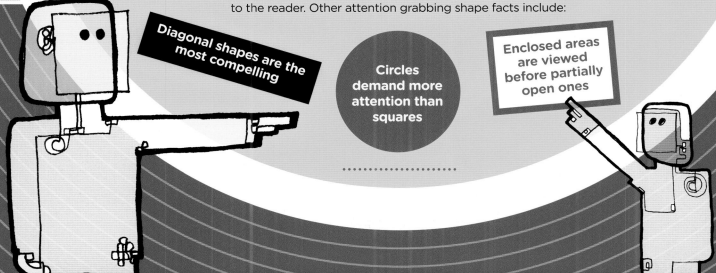

Diagonal shapes are the most compelling

Circles demand more attention than squares

Enclosed areas are viewed before partially open ones

115

e-newsletter—monthly

People get so many emails every day, but how many of those are interesting and relevant to the recipient? You can really stand out by producing an email with engaging content, that fits your target audience.

friendly tone
of voice

images of Andrew Peace
brings brand to life

interactive competition involving
customer with the brand and product
in return for a case of wine

links to enter
competition

unsubscribe
message

relevant terms
and conditions

online/offline techniques

Emails are incredibly versatile, so consider your target audience before producing one. There's no excuse for sending out an email that isn't fit for purpose. If you have a very close and engaged community then an email with plenty of content is probably going to give you some great results.

clear branding

build interest

strong price proposition

relevant terms & conditions

necessary broadcast elements

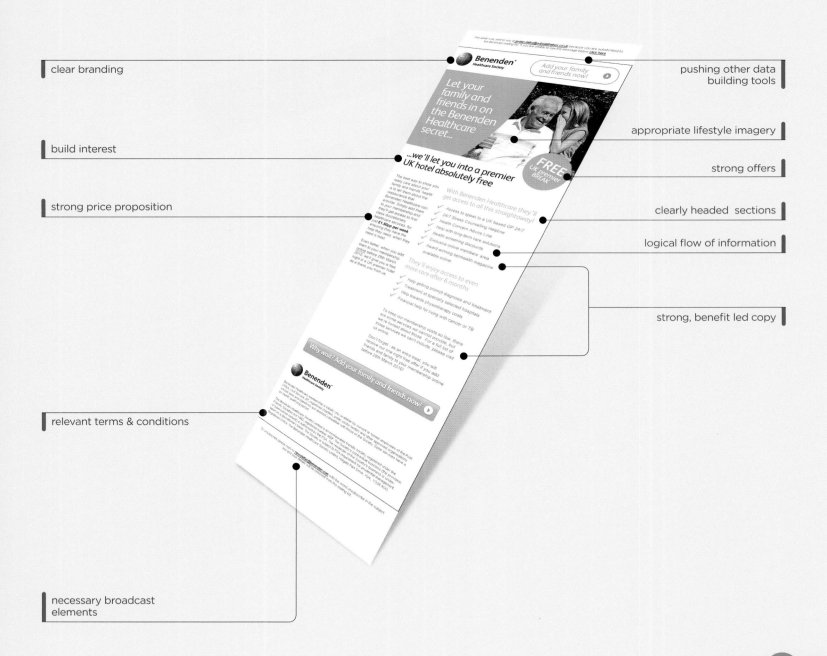

pushing other data building tools

appropriate lifestyle imagery

strong offers

clearly headed sections

logical flow of information

strong, benefit led copy

e-shot—tactical offer

Email is great for delivering a single, specific message. Keeping it simple,
with an offer, call-to-action and some attractive imagery, can have a big impact.

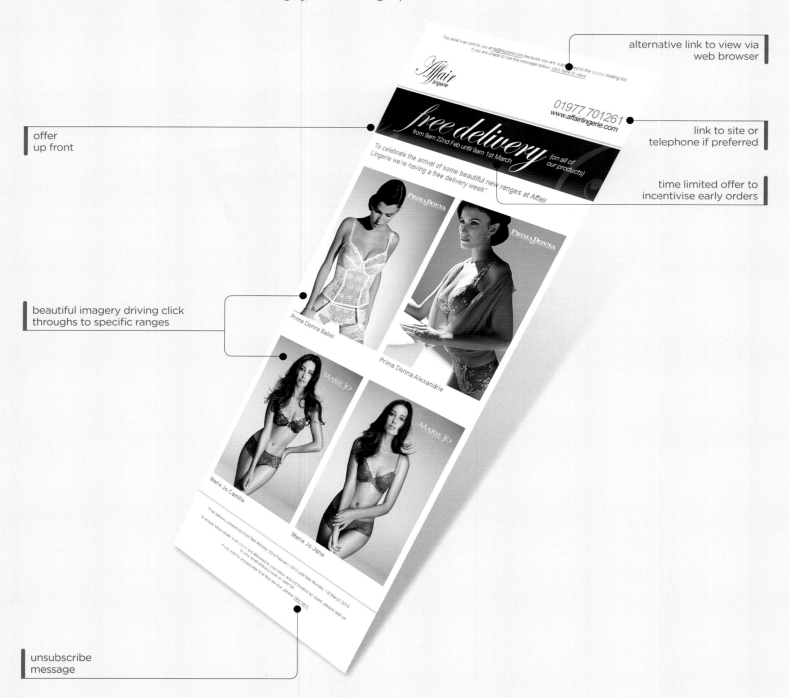

alternative link to view via
web browser

offer
up front

link to site or
telephone if preferred

time limited offer to
incentivise early orders

beautiful imagery driving click
throughs to specific ranges

unsubscribe
message

email—seasonal promotion

Speed is a real strength of email, both in delivery and conversion, making it perfect for time-relevant messages and limited offers.

clear positioning

message creates urgency

product links

promote new products

deep link

friendly tone of voice with a personal touch

additional calls to action

promotes additional links

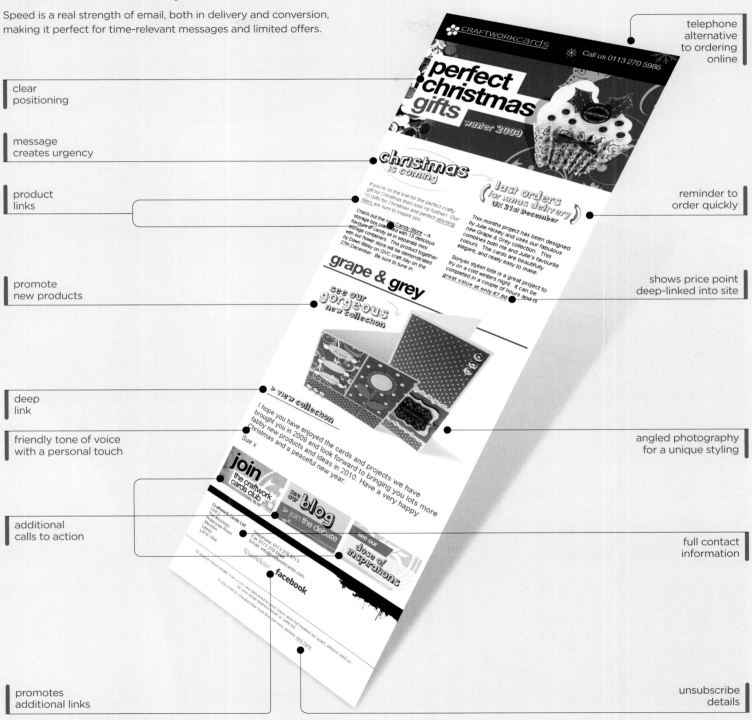

telephone alternative to ordering online

reminder to order quickly

shows price point deep-linked into site

angled photography for a unique styling

full contact information

unsubscribe details

website design

How do you win the hearts and the minds of your customers?

e Project
l" content="ge
d="otb_
' /><meta name
Gazpm
'favicon.ico"
rtcut
neet" type="te
nk
:/css" media="screen" /><li
ef="common/css/
' />
aKeywords"
qCvz4at
><link
/css/
eet"

A website allows a business to reach and engage with a huge amount of customers and has become a prerequisite for any enterprise, but it is amazing how many utterly useless websites litter the internet. They can be useless for a variety of reasons: they can be over complicated, poorly designed, inaccessible or they may just not do anything. In the online world, people have a vast range of choice and are able to read reviews, forums and message boards to discern the quality of almost anything. As such, a poor website will rapidly disappear into obscurity as internet users identify all of the sites that do the same thing but better. However if you build a customer focused website that works well, engages the user and continues to be dynamic and up to date, then there is a very good chance that it will attract an ever larger number of users who will continue to visit and recommend others to do the same. This chapter runs through the main features that you should be aware of if you are revamping an existing website or creating a new one.

Usability

If a website is too confusing or complicated, users will become frustrated and leave, with little chance of returning. A site should be designed so that it works almost intuitively for the user, allowing them to perform any action or task efficiently. Improving the usability of a site in this way will result in a more satisfying customer experience, an increase in the number of return visits, and an improvement of visitors' opinions of the brand. It can also lead to higher conversion rates as a greater proportion of visitors will be willing to stay on the site long enough to see a transaction through to completion.

The key factors related to the usability of a website include the **Information Architecture** of the site, the **Accessibility** of the site for people with disabilities or uncommon computer equipment, and the **Navigation Tools** contained on individual pages.

Information Architecture

The term **Information Architecture** broadly refers to the way in which the different pages and sections of a website are structured. If a site is structured logically and efficiently, and in a way that reflects its users' expectations, then this can facilitate and enhance the customer experience and increase conversion rates. Information architecture can also have an impact on search engine optimisation by helping search engine robots – take a look at our **SEO Chapter** – find all of the pages on a site.

> ### Hint
> When creating a site you should design a site map; a flow chart mapping each webpage and how they connect to one another. These can be used to visually represent the grouping and hierarchy of all of the different pages on a website, and should be made available to visitors to help them find the pages that they are looking for.

The basic process of developing the information architecture of a site is quite simple. You should start by deciding what the main themes of the site will be; if it is a site selling clothing then the main themes might include women's, men's and children's clothes. Having done this, you should then determine which pages should be grouped into which theme, though keep in mind that a single page can be assigned to more than one grouping if appropriate – for example, unisex accessories could be included in both men's and women's clothing. You can now sort the different pages within each grouping into a hierarchy of sub-categories. You should ensure that the information hierarchies are not too intricate; ideally, a user should never have to follow more than three or four links to get to any page on the site. In addition, you should be very careful when deciding how to group information as it might seem obvious to you that a page belongs in a particular section but visitors might think otherwise and, subsequently, look in the wrong place. This can cause visitors

considerable frustration and will affect the website's conversion rate. It can, therefore, be worthwhile consulting visitors – through questionnaires, feedback forms, forums and message boards – to assist with the structuring of the site in a way that reflects their expectations and behaviour.

Accessibility

Making a site accessible to everyone regardless of disability, browser, platform or operating system is a central consideration when designing a site. In the UK, the **Disability and Discrimination Act** has created a legal requirement for websites to be accessible and similar legislation exists in most other countries. But irrespective of any legal obligations, it also makes commercial sense to ensure that no potential visitors or customers are prevented from accessing a site. Detailed information on all the possible accessibility options is available at **www.w3.org/WAI** or **www.makingwaves.co.uk**

Some of the basic accessibility features include:

- Allowing users to change text size

- Making use of the appropriate html tags including alternative text for images and graphic content to help define the content of the page to those using Screen Readers – a form of assistive technology potentially useful to people who are blind, visually impaired, illiterate or learning disabled. This is also beneficial for SEO.

- Ensuring that the colours used will not cause problems for people with one of the three forms of colour blindness.

- Providing a high contrast version of the site.

- Supporting as many web browsers as possible, these will include Internet Explorer, Firefox, Safari and Google Chrome, as well as more specialist browsers such as the text-only Lynx.

- Creating Fluid Pages that will stretch to fill the entirety of a browser window. This means that users with larger monitors or higher screen resolutions will not be presented with large areas of white space and that more content will appear Above The Fold – the top part of the page that will be visible to visitors without them scrolling down.

- You should allow users to indicate their specific accessibility requirements and make sure that these are provided on all pages throughout their visit and, preferably, on their return visits as well. You should have a page dedicated to accessibility which provides an explanation of the different features available and allows people to select what they need. However, particularly important features – such as changing the text size – should be made available on every page.

Cloud computing helps collaboration across devices and facilities

Navigation Tools

As well as having an efficient information architecture and comprehensive accessibility features, you should also aim to make it as easy as possible for visitors to navigate quickly to the page that they are looking for by including sufficient, useful, navigation tools across the site.

Navigation bars

The primary navigation bar is commonly situated in the header or in a sidebar down the left side of the page. It should appear on every page and contain links to each of the main sections of a site. Some navigation bars will allow you to roll over each of the main options to reveal links to the subsections within that category; this can save visitors time by enabling them to bypass an intermediary page. You could also indicate a visitor's current position in the site by highlighting the appropriate part of the navigation bar. Secondary navigation bars can be used within each section of the site to link to each of the appropriate subsections.

Page headings

Every page of a website should have an illustrative main heading as this works essentially as a sign to orient browsers. It is important to make sure that these headings are easy to find and identify so it is a good idea to make them at least two point sizes larger than the site's body text; use a different colour for the text or background to make them stand out and ensure that they are bordered by plenty of white space.

Breadcrumbs

Breadcrumbs allow users to keep track of where they are within a site and how they got there. They will usually take the form of links, offering an easy way to get back to previously visited pages. They will typically show the path to the current page from the home page and are normally situated below the header. They can be particularly useful if the site has a very deep hierarchy, and can help with SEO by increasing the number of internal links.

Footers

The footer can provide another opportunity to link to each of the main sections included in the main navigation bar as well as less important pages such as the Privacy Policy, the Terms and Conditions and the Site Map. You could also include a Back to Top option.

Hyperlinks

Hyperlinks can be used within the body copy of different pages to direct users to other information that may be of interest to them. The link anchor text should be clear and easily understandable and should, ideally, also make use of carefully selected keywords to help your SEO efforts. Be careful not to make hyperlinks too small, as larger links will be more noticeable and easier to click. To make text hyperlinks immediately apparent, you need to differentiate them from the rest of the text. This can be achieved by underlining the hyperlinked text, or changing its colour or size; just make sure that hyperlinks are denoted in a consistent manner throughout the site.

Image hyperlinks can be used as an alternative to text. However, because users tend to scan web pages for text, they will pay less attention to images and you should, therefore, ensure that image hyperlinks are particularly eye-catching and immediately identifiable as hyperlinks. You should also remember to use alternative text for images as this is important both for accessibility and for SEO.

Sitemaps

As mentioned above, a sitemap is a tool to help users navigate around a website and should be linked to on every page of the site, usually in the header and/or footer. Sitemaps visually represent the structure and hierarchy of a site and provide links to many or all of its pages. Having a clear and effective sitemap will provide visitors with a quick and easy way to find what they are looking for. Once again, SEO is helped by providing a lot of internal links and increasing the number of pages indexed by the search engines. You may wish to use a single sitemap for the whole site or, if the site is very large or complex, you can have a range of different sitemaps dedicated to each of the main sections of the site. Make sure that you pick the link anchor text carefully; it needs to be clearly understandable for visitors and should make use of keywords to help with SEO.

Sitemaps can also be a great tool for pre-empting usability problems. Once a sitemap has been created you can use it to follow the customer journey and see if it flows naturally or comes across any unforeseen errors or dead-ends.

On-site Search

All sites should have an on-site search tool included in a prominent position on every page to help users find specific information quickly and easily. You could also include an **Advanced Search** option – usually a link next to the standard search box – to allow users to search within specific criteria. Remember to provide instructions on how to use the advanced search facility properly.

Make sure that the search engine results pages are presented in an easily scannable format and that you enable users to sort the results according to different criteria – date, relevance, etc. – and change the number of results presented on each page.

Hint

A good search analytics tool – such as Google Analytics – will aid in assessing the effectiveness of the on-site search engine across a range of criteria, and will enable you to make appropriate alterations and improvements.

URLs

Another way to make a site easy to navigate is to have URLs that are simple, clear, and easy to remember – for example, www.homefitnessdirect.com/treadmills – so that people will be able to type them in directly without having to go via the home page. In addition, the use of keywords within URLs can have a significantly positive impact on SEO and you should, therefore, be very careful when deciding on URLs for the most popular pages on a website.

Consistency

The most important thing to achieve if you are going to make a website easily navigable is consistency. Page titles, breadcrumbs, main headings, and link text should all match one another when appropriate so that, for example, the breadcrumb label is worded and formatted in exactly the same way as the main page headings that they refer to. Consistency not only helps visitors to orient themselves within the site, but also works to reassure them that they have arrived in the section of the site that they wanted to get to.

Website Creative

The creative side of building a website is every bit as important as the functional side. It isn't enough that a site is accessible and easy to use, it also has to be effective in attracting and retaining visitors and persuasive enough to maximise purchases, sign ups, etc.

Site Personality

First of all, you will need to decide on the type of site that you are trying to build. Clearly, you will need to know the purpose of the site – transactional or brand-building – but you will also have to decide on the site's personality. The personality of the site will, of course, be a reflection of the personality of the brand as a whole which, in turn, will often be heavily influenced and constrained by customer demographics and the industry that it belongs to; a business-to-business site in the financial services industry will necessarily be very different to a computer games site aimed at teenagers. However, even within a particular area, it is possible to differentiate a brand from its competitors with a distinctive character. Having a specific, well-defined brand personality will enable all marketing activities to be consistent in projecting the right qualities and can help both in acquiring new customers, and in creating loyalty and affection for the brand from the existing customer base. For more brand building information, head to our **Strategy Chapter.**

One of the best techniques for determining a site's personality is to think of the relationship between the company and its customers as being analogous to a relationship between two people. You will know a wide range of different types of people and each will serve a different purpose in your life – for instance you might have a grandfather who is old-fashioned and knowledgeable, a friend who is exciting and unpredictable, and a business partner who is hard-working and competent. Each of these people are good to have in your life and each can be very useful to you in different ways depending on whether you are looking to have fun, seek advice, or solve a complicated problem; you could even decide on a specific real or fictional person as the personification of the brand. By engaging in exercises such as this, and thinking hard about the different qualities that you want people to associate with the brand, you will not only help to make sure that you portray those qualities across the website and other marketing materials, but you will also be able to compare the personality that you want the brand to have, with the personality it has at the moment. This will allow you to more easily identify the ways in which you need to change the presentation of the company.

You should also bear in mind the personalities of competitors as you may be able to identify an online niche to help differentiate the brand that you are promoting. The recruitment site for corporate law firm **Morrison and Foerster – http://www.mofo.com/career/index.html** – is a great example of this. Their use of fun and unusual methods to present their information to potential applicants – including referring to themselves by the abbreviation MoFo – sets them apart as being fun, innovative and quirky compared to their more conservative competitors while still managing to appear highly professional.

```
<html>
<head>
<title>Your Page
Title</title>
</head>
```

Colour

Colour can help visitors to understand a website by giving them clues about the site's navigation and grouping of content, and can also be used to communicate the personality of the site. A poorly chosen colour scheme can make an otherwise well-designed site appear cheap and unprofessional. For these reasons, colour is a crucially important consideration when designing a website.

Different colours are associated with different feelings and emotions, with green being associated with nature and the environment, red with passion and excitement, pink with femininity, blue with calm and tranquillity, and so on. Fashion also plays its part in website colour schemes, with certain colours going in and out of style on a regular basis. You should aim to select a small number of colours to form the basis of the colour scheme; pick a base colour that reflects the personality of the brand and then add several complementary secondary colours.

Hint

Adobe provide a free tool to help create and share different colour schemes – **http://kuler.adobe.com/** – that you might find useful.

You will need to test your desired colour scheme on a colour-blindness simulator and provide a high-contrast version of the site in order to ensure it is accessible by the visually impaired. Another issue to consider is the proportion of **White Space** that you should use; white space can make a page appear less cluttered and helps focus the users' attention on the most important aspects of the page. On the other hand, too much white space makes a site look sterile and can be better used in providing more information to visitors. You will therefore need to find the right balance which is neither too minimalist nor too busy.

Typography

It is vitally important that the site is clear and easy to read and an important factor in this is the typography that is used. Typography should be consistent throughout the site, and you should, therefore, be wary of regularly changing its size, colour or font as the site will look and feel more professional if it has a degree of uniformity across all of the different pages. Be careful about using text formatting; underlining, bold and italics can be used sparingly for highlighting key points and helping to disaggregate large blocks of text but too much can look amateurish. Similarly you should try to limit the use of full capitalisation of words as these are more difficult to read – **WE ARE USED TO READING IN LOWER CASE AND IT CAN THEREFORE TAKE US LONGER TO RECOGNISE CAPITALISED WORDS** – though some moderate usage of capitalisation can be helpful for emphasising important words or phrases. Another important point to remember is to try to use relatively narrow columns of no more than half the width of the screen when writing large blocks of text as these are easier to read and quicker to scan. You should also be careful using reversed-out text – for example, white text on a black background – as these are more difficult to read, and can make it problematic for visitors to print pages from the site. Finally, in HTML, try to choose a common font that is likely to be installed on the vast majority of computers such as Verdana, Helvetica, or Times New Roman.

Hint

Typography can be very effective in building brands. Many companies – such as Coca Cola and the BBC – can be recognised through their text alone. This is, however, far more difficult online as certain fonts may not be installed on all user's computers. The more uncommon fonts should, therefore, be used with caution, while bespoke fonts are mostly unusable.

Copy

Writing copy for websites is, to some extent, much like writing copy for other media such as direct mail or email. It is, however, worth stressing two very important points. First, on websites more than any other medium, it is vital that readers are not presented with large blocks of undifferentiated copy as these are difficult to scan and will immediately deter many online users. You should, therefore, concentrate your copy as much as possible by moderating the use of superfluous, elaborate language and by writing in a more informal, to-the-point style, provided that this is consistent with brand personality. To make the copy scannable, divide any page that needs to contain a lot of copy into several small sections, each with a different header, while also highlighting key words or phrases by using different colours, or bold or italic formatting. You can also use bullet-points and numbering to separate large blocks of text. If possible, you should try to spread out copy across lots of different pages in order to avoid having any pages that are too long. This will also help you to make sure that the most important information is contained above the fold.

The second major factor to bear in mind when writing website copy is search engine optimisation. As described in the **SEO** chapter, you should identify a small number of keyphrases for each page and ensure that these are included in the body copy as well as the appropriate meta-tags. You should ensure that you continue to write in a natural way as, if you repeat chosen keyphrases too many times, you could be penalised by the search engines. Including hyperlinks within copy to other pages on the site is another great way to improve your position in the search engine results pages, though you should only do so when it is appropriate and relevant to the information on that page. The best approach to help your SEO efforts is to get people linking to the site, and the only way to achieve this in a sustainable and honest way is to write engaging content that people will find valuable and which they will want to share with visitors on their own site. This can be done in a number of ways, such as writing instructional how-to guides, or by writing articles or blog posts offering interesting and contentious opinions on current industry developments.

Common Pages

Home Page

A **Home Page** will serve two main purposes. Its primary function is to act as a gateway to the site and provide a space that visitors can return to as and when they want to navigate to a different section. The second purpose is to introduce visitors to the brand, company and product/service and persuade them to buy into it. You should, therefore, focus on ensuring that the home page is built in such a way so as to enable visitors to navigate as quickly and easily as possible and to persuade them to go to the pages that are most likely to deliver value from each individual.

As well as the usual, aforementioned, navigational tools, the home page could provide personalised links to products or pages that the visitor has most recently viewed and links to products or pages that are recommended to each visitor based on their browsing and/or purchasing history. You should provide information of any particularly attractive special offers, and perhaps also include links to the top-ten highest selling or most frequently viewed products.

Hint

In most cases try to avoid using **Introductory Pages** – i.e. pages that come up before the home page that contain flash animation with a 'Skip Intro' button – as most visitors will be interested in finding specific information and will not take the time to view an introduction, however attractive it may be, and it is likely that many people will find it more annoying than impressive.

About Us

The **About Us** page is very popular with first time visitors and is a great opportunity to explain, in greater detail, the values and ethos of the company and why people should choose to buy from the brand. This space is normally used to explain the history of the company and the experience of some of the key individuals as a way of humanising the brand and highlighting its expertise and the esteem in which it is held by peers and clients. It is also a good idea to include details of any awards, positive reviews or testimonials that the brand has received from independent sources. A good approach can be to talk about the company's goals for the future as most About Us pages tend to be backwards-looking so, by looking ahead and discussing where the brand is aiming to be in five or ten years time, it can appear more motivated and forward-thinking than the competition.

FAQ

The **Frequently Asked Questions** - FAQ - page is also very popular, and important in helping visitors find key information about the services that are provided. With e-commerce sites, the fact that a visitor has gone onto the FAQ page will mean that they have a degree of interest in buying something and are trying to find out more details before they decide to complete their purchase. The quality of the FAQ page can, therefore, be a very significant factor in generating sales and it is vital that you get it right. Start by anticipating potential queries that customers might have, and go on to the FAQ pages of similar websites to research the types of information that they have included. You will want to provide details of everything a visitor will need or want to know in order to make a purchase, including details regarding the different payment options available, returns policy, expected delivery times and costs, and so on. You will also want to address any questions people might have regarding the accessibility features available on the site. If, after doing this, the FAQ page becomes overly large, then you should divide the different questions into sections to facilitate searches for a specific topic.

For all your efforts to achieve as comprehensive a FAQ page as possible, it is impossible to cover every query that a customer could conceivably devise. As such, it is worth providing contact details for customers to get in touch with customer services, and also linking from the FAQ page to a forum or message board where people can consult one another for the answers they need.

Product Detail Pages

Product Detail Pages are the major arena from which to persuade visitors to purchase specific items. How you go about this will vary greatly according to what is being sold but, in most cases, they will include some imagery and sales copy, as well as attempts to cross-sell. One of the concerns that many people still have about shopping online is that they don't have the chance to see and feel the products that they are buying, so you will have to compensate for this by providing high-quality photography of the product – preferably from several different angles – and, if necessary, make use of illustrations or embedded videos to show the product in action so that the visitors can see how it is used. There are more creative ways to achieve this as well, a la **Amazon's** 'look inside' feature which allows the reader to browse as they would with a physical book, and flick through the first few pages.

Hint

Augmented Reality – where the virtual world interacts with the real – is an interesting way to bring online products closer to the customer. For instance, the customer could hold a piece of card in front of a web cam and have the product superimposed onto the card so that as they turn it, the product displayed on their screen also turns, allowing the customer to manipulate the product in order to see it from every angle.

In addition, the copy should provide all of the detailed technical specifications of the product that the customers could possibly want to know.

As well as providing the essential details of the product, the copy should try to persuade people to make a purchase by explaining the main benefits of the product in a concise and easily-scannable way. Try to include a prominent call-to-action such as a large button containing the text **Buy Now** or **Add to Basket**. If appropriate, you should also enable customers to customise a product by offering a range of different colours, sizes, and other alternatives. Endeavour to allow customers to select their exact desired specifications on the product page itself – preferably without the need for any pop-up windows – and to see an updated image of their product in the colour that they have selected. Finally, you should attempt to cross-sell on the product detail pages by recommending alternative products that people may be interested in as well as, or instead of, the product that they are currently viewing, and perhaps offer a special discount if they choose to make additional purchases. However, you should be careful not to clutter the product detail pages with too much cross-selling; the focus should be on trying to sell the product being viewed.

Checkout Pages

The **Shopping Basket** and **Checkout Pages** are all about trying to make the payment process quick and simple to understand so that as many people as possible go on to complete their purchase. You will usually need to require everyone to either log in as a previous customer or to register as a new customer. When doing this, try to avoid diverting people to a pop-up registration window and, instead, try to make the registration form fit in seamlessly with the rest of the purchasing process. Try to encourage people to opt-in to the email newsletter during the registration process so that you can contact them in the future with details about special promotions.

You should try to minimise the number of steps that the customers have to go through in order to complete their purchase. Aim to have no more than 4 or 5 stages in the checkout process; at its most basic, a checkout process will include a **Register/Log** In section, a **Payment Details** section, and an **Order Summary** section where the customer can confirm their purchase. You may find it necessary to include additional sections, but keep it as simple as possible as the easier it is to complete the transaction, the more people will do so.

Customers can be reassured throughout the process by a display of the key details of their order so that they know that they are buying the right product. Emphasis should also be placed on the security of the payment system as some people will be wary about making purchases online so you should provide details of the reliability and safety of the system. After the transaction has been completed, you should display a page confirming that the payment has been made successfully, thanking them for making a purchase, and reiterating the details of how and when the goods will be delivered to the customer and perhaps also recommending other products that the customer may be interested in.

Landing Pages

A landing page is a page that people are directed to when responding to a specific marketing campaign – PPC search marketing, banner ads, etc. The purpose of a landing page is to persuade the visitor to take a desired course of action, which usually will mean making a purchase or entering their contact details to enable you to get in touch with them at a later stage. Landing pages differ greatly according to the marketing budget available, and what is being sold. A landing page can involve just a single page or an entire microsite designed specifically for a marketing campaign; a famous example is the **comparethemeerkat.com** site. If necessary, you can simply direct people from the marketing campaign to one of the regular pages, such as an appropriate product page or the home page. However, if the budget is available, we would strongly advise that you create bespoke landing pages that are fully optimised to be as effective as possible in generating sales. Landing pages should aim to be as relevant and targeted as possible; make sure that the sales copy on the page matches the information contained in the marketing promotion that has led the visitors to that page and that there are no discrepancies regarding the details of the offer. By creating a bespoke landing page, you can produce a layout that is more focused on the specific promotion and does not need to be cluttered with the usual navigation bars, headers, footers, etc. that take up so much space on the average webpage.

CROSS MEDIA

Spreading Content

If you have spent the time, effort and creative juices on generating quality content, then your next step should be to make sure that as many of the right people see it as possible. Websites are great facilitators of this as they can link to or embed any number of media from anywhere else on the internet. For example, **YouTube,** and many other video content sites, allow you to embed their videos in your websites or blogs so that it can be easily accessed by your users. Web makes this interlinking, cross-pollination of content incredibly easy but if you have great, engaging offline content then you should be looking to facilitate its spread in much the same way by putting your latest experiential campaign on **YouTube,** and spreading it through social media or uploading your catalogues and mailers as PDFs to be hosted on your website. You can also bring web content into the real world with augmented reality, Near Frequency Communication — a wireless way to transmit data between two devices and QR Codes — a type of barcode that contains information that can be accessed through scanners and Smartphone apps — so that all of the channels you use are connected to one another. By creating the links between media, you ensure that you are engaging as wide an audience as possible, who can view your content in whichever medium they feel most comfortable with.

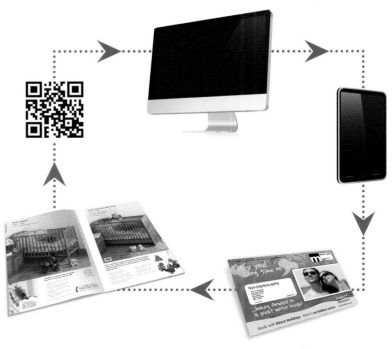

information architecture

When it comes to web design, preparation is key. A good sitemap should address the natural flow of information to the user and provides you with a logical plan for your team to buy into.

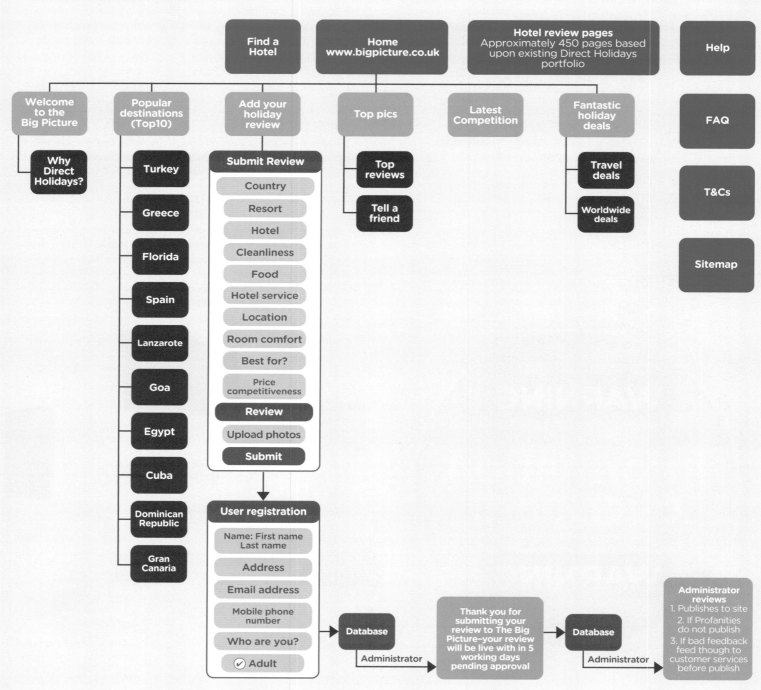

information architecture

Visitors to a website want, information and they will often turn to the search function to find it. Getting your search function right can be difficult, but getting it wrong will ruin the site.

free text search with
predictive text option

banner advertising
space to generate
additional revenue

search by
destination
by clicking
on the map

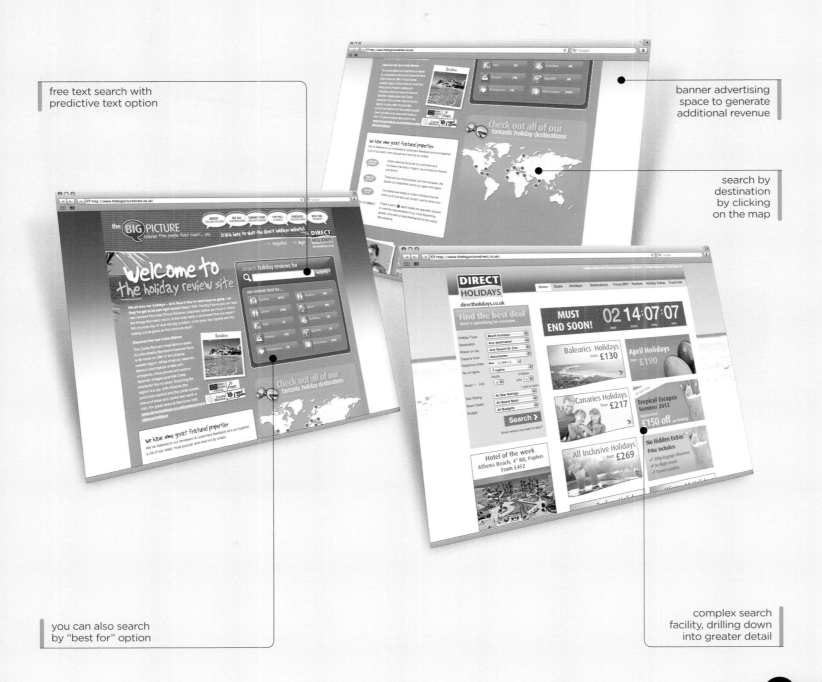

you can also search
by "best for" option

complex search
facility, drilling down
into greater detail

information architecture navigation

Web pages need to be easily navigable. Delve into your target audience's psyche and work out what they need and where they need it.

colours change on rollover

clear primary navigation

clear
typography

clear page
headings

information architecture content

Don't be tempted to go overboard on imagery and copy. Keep every page simple and balanced, so that nothing confuses or gets in the way of the user's experience.

good balance of
imagery & text

provides impact & interest
without over-complicating

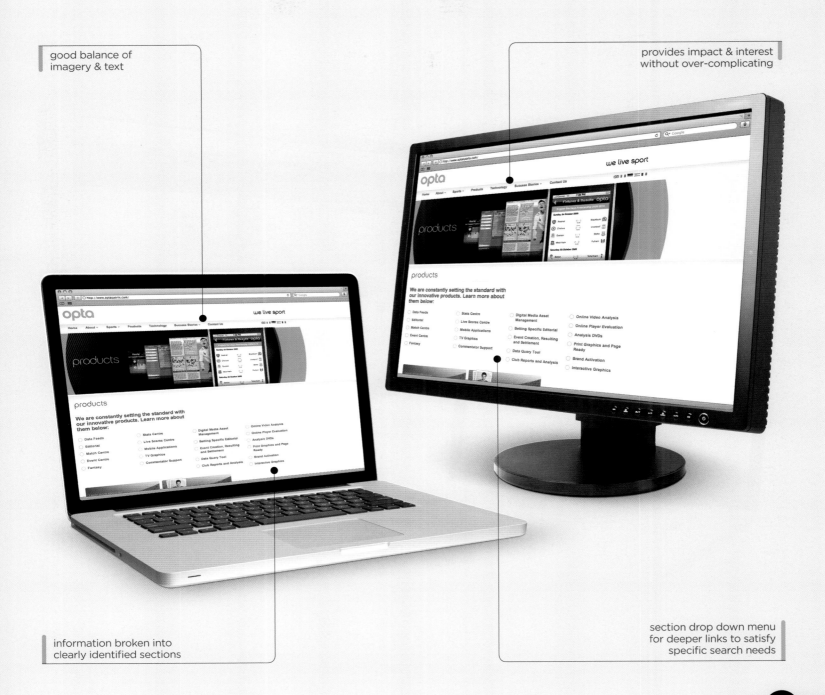

information broken into
clearly identified sections

section drop down menu
for deeper links to satisfy
specific search needs

information architecture—accessibility

Website accessibility might be a legal requirement, but that doesn't mean that you should bolt it on as a token afterthought. A well thought out and accessible design could give your website a real edge.

various colour options for the colour impared

low graphic optopms for screen readers

various text size options for visually impared

clear proposition

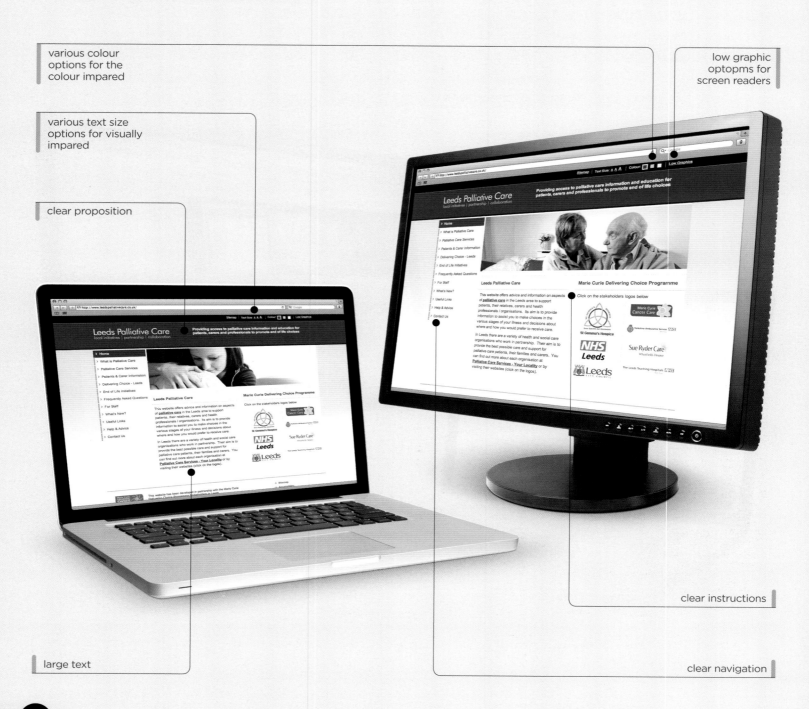

clear instructions

large text

clear navigation

information architecture—accessibility—colour and low graphics

Don't forget that there's an ageing population, and it's unwise to believe that the internet is only viewed by the young. Designers might prefer small text, but your audience might think otherwise.

different colour option

low graphics

information architecture—interesting design

Think of how many websites there are out there. To make yours stand out, you need to think differently and supply the user with interesting design to catch their attention and interactive elements that engage them.

low graphic
optopms for
screen readers

powerful
graphics really
attract interest

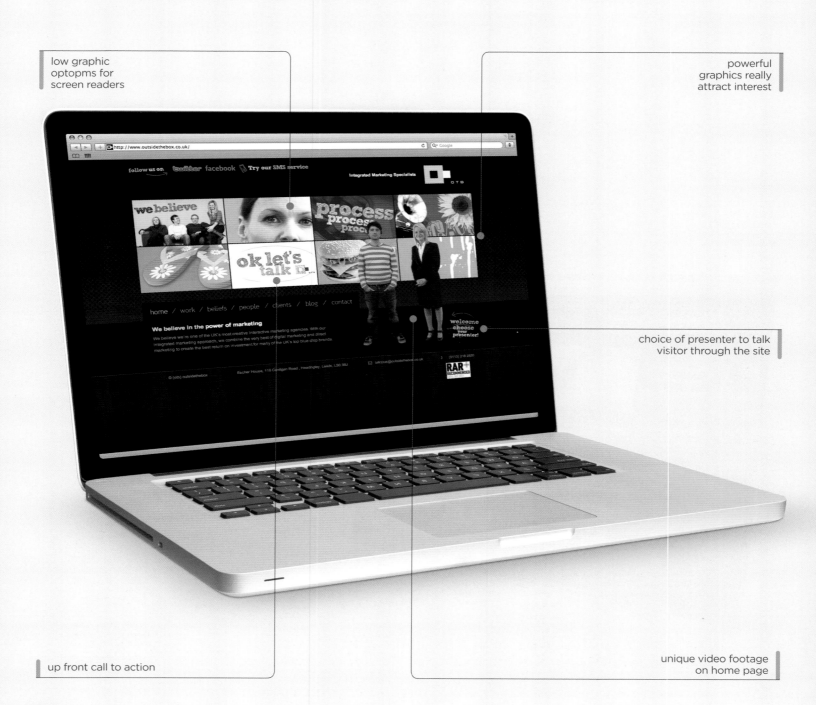

choice of presenter to talk
visitor through the site

up front call to action

unique video footage
on home page

information architecture focus

Think about your audience. Are they interested more by the product/service, or the company that supplies it? Make sure that your site is focused on shining the best light on whatever is most important to the user.

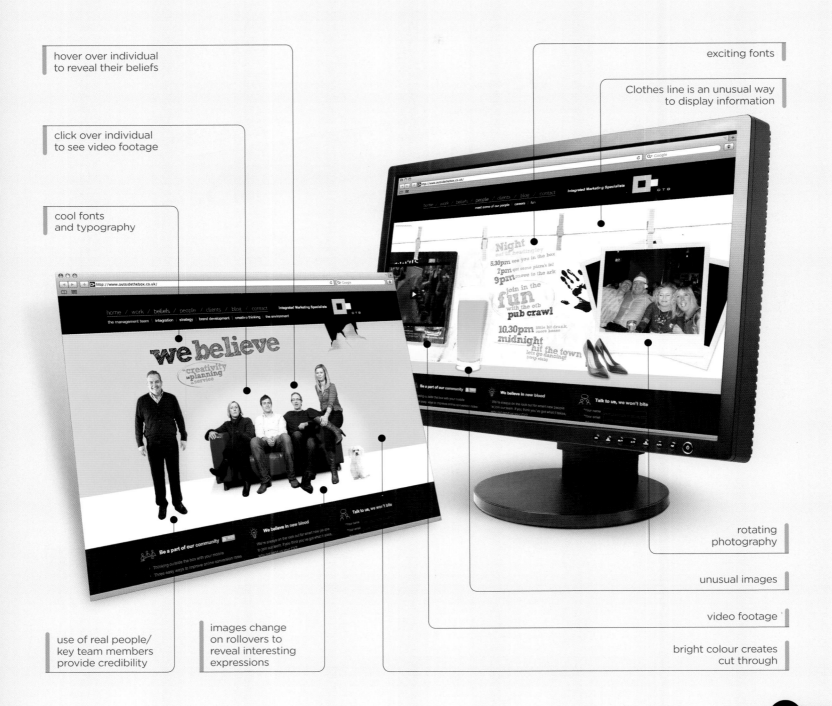

hover over individual
to reveal their beliefs

click over individual
to see video footage

cool fonts
and typography

use of real people/
key team members
provide credibility

images change
on rollovers to
reveal interesting
expressions

exciting fonts

Clothes line is an unusual way
to display information

rotating
photography

unusual images

video footage

bright colour creates
cut through

landing page

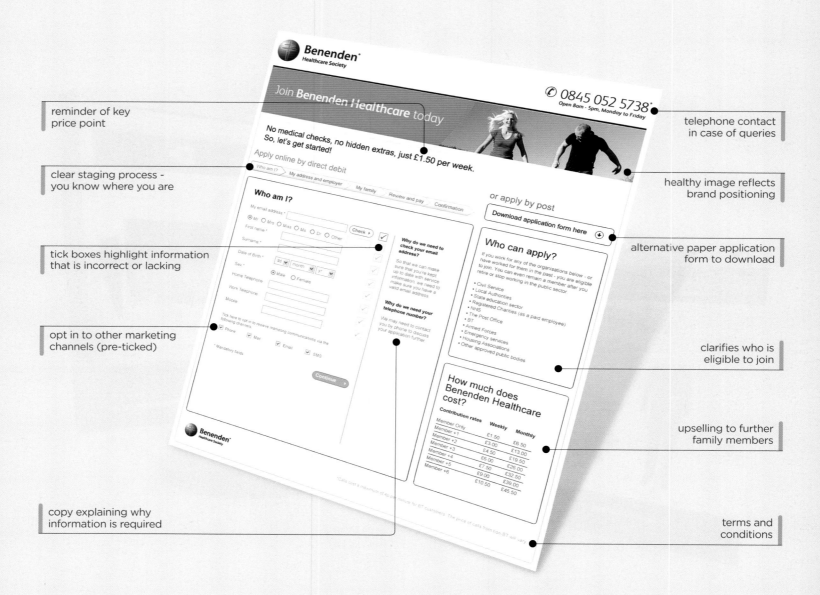

reminder of key
price point

clear staging process -
you know where you are

tick boxes highlight information
that is incorrect or lacking

opt in to other marketing
channels (pre-ticked)

copy explaining why
information is required

telephone contact
in case of queries

healthy image reflects
brand positioning

alternative paper application
form to download

clarifies who is
eligible to join

upselling to further
family members

terms and
conditions

information architecture—basket and billing page

Conversion pages are the last hurdle that the customer has to jump, so make sure that it is as easy as possible, and reassure them that everything has gone to plan.

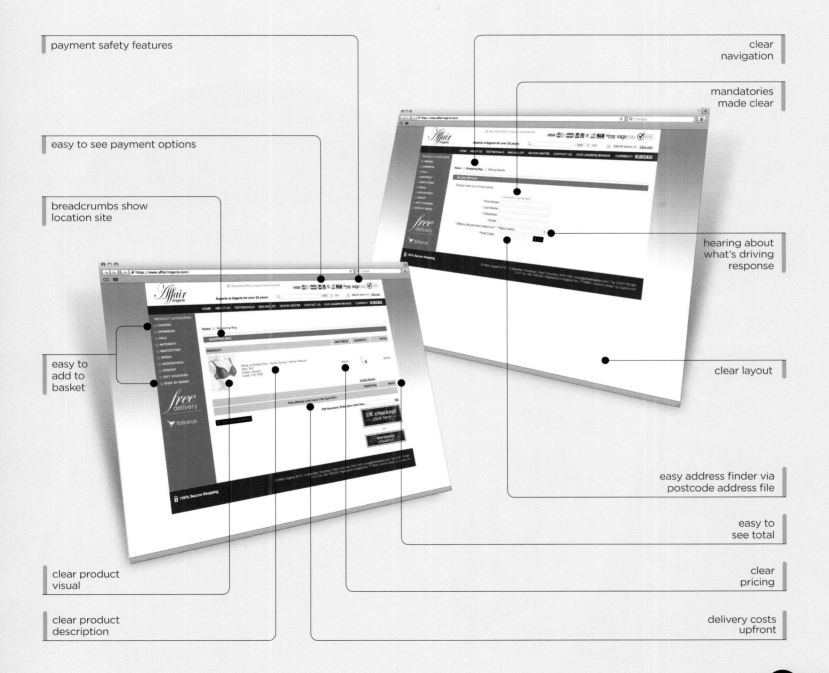

payment safety features

easy to see payment options

breadcrumbs show location site

easy to add to basket

clear product visual

clear product description

clear navigation

mandatories made clear

hearing about what's driving response

clear layout

easy address finder via postcode address file

easy to see total

clear pricing

delivery costs upfront

search engine optimisation

Connect to customers, be ahead of your competitors

Search engines are hugely important in encouraging traffic to a site. One way to attract visitors is to persuade people to specifically seek out a website through various promotions. However in order to receive a significant boost to traffic, a website needs to achieve a good position in the Search Engine Results Pages – SERPs – through Search Engine Optimisation – SEO. Achieving a high SERP position is not a simple task, but by taking the time to understand how search engines work, and adjusting online strategies accordingly, considerable improvements can be achieved very quickly.

While the technology behind search engines is extremely complex, the essence of how they operate is quite simple to understand. The search engines follow links to **Crawl** – a methodical scanning of pages, also known as **Spidering** – web pages using software known, amongst other things, as a **Spider** or **Robot** to build up an index of every readable word on every page. When a search is made, website pages are ranked in order of relevance calculated by a complex algorithm which takes into account many different criteria including the number of times the words or phrases occur on the page and the number of **Backlinks** leading to the page from elsewhere on the web. The search engine algorithms are not released to the public, but it is possible to deduce the key criteria on which search engines base their rankings. These algorithms are, however, known to change regularly requiring you to alter your SEO strategy from time to time.

This chapter will cover the most important aspects of SEO, including getting a site indexed, optimising a site through the use of Keyphrases and an organisational structure amenable to spiders, encouraging links from external sites and avoiding unethical **Black Hat** techniques.

Submitting a site

The first step in SEO is making sure that all of a site's web pages are included in the search engine indexes. There was a time when it was necessary to manually submit a site to the various search engines and to resubmit them when significant changes were made. Thankfully, the search engine robots now perform this action automatically, by following links to find a site and then frequently revisiting it to check for updates. Any new or modified pages are, therefore, usually added to the index of the main search engines fairly quickly with the length of time dependent on the site's popularity. Encouraging external backlinks is, therefore, worth concentrating on in order to make a site conspicuous to the search engine robots which, in turn, will ensure that all updates make it onto the search engine as quickly as is robotically possible.

If you want to make sure that all of the pages on a website are indexed then you should think about submitting an **XML Sitemap**.

Gloss
An XML sitemap is a file placed on your site but hidden from visitors – in the **Root Directory** – which contains an index to help search engines navigate a site.

This can help in getting more pages indexed and can encourage the search engines to crawl a site more frequently. After the sitemap has been created, it can then be sent to the search engines so that they know where to find it. Sitemaps are especially important for large, complex sites, particularly if there are pages which are not easily found by robots; for instance, if they are not well linked to each other or include content such as PDF Documents or Flash which is not crawlable by the search engines.

Hint
You may also want to submit a site to directories such as *Yahoo!*, which rely on sites manually registering their URLs rather than actively sending out robots. This can attract traffic to a site and is a great way to get links. The directories are also regularly crawled by robots, so it can be a good way of getting a site indexed and updated regularly.

Keywords and Keyphrases
One of the main criteria which determine a site's search engine ranking is the relevancy and density of the keywords and keyphrases contained within the content of the website. This means that you should try to predict the search terms that potential customers might use and then optimise all of a site's pages for those keywords or keyphrases.

Selecting the Right Keyphrases
The first stage is to determine which keyphrases to target. There are various ways of formulating potential keyphrases and the easiest, and most obvious, option is to have a creative session; put yourself in the position of potential customers and establish which words or phrases you would use if you were searching for a particular service. You should include words related to the products or services, geographical location, indications of price – cheap, budget, etc – brand name, or even competitors' brand names.

Another useful technique is to examine the keyword tags on competitors' websites. These take the form:

<META name ="keywords" content="keyword1, keyword2">.

You can usually find these tags by clicking on the 'View' tab and then 'Page Source' within the browser window when viewing the desired website.

Once you have compiled a list of keyphrases, you should expand this further by adding similar or related keyphrases such as plurals, synonyms, different combinations of words, and hyphenated or dehyphenated versions of phrases. You can also abandon keyphrases if they are too broad or ambiguous.

Once you have compiled a sizeable list of potential keyphrases, you should use an online tool to assess their popularity and to suggest alternatives.

There are various free services including Google's keyword tool: *https://adwords.google.co.uk/select/KeywordToolExternal*

However, it is advisable to pay for a fee-based service such as **Wordtracker.com,** which will not only analyse keyphrase popularity across each of the main search engines and suggest alternatives, but will also provide details on how competitive each keyphrase is.

> **Hint**
> The information you gather regarding how potential customers search can be used in all marketing activities, on and offline. Find the key words or key phrases most commonly searched and see if they can be used in headlines in other media.

On-page optimisation for keyphrases

Keep Focused
By this stage, you should have a list of dozens, or perhaps hundreds, of good keyphrases which you can prioritise by order of importance, determined by the relevance, popularity, and competitiveness of each keyphrase. Try to focus on one or two keyphrases for each page, but also try to work other keyphrases into the page as well, if doing so does not detract from the quality and readability of the content.

> **Hint**
> Always keep a copy of your list of keyphrases handy while writing copy for a web page and look for opportunities to apply them.

Keyphrase Density
It used to be that keyphrase frequency was one of the most important factors in ranking pages. However, due to widespread spamming techniques in which disreputable sites would repeat keyphrases an unnatural number of times, most search engines now concentrate more on **Keyphrase Density** rather than frequency, and a moderate density is considered optimal. This is designed to reward websites that are written naturally rather than those crammed with keyphrases.

If a keyphrase appears five times in a 100-word page, its density will be 5%, which is clearly higher than if it appears ten times in a 500-word page – 2%. One danger is that keyphrase density may be too low in large documents with a high word-count so, to avoid this, large documents are best spread across several interlinked web pages. Ideally, you should be aiming for a density of between 5%

and 10%, but be careful as you may face a penalty if the density rises too far above 10%. If a page is in danger of becoming too keyphrase heavy, you can use synonyms or rearrange the words within the phrase, to alleviate some of the density.

Search engines now attach great importance to synonyms as a means of identifying and avoiding web pages that have made use of keyphrase stuffing, and rewarding those written in a more natural style involving the use of synonyms rather than repeating the same phrase ad infinitum. You should aim to include keyphrase synonyms not just in copy but also in the meta descriptions and title tags of a website, though this is something that is best left to an SEO specialist or web developer.

Text formatting
There are several ways in which you can highlight the importance of a particular word or phrase to the search engines. You should position keyphrases in different headings and sub-headings, making use of different HTML header tags – <H1>, <H2>, etc. – and you can also use bold, italic, and bullet-point formatting to indicate the importance of specific keyphrases. The impact of measures such as these is likely to be quite small, but they will have a cumulative effect, which could make all the difference. A related factor worth paying attention to is the position of the keyphrase on the page. It is usually best to make sure that the keyphrase is included near the beginning and end of the copy and then repeated throughout the document in ever decreasing quantity, so that there is a higher density towards the beginning.

<TITLE> Tag
Using keyphrases in a page's **<TITLE>** Tag can have a significant impact on its SERP position. The search engines pay a lot of attention to the <TITLE> tag, so be careful not to squander the opportunity with a generic welcome message. Instead, you should include the chosen keyphrase for that page at the beginning of the tag, followed by any additional keywords or phrases that might be appropriate for that page. The <TITLE> tag should be no longer than 60 characters, and should be placed directly below the <HEAD> tag.

> **Hint**
> Remember that the <TITLE> tag will be displayed as the link anchor text in SERPs, so make sure that it acts as an accurate page description and preferably also as an effective call-to-action.

Description Meta Tag
The **Description Meta Tag** is often displayed in the SERPs under the hyperlink to a site, and can therefore have a significant impact on click-through rate. Where possible, you should aim to produce a different description meta tag for each individual page containing target keyphrases, otherwise the search engines – especially Google –

might, instead, display a **Snippet** in the search results which is likely to be less successful in persuading people to click through. You should make sure that it acts as a compelling call-to-action, though only approximately 20 words of the tag will be visible in the search results, so make sure that your message is concise and to the point.

Keywords Meta Tag

The **Keywords Meta Tag** is relatively unimportant compared to the title and description tags as it will be entirely hidden from visitors, and will have little impact on SERP positioning. However, it may be used to inform the search engines of the nature of the content on each page which can be useful for pages that are difficult for search engines to read. You should, therefore, include short keyword tags of between 10 and 12 words incorporating specific keywords to indicate the content of each page.

Site Design

Just as important as the use of keyphrases is the optimisation of the design and structure of a site, including the navigation system and the use of images and rich media content. These factors can have a major impact on SERP positioning – either good or bad – so it is important to be aware of common best practices in this area.

Navigation System

Search engines will not be able to find their way through sites which only use a JavaScript navigation system, which means that many pages may not be indexed unless they are linked to from elsewhere. You should, therefore, make sure that you include a basic HTML navigation system which makes it easier for search engine robots; for example, including various simple text links at the bottom of each page which, in turn, may also make it easier for visitors to navigate around the site.

Framed Sites

In a framed site, a single browser window is divided into different parts, each containing a different web page. These are now very rare and you definitely should not be adding frames to a site as they make it very difficult for search engines to understand the content. This is because search engines are designed to index web pages rather than framesets, and individual frames may not make much sense without their 'parent' frame. Frames can also create problems with printing and bookmarking and should be avoided. To summarise; framing = bad.

Plug-ins

Flash and other **Plug-ins**, such as Java, can be used to produce content which is particularly attractive and interactive. Text within these applications can sometimes be indexed by search engines, but generally not as well as HTML-based text. It is, therefore, strongly advised that pages that comprise only of Flash, or other plug-in

content, are to be avoided and instead, include at least some basic HTML while also making full use of the <TITLE> tag and description meta tag to indicate the content on the page.

Embedded Text

It is not uncommon to find whole web pages made entirely of images, with any text embedded within the images themselves. This can give the designer more freedom over the presentation of the text and can be simpler to create than using HTML coding. However, the embedded text will be invisible to search engines and SERPS positioning will suffer as a result; also, these pages can be very slow to load.

Dynamic Content

Dynamic Pages are created from a database in real time so that the same page will appear differently in different contexts. Search engines dislike dynamic pages for various reasons, and will often refuse to index them at all. The primary reason for this is that the search engines are concerned that they may have to index large numbers of nearly identical pages. Search engines can usually spot dynamic pages as they tend to contain unusual characters such as **?**, **&**, and **!**. However, you can use URL rewriting to make dynamic pages appear Static to the search engines; different servers have different URL rewriting instruments to help you with this and it is worth doing if you want dynamic content to be indexed properly in the main search engines.

Session IDs

Session IDs are used to identify individual visitors and to track them as they navigate through a site. This usually results in a unique identifier for individual users being included in the URL of each page which can confuse the search engines and result in pages being indexed improperly or not at all. To avoid these problems you can choose to store the session ID in a **Cookie** rather than in the URL itself, or a site can be programmed so that session IDs are removed for search engine robots but still used for ordinary users.

> ### Gloss
> A Cookie is a small text file stored by a user's web browser which can be used to effectively 'remember' shopping basket contents, site preferences, or anything else that can be accomplished through storing text data.

Internal Linking

Internal links from one page on a site to another will be given less weight in the search engine rankings than links from external sites, but you are in complete control of internal links and, if utilised properly, they can provide substantial results. Navigation bars are placed on every page and can, therefore, significantly increase the number of links to their target pages. You can also include **Breadcrumb Trails** and **Footer Text Links** containing a more comprehensive collection of links on each page, to aid navigation and boost the number of internal backlinks. Having a **Sitemap Page** containing links to all of the main pages on a site can also be useful, and you can try to include links within the body copy of web pages, where appropriate. Always try to use text links rather than images as these can be followed more easily by robots, and make sure that the link anchor text uses appropriate keyphrases for the target page where possible.

Duplication

Most of the main search engines operate a **Duplicate Content Filter,** meaning that, if different web pages are sufficiently similar to one another, then one or more of them could be removed from the search engine indexes. This commonly happens when different pages on a site are very similar for some reason – for example, if they are displaying very similar products – or if somebody else has copied a page – usually through a process called **Screen Scraping** – and added it to their own site. You should, therefore, ensure that unique content is added to each page and make use of meta tags to differentiate very similar pages. You should also regularly check to see if any other sites are plagiarising content; **copyscape.com** is a useful tool for this.

The Importance of Links

Search engines regard each link to a page as an indication of the quality of the content; each link is essentially a vote for that page. Links also make it easier for search engine robots to find pages and help the search engines to understand more about the content of a site; if a lot of classical music sites are linking to a site then the search engines will ascertain that that site is probably related to classical music.

All of the main search engines have different systems for ranking pages according to the quantity and quality of backlinks, but the **Google** system is called **PageRank** and, given that Google is by far the most popular search engine, the best course of action is to focus efforts on boosting PageRank. The measures necessary to achieve a high PageRank are also likely to lead to a high ranking in other search engines.

You can establish an estimation of the PageRank of any web page very easily; simply install the Google toolbar from **www.toolbar. google.com** onto an appropriate ISP, such as Firefox or Internet Explorer and the PageRank of each page that you open will be displayed in a bar – the PageRank is 0 if the bar is white, and 10 if the bar is green.

Hint

It is likely that PageRank is calculated on a logarithmic scale, so the difference between a score of 1 and 2 will be much smaller than the difference between 7 and 8.

Link Value

Some links are more valuable than others as the search engines seek to reward relevant links and penalise the more reprehensible link building activities.

Links from pages with a high PageRank are more valuable

A site's PageRank will benefit more if the sites linking to it are, themselves, heavily linked to and you should therefore target link-building activities towards popular, reputable sites. It is also a good idea to encourage these sites to link from pages with a high PageRank.

Links from pages with few other links are more valuable

The number of votes that a single page can allocate is limited, so the more links on a page, the fewer votes will go to each of the individual linked pages. This means that you should encourage other sites to link from pages with few other links, and avoid large Links Pages like the plague.

Links can impact on PageRank

Only individual web pages have a PageRank, not websites as a whole. You will probably find, therefore, that particular pages within a site have a much higher PageRank than others. This can be addressed by making sure that pages are as highly interlinked as possible, thereby distributing PageRank to the whole of the site. When a site links to external sites it will leak votes which could have been used to boost its own pages. This shouldn't deter you from linking to other sites but you should try to concentrate as many of these links as possible on a small number of pages with low PageRank in order to minimise the leakage. You could also apply the **Nofollow** HTML attribute when coding external hyperlinks which will prevent search engine robots from following these links and so prevent PageRank leaking to external sites.

One caveat to this is that having outbound links on a page may actually increase its PageRank if it is identified by the search engines as a **Hub**. A Hub is a page that links to a lot of other external pages, all concerning a specific topic and search engines favour this class of page and reward them with high rankings. In reaction to this, you could divide main links pages into several smaller topic-specific pages so that these may be classified as Hubs. You could also encourage other sites to link from Hub pages rather than a large general links page.

Links from pages with relevant content are more valuable

Also important, is the context in which links to a site are placed. Search engines identify context by assessing the use of keyphrases or synonyms on that page – particularly in the title tag and headings – and also by the use of keyphrases in the link anchor text. Links from pages with content similar to a site's own will be considered more important than links from pages or sites that focus on different areas and you should, therefore, concentrate your efforts on having links posted on sites that are relevant, and also encourage anchor link text which includes your chosen keyphrases rather than just the brand name or a generic phrase such as 'Click Here'.

The rate at which you attract links to pages can affect PageRank

If a page attracts large numbers of links from relevant sites in a short period of time then this suggests that it contains material that is highly topical and good quality and will therefore be rewarded by search engines. On the other hand, if new links have slowed down this indicates that a site is becoming less popular and will negatively affect PageRank even if old backlinks are kept in place. Link-building must, therefore, be a continuous process.

Some links will contribute little or nothing to PageRank

Websites used to have online **Guest Books** which allowed visitors to post their own links, but search engines quickly caught on to this practice and links from pages such as these are now of negligible value.

    Link Farms are automated systems which large numbers of websites join in order to exchange links. They are an audacious and highly unnatural method of boosting link popularity and using them will not only fail to improve PageRank but may also result in more serious penalties from search engines.

    A **Free For All** – FFA – page is one that allows anybody to post a link back to their own site. Given that these pages will tend to include large numbers of unrelated links, backlinks on these pages will not significantly improve PageRank.

    The **Nofollow** attribute already mentioned above can be included in a hyperlink's HTML coding, and prevents the link from contributing to the target site's PageRank. You should check to see if any of the links to a site contain the Nofollow attribute and, if so, either request that it be removed or concentrate your efforts on sites that do not use Nofollow.

Places to get links

Concentrate on content

Great content – or **Linkbait** – is the best and most natural way to consistently attract large numbers of backlinks from relevant and popular sites. Generic content is unlikely to draw much attention, so when adding new material to a site you should try to create something genuinely useful, original or entertaining. Some good ideas for link-generating content include using instruction guides, news items, blogs expressing original and controversial opinions, reviews of new products, videos and podcasts. This is the key element when looking to make waves.

Capitalising on relationships

If you are developing the SEO for your own site, then the first thing that you should do is ask everybody that you know who has a website of any kind – whether it is a business or a blog – to link to your site. Use any of your social network sites such as Facebook or

optimise to **increase** the quantity and **quality** of traffic

Twitter to inform all of your contacts about your site and request a link. It is also always worth contacting any trade associations of which you are a member to see if they can link to your site, and if you are not a member of any you should consider becoming one. Industry association websites may have a member directory or a page dedicated to linking members' sites and, if so, you should make sure that you are included. Finally, you should consider contacting all of your major suppliers and clients to request a link. Your suppliers will probably be the most persuadable; if they really value your business they should be willing to provide a link somewhere on the website and if you are a particularly important client they may even agree to display it on their home page where it will have the biggest effect on your PageRank.

Social Bookmarking

Social bookmarking sites, such as **Delicious** and **Digg**, allow people to record their online bookmarks and access them on any computer, while sharing them with other online users. When a bookmark is created on a user's homepage, a link is created to the bookmarked page which can have a positive effect on its PageRank. You should, therefore, include links to the main social bookmarking sites at the bottom of all pages where appropriate. However, the importance of social bookmarking to SEO may be on the decline as some sites such as Delicious now use Nofollow on all of their external links so, as a result, their backlinks will no longer boost PageRank. They can, however, still be useful in driving traffic to pages from other users of the social bookmarking sites.

Finding other sites

You should use an online service such as **Yahoo Site Explorer** to research who is linking to competitors and, if appropriate, request links from them. You can also research which types of sites are already providing links and try to find similar sites that may also be interested in doing the same.

Reciprocal links

It is usually preferable to receive links from other sites without having to link back to them but, if necessary, you can propose a reciprocal link exchange with a small number of high quality sites. These can be very effective, as you can usually influence how the other party presents your link and you can target sites that are particularly relevant.

Hint

It is likely that reciprocal links are less helpful than they used to be and that the main search engines attach less importance to these links than to spontaneous, non-reciprocal links. One way to increase the impact of reciprocal links is to establish a three-way or four-way linking arrangement, in which a site links to a second party's site, which links to a third-party's site, which links back to the first. This arrangement may be difficult to organise but if done effectively, it will be difficult for search engines to detect and will, therefore, have a greater impact on PageRank than traditional one-to-one link exchanges.

Contributing to forums and blogs

There are millions of blogs and discussion forums on the internet, covering every conceivable area of business. You should find the most popular and highest-quality blogs and forums and start following them and posting responses with backlinks, making sure that they are genuine responses to the discussions rather than simply spamming, as this is likely to lead to deletion and can have a negative impact on brand.

However, because of the prevalence of spam responses to forums and blogs, search engines are attaching less and less weight to links from these sites, and many blogs and forums automatically attach the Nofollow attribute to any external links. It is, therefore, worth focusing on the company's website's blog, before adding content to others.

Buy links

There are several different ways in which you can go about buying links, and not all of them are recommended. The safest method involves paying for inclusion in certain online directories such as **Yahoo.** It is also possible to pay other sites for links; this can be done either on a pay-per-click or fixed fee basis and is relatively low risk as it is difficult for the search engines to detect. One method that you definitely should not use is to go through a broker as this practice is strongly discouraged by search engines and you are likely to be penalised if caught.

Online press releases

There are a lot of good quality online press release services through which companies can publish news about themselves which is then likely to be picked up by large, reputable news services such as **Google News.** This will help to drive traffic to the company's site as well as generating links and improving SERP position. Some good services include **businesswire.com** and **prweb.com.**

Black Hat Techniques

All of the main search engines have measures in place to filter out web pages using unethical **Black Hat** techniques to climb the search engine rankings and you need to make sure that you don't inadvertently or deliberately engage in any of the prohibited activities.

Keyword stuffing

This involves the repetition of keywords or phrases over and over again on the same page. This technique is now easily spotted by search engines and will inevitably have a negative impact on SERPs.

Keyword masking

This is the practice of adding keywords or phrases to a page which are visible to the search engines but hidden from the user; for example, by using the same colour for the text and the background.

Cloaking

Cloaking is a technique which involves showing a user-friendly page to ordinary visitors and a different, SEO-friendly page to search engine robots. This makes it impossible for the search engines to accurately assess the relevance and quality of the page. Cloaking can also be used to trick users to visit a web page based on an inaccurate description in a search engine and this is often used to hide pornographic content.

Interlinking

Interlinking describes the practice of building multiple websites and linking each of them together to boost their link popularity.

Doorway Pages

A **Doorway Page** is one which is highly optimised for SEO and which automatically redirects to a different, more user-friendly page.

Types of penalties

If a site is caught using a black hat technique then it may face one of a number of penalties which can be applied either automatically or manually by the search engines. These range in severity from a decrease in ranking for a specific page to the complete removal of the entire site from a search engine's index.

Negative SEO

Some unethical businesses may try to deliberately damage competitors' SERPS rankings. This can often involve tricking the search engines into thinking that they are using black hat techniques; by linking to the targeted site from obvious link farms, for example. This practice is fortunately still quite uncommon but you should be aware of it as a potential risk.

The Benefits of a Professional SEO Consultant

SEO is certainly something that can be performed in-house and following this chapter should give you a good start to provide a website with a boost to its PageRank. However, if you are less than confident about being able to keep up with the demands of SEO, then it is best to employ a professional. It is important to know one's limits and it is often far more cost-effective to outsource work to experts, whose efficiency and knowledge can provide the returns that in-house efforts cannot hope to achieve.

SEO experts can streamline the SEO process by spotting technical issues early and having the knowledge to deal with these swiftly. There is also the issue of keeping up with the mercurial search engine algorithms. This can be a seriously challenging task, but SEO consultants will constantly monitor any changes and adjust your strategy accordingly. Finally, a consultant can offer an integrated PPC and SEO strategy supported by accurate reporting which will allow you to see whether hiring a consultant is cost-effective.

seo case study

search engine

It may be an incredibly competitive business, but Search can drive a lot of traffic to a site so do everything you can to get to the top.

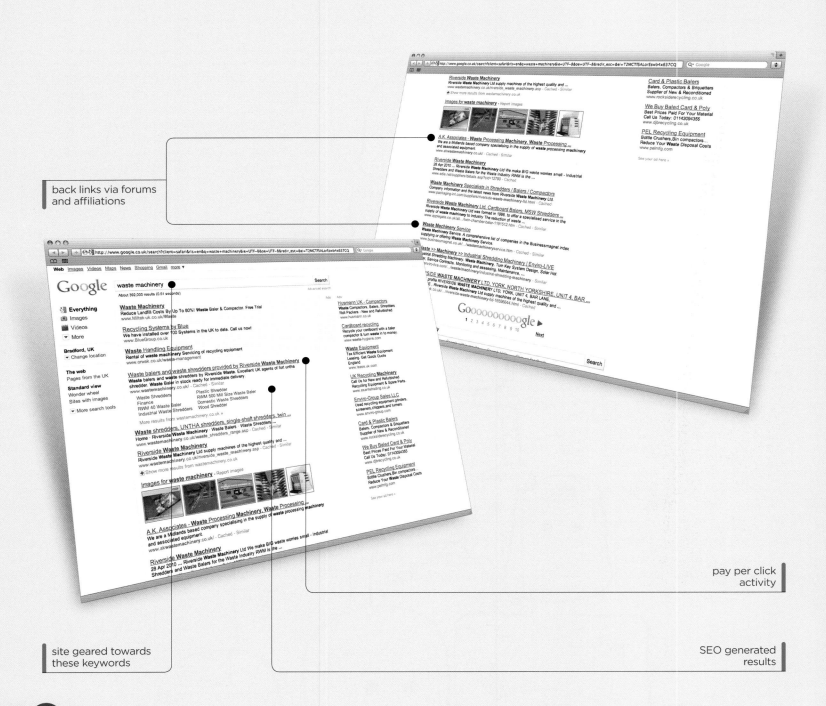

back links via forums
and affiliations

pay per click
activity

site geared towards
these keywords

SEO generated
results

content creations

SEO requires a dynamic multi-layered strategy of link building, keywords and content. It is in the search engines' best interests to champion the best sites and they keep getting better at it, so the most reliable approach to succeeding in search is to build a great website and fill it with up to date, engaging content.

homepage populated
with recent blog posts

Social media feed
adds more content

paid search marketing

People don't search for things they don't want

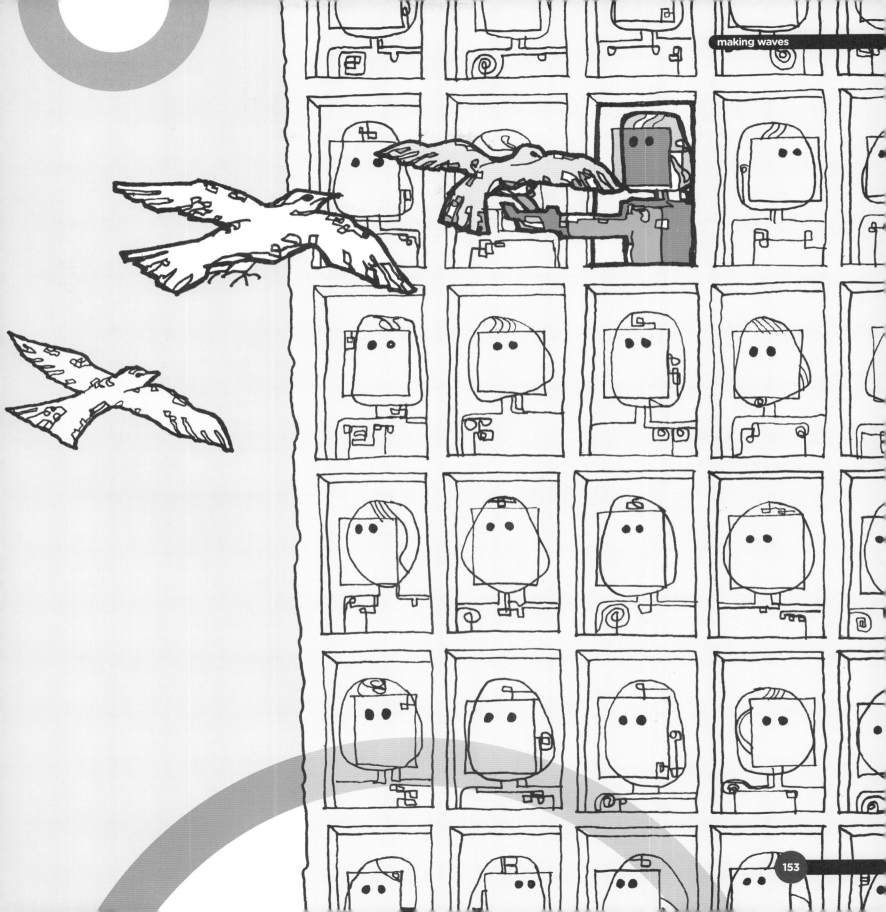

Paid search usually manifests as **Pay Per Click – PPC –** which involves small adverts that are displayed when a particular phrase is entered into a search engine, with the advertiser paying the search engine a certain amount whenever a user clicks on their advert. It is highly targeted, quick to establish, provides near-immediate results, and offers effective ways to keep track of ROI.

PPC can be very useful, especially for sites that are finding it difficult to achieve a high organic ranking in the Search Engine Results Pages – SERPs – and it can also aid new sites where the organic SEO strategy is still in its fledgling stage. That is not to say that PPC should be abandoned once SEO has taken off; PPC is often continued by many companies in parallel to a successful SEO strategy as it can provide further benefits, such as creating further leads, sales, footfall – which in turn bolsters SEO – and brand exposure.

There are a lot of different PPC advertising platforms, but it is a good idea to start with **Google AdWords** as **Google** is, of course, the most popular search engine and is, therefore, likely to generate the highest volume of clicks. Furthermore, if you can establish an effective PPC campaign on Google you will be able to apply the same principles to other PPC systems such as **Yahoo!** and Microsoft's **Bing**.

The advantages and opportunities of PPC are enormous. As a PPC advert is only ever shown to somebody who has typed specific terms into a search engine, the campaign becomes extremely targeted as it is generally only seen by a person who is interested in the advert's product or service and at the time that they are interested. PPC adverts become even more targeted when they direct the searcher to specific **Landing Pages** – the details of which we cover in our **Website** chapter – which can be optimised and, effectively, personalised depending on an individual's searches. There is, therefore, much less waste of time and money advertising to people who are entirely uninterested, while those that are interested are appropriately engaged with relevant content.

In addition, PPC is relatively low risk – there is no upfront fixed fee and, if set up independently, the only expense comes when the advert is clicked; so if you put out an ineffective advert which receives little response – not that you will. We believe in you – there is a good chance that the cost of the mistake will be minimal. PPC can also be handled by an agency, who will charge a start-up fee and an ongoing – usually commission based – management fee, but should more than make up for this expense with their expertise.

PPC advertising is also highly suitable for testing, so it is quick, easy and cheap for you to try different techniques in order to optimise a PPC strategy. However, PPC is not without its difficulties; creating and organising a keyword list, keeping costs under control and producing effective adverts are just some of the major challenges that you will face.

Keyword selection

While the keyword lists for SEO and PPC will necessarily be different, – PPC keywords tend to be more specific, so as to minimise the amount of useless clicks – the process by which you create them is broadly similar and described in more detail in the **SEO Chapter.** The main points are summarised below:

- Put yourself in the position of the customer and deliberate which words or phrases you would use if you were searching for a particular service.

- Research the keyword tags on competitors' websites.

- Look at the website's access logs to see which keywords are currently leading users to it.

- Add similar or related keywords, e.g. plurals, synonyms, common spelling mistakes, etc.

- Use an online tool such as **WordTracker** or **Google Trends** to assess the popularity and level of competitiveness of keywords and to suggest alternatives.

With PPC you will also need to take into account the price of keywords, which is, of course, related to their popularity and competitiveness. Always remember that you will need to be much more careful in PPC campaigns to avoid any keywords that are too broad or ambiguous.

Keyword Matching

You can also help to make a PPC campaign more highly targeted by using **Keyword Matching.** Keyword matching is the process by which you determine how broad or narrow your targeting should be. There are four different keyword matching options offered by Google: **Broad, Phrase, Exact and Negative.**

Broad matching — keyword

Broad matching is the default option on Google Adwords and results in an advert being displayed when the keyword or a similar phrase are searched for. So if your targeted keyword is 'cheap guitars' the advert may appear on a SERP for 'cheap electric guitar'. Broad matching is usually quicker and easier to set up than the other keyword matching options and will give an advert a greater reach and should, therefore, attract a higher number of clicks. However, you will have less control over the keywords being targeted and adverts may consequently appear on irrelevant SERPs which can negatively affect click-through and conversion rates. This can be remedied through the use of negative matching which will reduce the risk of this happening.

Exact matching — [keyword]

Exact matching is notated by brackets around the keyword. An advert will be triggered only when the exact phrase is used in a search query, so if your keyword was [cheap guitars], the advert would only appear when someone searched for that exact phrase and not for searches for similar phrases such as 'cheap guitar' or 'very cheap guitars'. This can result in a more specific targeting of keywords which can lead to higher click-through and conversion rates, but using exact matching can result in a lower volume of clicks and takes more time to put together.

Phrase matching — "keyword"

Phrase matching is notated by quotation marks around the keyword. An advert may appear when someone searches for the exact keyword or for the exact keyword with other terms before or after the phrase. For example, for the keyword 'cheap guitars', the advert may appear on a SERP for 'very cheap guitars', or 'acoustic cheap guitars', but not 'cheap acoustic guitars'. This can be useful because sometimes the broad matching option can be too broad while the exact matching option can be too limited and specific; the phrase matching option can be a happy balance between the two.

Negative matching — keyword

Notated by a negative sign before the keyword, this is used to make sure that adverts do not appear in the SERPs when a particular word or phrase is used as part of the search query, so that the advert is not shown to people unlikely to be interested in what it is offering. So, for example, if you – or the company that you are marketing for – only sell second-hand guitars, you may want to stop adverts being triggered by searches that include the word 'new'. It can take some time to think of all the negative phrases to be excluded but if done effectively, the negative matching option can be highly effective in achieving more specific targeting and can have a significant impact on click-through and conversion rates.

Ad Copy

Writing compelling copy for a PPC ad can be a challenge. While each PPC system is different, they all have strict limits on the number of characters that you can use, so you have only a very small space in which to persuade potential buyers to click on a link. Another challenge is that many of the different search terms that you are targeting will require different copy as they may relate to completely different services – this can prove to be a real problem if you are targeting hundreds or even thousands of different search terms. The solution to this is to sort your different keywords into small Ad Groups, where each group is focused on the same broad theme and so can use the same ad copy.

This will cut down on your workload while still enabling you to give each search term relevant, effective and targeted copy.

A PPC advert will consist of a headline, followed by one or two lines of supplementary text and a target URL. Given the strict character limitations you will need to make every word count – Google, for example, will allow just 25 characters in the headline and 35 characters for each of two description lines.

Headline

You should use the **Headline** to grab the user's attention, and one of the most simple and effective ways of doing this is to include all or part of the search term that they have just used. So if they have searched for 'vintage shoes' your headline should ideally be 'vintage shoes' or something very similar. This will not only help to catch their eye but will also make them more likely to click through as your advert will appear more relevant to their search.

> ### Hint
> It can be a good idea to word the headline in the form of a question which is then answered in the description – 'Want vintage shoes?', for example.

Description

Once you have caught the user's attention with your headline, you can use the **Description** to highlight the benefits that the site provides. This could include information on sales or promotions and/or details about the wide range and quality of the products in comparison to competitor products. Try to be specific about what is on offer as this will have the double benefit of attracting people who are genuinely interested while discouraging

Consider Consumer Relevance

those who are not from clicking on the link and adding to costs. It is usually a good idea to try to highlight keywords, and you can use capital letters for this purpose, though most PPC systems have restrictions on the amount of capitalisation that you can use. If possible you should also try to find some way of making your description stand out from other adverts, most of which tend to be fairly homogenous using very similar language to make very similar claims; try making use of humour or using unusual words or characters, or anything else that you can think of. You should also aim to end the description with a clear call-to-action such as 'Buy now!' or 'Sign up today!'.

Display URL

The **Display URL** is simply the version of the web address of the landing page that is visible as part of an advert; most PPC systems specify that it must be similar to the actual URL but because of space constraints you will often have to use a shortened version. You are advised to use all or part of the keyword in the display URL in order to emphasise the relevance of the target page. You could also capitalise the start of each word and use hyphens to separate different words in order to make it more easy to read. If necessary remove the 'http://www.' part of the domain to allow more space for the domain and directory names.

> ### Hint
> If appropriate try to use a country-specific domain such as '.co.uk' to highlight the fact that the business is local to the user.

Dynamic Keyword Insertion

Dynamic Keyword Insertion – DKI – allows you to specify a position in an advert where a keyword will be placed when that keyword is included in the search query that triggers it. This allows you to write a generic advert for a particular ad group, and then use DKI to make the advert more specific and targeted to each individual user. All of the main PPC systems allow some form of dynamic content but they operate in slightly different ways. The following example is based on Google Adwords:

If you have an ad group that consists of ties, cufflinks, aftershaves, electric razors, you could write the following generic advert:

Great {KeyWord:Gifts For Men}

Top {KeyWord:presents} ideal for Father's Day.

20% off for new customers!

example.com/{KeyWord:Fathers-Day}

The relevant keyword from the advert group would be inserted where the {KeyWord} codes have been positioned, unless this would make the advert too long in which case the default words would be used, which in the example above are 'Gifts for Men', and 'presents'. So the advert might appear as follows:

Great Aftershaves

Top presents ideal for Father's Day

20% off for new customers!

www.example.com/Aftershaves

The keyword 'aftershaves' has been included in the headline and display URL, but the default text 'presents' has been used in the description because 'aftershaves' would have taken the first line of the description over the character limit.

> ### Hint
> It is possible to control the capitalisation of your keywords as follows:
>
> KeyWord will capitalise each word, e.g. "Tennis Racket"
> keyword will lower case all words, e.g. "tennis racket"
> Keyword will capitalise the first character only, e.g. "Tennis racket"
> KEYWORD will capitalise the whole thing, e.g. "TENNIS RACKET"

Bid management
Deciding how much to bid
Before you start bidding for keywords you will first need to ascertain the maximum cost per click. This can be easily calculated by following a simple four-step process:

1. Work out the **Gross Profit** of the product that you are advertising or, if you are simultaneously advertising a range of different products, the average gross profit. This is calculated by taking the total costs associated with the sale of the product, which will principally include the cost of purchase, cost of shipping, and any transaction costs, and subtracting them from the total sale price including shipping charges. If total sale price is £50 and total costs are £35 the gross profit will be £15.

2. Having calculated gross profit you then need to determine the **Maximum Cost Per Conversion**. Cost per conversion is the total amount of money spent on clicks divided by the number of conversions, so 100 clicks at £2 each

resulting in twenty conversions would mean a cost per conversion of £10. Your maximum cost per conversion should never be greater than your gross profit as this would result in a loss; ideally, it should be significantly less than gross profit in order to maintain a healthy profit margin, so if gross profit for a particular product was £10 you might set the maximum cost per conversion at £5.

3. You now need to calculate the **Conversion Rate** – this is simply the proportion of clicks that ultimately result in a conversion. A conversion is the action that you want website visitors to take, which more often than not will be a purchase of products or services. So if an advert produces 1,000 clicks, and ten of those clicks result in a purchase the conversion rate would be 1%.

4. Finally, in order to calculate **Maximum Cost Per Click**, you simply multiply the maximum cost per conversion by the conversion rate. If the maximum cost per conversion is £5 and the conversion rate is 1%, the maximum cost per click that you should be prepared to pay would be £0.05.

measure
success
through
ROI

Hint

If a business is new to PPC advertising and doesn't yet have the appropriate data to be able to accurately calculate conversion rate, it becomes something of a guessing game — it would normally be in the range of 1% to 5%, though different types of website and different industries will have different average conversion rates.

The Bidding Process

When you want to bid for a particular keyword you take part in a large auction, and if the keyword is particularly popular the competition will be intense. While a lot of different adverts can be displayed on the same SERP, the higher an advert's position, the more clicks it is likely to get. Search engines base this position on both the level of the bid and the quality of the advert and site. For example, on Google AdWords you set a maximum bid – the maximum cost per click – and Google multiplies this figure by the advert's **Quality Score**, which in turn is based on a number of different criteria such as relevance and click-through rate. This calculation produces an **Ad Rank**, and those adverts with higher Ad Ranks get positioned higher. The amount actually charged is equal to the Quality Score divided by the Ad Rank of the advert ranked immediately below, rounded up to the nearest penny.

Initial Bidding Strategy

When deciding on how aggressive you should be when bidding for keywords or ad groups, a conservative strategy is probably best if the PPC budget is small or if you have time to start low and then analyse and optimise your bidding strategy. In this case you should bid high enough to obtain a reasonable position for your keywords so that they appear on the first page of the SERPs without paying a premium to appear in the very top positions. Over the course of the following weeks you should monitor the results closely and abandon or adjust adverts failing to produce conversions, while increasing the bid price of those that are bringing in conversions to increase the click-through rate until the cost per conversion reaches the maximum level. This strategy of starting off bidding low, then testing the results and making appropriate changes is low risk, but it can take a long time until you start seeing significant increases in sales.

As an alternative, you could adopt a more aggressive strategy in which you begin by bidding high. This has the effect of bringing in a greater number of clicks more quickly which provides more data to analyse so that you can start adjusting and optimising the campaign straight away rather than waiting days, weeks or even months for the results to trickle in. This can be especially important if you are targeting particularly obscure keywords with low search volume. Another benefit of bidding aggressively from the start is that the higher click-through rate should give you a higher Quality Score which will, in turn, push the advert position higher; this would then allow

you to lower the bid while still maintaining a high position. If you do choose to bid aggressively then be careful to monitor results closely to identify any low-performing keywords, whose cost per conversion is higher than the maximum level, and lower your bids accordingly.

Bid Management Tools

Bid Management Tools can aid in managing the bidding process across a number of different PPC systems by checking the status of each keyword or ad group and optimising the relevant bids to help achieve stated objectives. This can help to boost click-through rate and ultimately increase ROI. The bid management tools will examine the historical data on the performance of each individual keyword and recommend new maximum bid prices and target positions designed to optimise the performance of each keyword. They should also assess the relative performance of different keywords and recommend changes regarding which keywords should receive the highest relative level of spending. Bid management tools can be especially useful when launching a particularly large or complex PPC campaign with a high budget, though you will still need to intervene manually on occasion to make sure that it is running effectively and to keep an eye on the most important and expensive keywords. This is especially important in the first few weeks and months of using a bid management tool while its data on keyword performance is still limited. We are by no means suggesting that bid management tools are always the right choice as they can be very expensive, so you need to carefully assess whether the ROI increase that they will produce will cover the cost of the bid management tool itself. You will often find that you are better off running the campaign manually, especially for smaller campaigns; however, for the right kind of campaign and the right kind of company, bid management tools are an invaluable resource.

There are some very good bid management tools on the market and they often provide very different levels of service for very different prices. If you are exclusively using Google for your PPC activities then you could do worse than using the free **Google Conversion Optimizer.** Alternatively, **PPC BidMax** offers an effective bid management tool which will enable you to manage large campaigns across the three main search engines. **Omniture** is more expensive but offers very high quality bid management services as

well as a range of other applications useful for PPC such as keyword generation tools. There are a huge number of other very good bid management tools out there and you will need to do your research to find out which is best suited to your particular requirements.

Quality Score

It is in the search engines' interests to ensure that the best quality adverts are displayed most prominently and, therefore, Google, Yahoo and Bing assess each advert's quality – Google has its **Quality Score**, Yahoo has the **Quality Index**, and Bing has **Quality Based Ranking** – and you can make this work in your favour. If you succeed in increasing an advert's Quality Score, you can achieve higher positions for less money and, luckily, the type of changes that you will have to make to get a higher score are generally things that you should be doing anyway and they will tend to make your PPC campaigns more effective in encouraging clicks and conversions, so everyone's a winner.

Each of the three major search engines determine their Quality Score/Index/Based Ranking differently, but there are several factors very important to all of them:

- The three search engines attach great importance to the relevance of the ad copy to the keyword, so adverts with copy that contains the keyword will be rewarded with a higher Quality Score.

- The quality of the landing page is taken into account, determined largely by its relevance and originality and, in Google's case, load time.

- Different criteria are used to determine the Quality Score of an advert on the Content Network - in this case search engines look at the relevance of an advert to the third party site and the previous performance of the advert on that site and similar sites.

- The inclusion of appropriate keywords in the advert copy and landing page, should always be a priority, though you should make sure to use them naturally – don't overdo it.

- DKI can be a useful tool if you are managing huge numbers of keywords but if your ad groups are too broad then your copy may be inadequately targeted to the search term by which it is triggered, and this can result in a lower Quality Score. You should therefore ensure that your ad groups are sufficiently small and focused so that the copy can be specific and relevant even where DKI is used, and remember to create a different landing page for each group tailored to be as relevant as possible.

- Another tactic to keep in mind is to focus on maximising your click-through rate. Too often advertisers will focus on increasing their conversion rate, but by increasing the click-through rate and thus boosting their quality score they can reduce the costs of their PPC campaign and increase their profit margin just as substantially as by increasing the rate of conversions.

Click Fraud

With a charge being incurred every time a user clicks on a link, an obvious danger with the PPC system is that someone could run up costs repeatedly by clicking on links with no intention of purchasing anything. There are a number of reasons why someone might want to do this. PPC advertisers generally have a daily budget and they will stop showing adverts each day as soon as that budget has been exhausted. A company looking to reduce the number of adverts running alongside their own may, therefore, try to use fraudulent clicks to sap competitors' daily budgets and so prevent them from displaying their adverts, which would generally help to increase their own click-through rate. A different type of click fraud involves **Content Placement** PPC adverts which essentially involves an advert being placed by a search engine on a third-party site. In this situation, the owners of the third-party site may try to artificially increase the number of clicks on the adverts on their own site in order to boost their advertising revenue.

While the risk of click fraud should of course be taken seriously you should not let it deter you from getting involved with PPC. All search engines are incentivised to tackle the problem of click fraud in order to minimise the risk associated with PPC and encourage greater levels of advertising spend, and as such they have become increasingly active in detecting and preventing fraudulent clicks. If such clicks are identified then, provided that you are using a reputable PPC system, you will not be charged for them. It is generally safer to stick to the main search engines such as Google, Yahoo, and Bing for PPC activities as these tend to be the most reliable in dealing with click fraud.

Hint

Keep an eye on your analytics tools for any unusual patterns in clicking activity that may be indicative of fraud, such as a large number of clicks coming from a specific IP address, sudden changes in your conversion rates, or an unusually high number of clicks for a particular keyword. If, after assessing the data, you have grounds to believe that one of your adverts has been subjected to fraudulent clicks, you can inform the appropriate search engine and try to recover the cost of the clicks.

Content Placement

As well as placing adverts on SERPs, you can also place them on third party sites. Clearly no search terms are involved here so adverts are placed according to the context of the page – the owner of a site agrees to host adverts on one of their pages, the search engine then reads this page, decides what it is about and then finds relevant adverts to place on the page. Alternatively, the advertiser may try to operate greater control and specify the particular type of sites that they wants to host their adverts, and may even identify specific sites.

Content placement has a number of disadvantages compared with ordinary search engine PPC campaigns. Firstly, when people use a search engine, they are actively looking for something – if someone searches for 'camping equipment' it is pretty likely that they are interested in buying camping equipment and by advertising to them on the SERP, you are targeting exactly the right person at exactly the right time – yet, with content placement you will inevitably find yourself advertising to lots of people with no interest in what you are offering and this naturally results in lower click-through rates. Conversion rates may also be lower as users on content sites are more likely to click impulsively because they are browsing content rather than actively looking to make a transaction. Secondly, it can be difficult to ensure that your ads are placed on pages that are relevant. It is very difficult for search engines to get a good idea of the nature of a particular page and to select an appropriate advert to display so it is likely that your adverts will end up getting displayed on lots of irrelevant pages and will suffer a corresponding decline in their click-through and conversion rates. There is also a greater risk of click fraud in content placement – the owner of the content page has a strong financial incentive to artificially increase the number of clicks on adverts which, if undetected, could significantly affect conversion rates. For these reasons you may find it simpler and safer to simply turn off the content placement option when setting up a PPC campaign.

Nevertheless there are some strong reasons why you might want to use content placement. Using content placement gives you greater reach and can therefore increase the overall number of clicks considerably and the cost per click will usually be cheaper because there is less competition. Return on investment will generally be lower because, although the cost per click is lower, your conversion rates are often adversely affected, but it is quite possible to have a profitable PPC campaign that incorporates content placement.

If you do choose to use content placement be sure to follow the advice below:

● Bid separately for content placement and make sure that you bid lower to reflect the less favourable conversion rates.

● Don't use the same ad copy from your search engine PPC adverts – content placement PPC targets a different type of person – someone who is not already looking to buy something – and this means that you will have to work even harder to grab their attention and convince them that they should purchase something. You should also be aware that the Quality Score is calculated differently for content placement and takes into account the relevance of the advert to the site that it is being advertised on.

● Where possible, you should exert control over the sites on which your advert appears in order to ensure that only reputable, high-quality and relevant sites are used. This will involve specifying the type of sites you want to advertise on, as well as identifying sites that are inappropriate or which are producing poor results and tell the search engine to exclude them from your PPC content placement campaign. You should be aware however that not all search engines allow this degree of control over the placement of ads.

Bear in mind, whatever you do
online, **somewhere, someone**
is sat behind a screen developing
an opinon on your brand

social media

The term 'social media' refers to online resources that facilitate interaction between different people and organisations.

transform
broadcast media
monologues
into social media
dialogues

Forget Spin
be Frank

Frank

Marketing has gained a reputation as the business for spin doctors who specialise in promoting the positives of a product/service while hiding the negatives; the best marketing would, of course, take the negatives and turn them into positives.

But things have changed. We have now become entrenched in what **outside the box** likes to refer to as **The Age of Frank.** That is being frank and forthright, being open about every aspect of a business, product, service, or anything else that you are expecting the public to buy into. If this information isn't made available by you then it could be discovered or leaked by one of the great mass of individuals that will scrutinise every aspect of a project in a completely uncontrollable way, generally to the detriment of brand perception.

The reason for this transparency is the rise of online **Social Media**. The term social media is a broad term used to describe online resources which allow people to interact with one another. Whereas traditional media typically involves the broadcast of a message to a passive and receptive audience, social media encourage two-way communication; a **dialogue** rather than a monologue. In its very essence, social media is a channel where participants can engage in a multi-way conversation with others who share similar interests or wish to engage in particular subject areas. Many online experts have hailed the proliferation of these media as a return to the grass roots of the origins of the Internet, a place where communities and content sharing sites are formed between like minded individuals.

As mentioned in our **Making Waves** chapter, we are all pack animals, reliant on contact with others to self-affirm: 'I have friends, therefore I am'. Social media was born from this need and has existed for some time now. It certainly did not take the creation of online communities to allow people to utilise media to socialise around a specific topic. The model car maker, **Corgi**, for instance, started **The Corgi Club** in 1986 to satiate the desires of the mass of hobbyist fans by starting a community where discussions could be pursued, events organised and news shared. There are a plethora of these communities, communicating through newsletters and events, spread across an unimaginably large range of hobbies and passions.

The traditional social media fulfilled the need for people to communicate with one another as long as they were willing to make travel, post or telephone, but it is undoubtedly the internet that has made it easy and accessible and, therefore, prolific. The offline media should not, however, be dismissed as antiquated and obsolete, but should instead be utilised in conjunction with online in order to provide users and consumers with a wide spectrum of ways to communicate to and around a brand.

> **Hint**
> We really like it when Social Media makes its way into the real world. Whether it's an impromptu disco or a massive pillow fight, constructing an experience around a brand gets people involved and can get you some great PR.

The adoption of the internet continues to expand across the world and so many of us will engage with some form of social media in our online experience, expressing views on just about everything it is possible to have an opinion about, creating and uploading videos, photos and blogs, and sharing knowledge and expertise with the world. In fact, social media is the #1 activity on the Web, surpassing all of the internet's more traditional uses. The rise of social media represented a fundamental shift in communication and, in doing so, created great opportunities – and potential dangers – for business.

Social media provides unprecedented scope to learn about customer behaviour and views, to enhance brand reputation by engaging constructively in the online conversation and to gain cost effective, extensive exposure to capture more customers and collect data; a particularly successful video on a video sharing site such as **YouTube** can receive millions of views, a level of coverage that would be extremely expensive to achieve using traditional channels. However, while social media create tremendous opportunities for greater exposure, research, and brand management, there are also great risks involved as disgruntled customers can inform hundreds, thousands or even millions of people about it through a blog, a social network such as **Twitter** or **Facebook**, or through an offline event. Luckily, these media also provide the means to learn from and deal with such dissatisfaction. If a social media strategy is proactive, dynamic and reactionary enough, it can address any customer issues in a way that presents the company as concerned, empathetic and customer focused; to be successful in social media, it is imperative to listen.

support the
democratisation
of knowledge and
information and
transform people
from content
consumers to
content producers

Developing a Social Media Strategy

As with any good campaign, it is vital to start with the development of a robust strategy. However, due to the fractious and diverse nature of **Social Media**, it is easy to get carried away; both with the number of media and the aims of a campaign. Doing too much can dilute or muddle the message and overwhelm or confuse customers. Therefore, the first step of any social media strategy is to define the circumstances and objectives of the campaign through the **Absorption**, **Explosion** and **Consolidation** model and then refine the campaign in order to provide a high degree of focus on precisely how and why social media activity is being performed, who needs to be engaged with and how to measure success. The best campaigns will use this information to find every facet of social media that can be utilised to effectively present a single message to the target audience.

Blogs and Micro Blogs
Blogging

Blogging represents an important medium for creative self-expression and an avenue for otherwise ordinary individuals to reach and influence a global audience on just about anything.

Gloss

A contraction of 'web log', a blog involves the online publishing of content by an individual or organisation featuring news or analysis on a particular topic, including anything from celebrity gossip to contemporary economic theory or simply the personal life of the author.

Most blogs – or at least most good blogs – allow readers to leave comments on individual posts and authors will often try to engage with their readers by responding to these comments. An online community of bloggers – **The Blogosphere** – emerged in the early 2000s and quickly set about having a real impact on society, with many of the more influential bloggers posing a threat to traditional media as a source of specialised news and analysis. Blogging is also extremely important for companies as a means of engaging and building a relationship with their existing customers, enhancing their brand, increasing their exposure and learning from other individuals and companies in their industry.

When starting a blog, the first step is to decide on its demographic and purpose. Think about the target audience and what particular type of customer is most likely to read the blog and then consider what information is most likely to interest that particular demographic. Once you have this in mind, you should be in a position to decide on the nature of the articles and the style in which they will be written. Generally speaking, blogs are written in a conversational, informal style that is entertaining to read and easily scan-able, but this style is not

necessarily appropriate for all blogs; if a blog is targeted at keeping its business clients abreast of the latest goings on at the company, it should have a suitable level of professionalism and formality.

The best posts are those that will be useful to visitors with some of the best options being detailed **How-to Guides** on various topics; expert **Insights** on major industry developments and how they might affect readers; **Interviews** with prominent industry figures; and **Case Studies** of recent projects. As a social medium, blogging relies on interconnectivity and interactivity so it is generally a good idea to link to interesting articles and blog posts from elsewhere on the internet and to directly respond to other bloggers as this can be a good way of attracting new visitors, especially if you are responding to more famous, popular bloggers.

Hint

If you are trying to build a more meaningful connection with customers in order to increase loyalty, you could think about including informal articles describing the human side of the company, focusing on the people rather than the work that they produce. Pictures of the respective bloggers will add further weight to this personal approach.

The frequency of posts is as important a concern as having a blog in the first place. Blogs will quickly become stale and void of readers if there is a consistent lack of new material as blog readers are often very discerning and rarely have the patience to continue visiting a site if there is little chance that they will be presented with something new. Conversely, regular posts breed a higher frequency of hits as readers integrate a visit to the site into their daily or weekly routine. So, if possible, new posts should be written at least once a day in order to encourage daily visits, while regular responses to any issues that have been posted in the comments section will also aid in showing that the blog is a dynamic, active and integral part of the site. Well written blogs are also handy for SEO, as they provide another means to populate a website with keywords and attract the links that are so vital for getting to the top of search engine rankings.

Microblogging

Microblogging services such as **Twitter**, **Tumblr** or **Plurk** act as both a social network and blogging arena by enabling users to send and read short messages. These messages – or tweets if you're using Twitter – can be sent and received from any device with internet access as well as conventional mobile phones and are, quick to write, easy to read and published in real-time. Most services also allow you to subscribe to specific microbloggers and have others subscribe to you making them highly targeted as well. This makes microblogging a valuable resource for many businesses, allowing for communications with customers casually and regularly, thereby developing stronger relationships with them. In addition, it enables a business to discover what people are saying about their brand, their competitors and their industry and to respond directly to their comments.

A business's microblogging strategy could have any number of possible objectives, such as learning more about their customers in order to improve service, developing better relationships to increase customer loyalty, or increasing exposure to help attract new customers. As we mentioned above, social media strategies should have a specific goal so the first step of a microblog campaign is to decide on its purpose. After choosing a focus and successfully setting up an account – a very simple process that can be completed through the respective services' homepages – it is time to start encouraging people to become followers. Search for people who are sending messages about the company, its competitors or anything else relevant to the industry. These services work both ways as well so it is also very beneficial to follow others; if you discover anybody who appears to be writing valuable or interesting messages, start following their accounts as this will instil the account into the right communities and will provide valuable information and insights.

reach a
broader range
of **consumers**

Hint
In order to help increase the number of followers, you should make use of company websites, blogs and email newsletters to promote the account and you should use offline methods as well. You could, for example, start including the account's URL on business cards.

If you are going to use microblogs to improve the perception of a brand, you need to focus on producing content that demonstrates the company's expertise and which people will find useful. This will encourage more people to become followers and discourage existing followers from unsubscribing. Every single message does not have to directly advertise the company – nobody is interested in reading mindless self-promotion – but can instead be a regular stream of hints, tips, news and links to articles or blog posts that followers will find interesting. Another method for creating better awareness for a business is to answer any questions that people might have posed in their messages that are related to the company or its area of expertise.

Certain services – such as **TweetWorks** for Twitter – can be utilised to set up groups with followers that can act as a platform for discussions on specific areas. This is a great way to facilitate the dialogue that is so important to social media; the aim is to become an engaged and trusted member of a community. When taking part in discussions, it is vital to express views and opinions so that followers don't start to think that you are bland and

boring but you need to retain a degree of diplomacy so as not to alienate anybody.

Another option is to offer incentives for people to follow and pay attention to messages by providing exclusive special deals or discounts to followers for example. Consistently engaging with people in a constructive way will encourage far more people to become followers and subsequently hold – and spread – a more favourable brand perception.

As with normal blogs, microblogging provides a great resource to uncover real opinions of a brand. As such every effort should be made to keep track of all of the main words or phrases related to the company that you are marketing, including abbreviations of the company name and any nicknames, references to prominent people within the organisation and to the specific products or services that they provide. Services such as **Monitter** can help you track various keywords in real-time rather than the long process of manually searching for each one. When you find people referring to the company you can start responding to them. If they are being positive, you can send them a message thanking them for their custom and recommending other products and services, and if they are complaining of an issue then you should contact them to offer a solution for their particular problem or to encourage them to contact you directly with any concerns. When dealing with complaints tone of voice is incredibly important; always be polite and respectful even when the complainer is being unreasonable.

Hint
Another way to use microblogs for research is to pose questions directly to followers as this can be very useful when looking for feedback on a new idea.

Video blogs

People are far more receptive to video blogs – sometimes called **vlogs** – than their text alternatives. They are likely to be more visually pleasing and are far more convenient than the text alternative, if only for the fact that it doesn't require the user to scroll down the page. With high speed internet being so common place, there really isn't any excuse from the consumers' point of view for not providing video content. From the position of the blogger, the only obstacle is having the resources, which at the most basic level consists of a camera, a video hosting site – such as **YouTube** – and possibly an editing tool. Video blogs do not need to be hi-tech, slick and perfectly edited; the best are succinct, interesting and presented with charisma and, as long as these features are present, there is no need for a green screen, graphics or props.

Not only can these videos be placed on a site's blog, they can also be attached to emails or embedded in other online literature, to add an extra eye-catching element; we found that when we included our latest video blog in emails sent to prospective clients, the click through rate rose quite dramatically. The other location that the videos can be viewed will be the site that hosts them, with people being able to come across them either through the host site's search function or a search engine. In fact, certain larger video hosting sites are used as search engines in their own right by a large proportion of web users. As such, it is vital to sufficiently label and tag videos – for more detail take a look at our **SEO** chapter – so that videos are easy to find and present themselves to anybody making a relevant search.

As we have mentioned before, it is important to provide for every channel by which the audience can experience a brand's content. It is therefore a good idea to create a balance between video, audio and text as people consume media everywhere and each medium suits different environments and circumstances. For example, while driving to work, a user can listen to an audio blog in a downloadable podcast form; after getting to work, they can continue to engage with blog activity by the more appropriately discrete text format; and can finish the day relaxing in front of video content.

Blogger Outreach

Within the **Blogosphere** there are always voices that garner more attention and respect with their comments and opinions on a certain field. A company's blog should, of course, aim to be one of those voices but it is extremely difficult for a company to achieve the required amount of trust due to the perceived lack of impartiality that will automatically be attributed to them. So it is vital to take

measures to ensure that blogs are balanced and unbiased, but it is also possible to win an audience through engaging with, and gaining the support of, those bloggers who are already well reputed. These bloggers typically gain their reputation by being informed, interesting, opinionated and, most importantly, independent. They may be heavily biased towards a certain point of view, but the trust that they achieve is based on the fact that their bias is their own and has not been manipulated by sponsors.

Gaining blogger endorsements is a valuable acquisition but it can require a high level of diplomacy as a blogger who has earned a good reputation will not want to risk it on a company or product that they are unsure of and they certainly would not want to be seen to be 'selling out'. Once a blogger has decided to accept an invitation to engage with a brand – through an event, demonstration or sampling – you should consider that they are likely to approach it with an element of cynicism and will need to be won over through the quality of the product and presentation so it is important to be confident that this can be achieved before starting any blogger-winning activities.

Hint
Do not be dissuaded from contacting the most cynical, belligerent and stubborn bloggers as. Although they may take more effort to win over, an approving blog post from one of the more cut-throat bloggers is an impressive indication of a product/service's quality.

Forums/Message Boards

Forums and message boards are online platforms for discussion, situated either on a dedicated site or a section of an existing site. They are a great opportunity to listen, target and create a dialogue with the public giving a company or brand a presence and voice amongst large numbers of individuals. Analysing the reaction to a product or service is a vital part of a company's research, while addressing that reaction is essential for customer relations. This presence can also be used to influence people's reading by using links to direct them to a brand's main site or other destinations on the web that reflect well on the brand.

To create and sustain a forum on a brand's site demands a massive investment of time and effort to attract a community if they are to function. Without a community to drive them, forums will become the internet equivalent of a wasteland, without even digital tumbleweed to break the silence. It is, however, possible to start smaller and provide site users with the means to comment on any news or announcements and they should already be able to respond to blog posts. Once there is enough activity in the comments sections, with a good number of regular users – this is best achieved through frequent, interesting content – it is worth adding a full-scale forum to the site but until that time a much more manageable method is to engage with those forums that already exist.

There is likely a multitude of forums or message boards for almost every industry imaginable and a quick investigation using a search engine will produce the most popular with the most activity. Once they have been identified, it is important to integrate the brand voice into the community and this can be accomplished by providing reasonable and well-informed opinions within discussions and initiate interesting discussion topics. This will take some time and effort but will probably have a degree of overlap with blog content so there can be an element of recycling. From an integrated platform it should be possible to start a systematic marketing strategy of identifying interested parties and providing them with news and product updates and gathering valuable reviews and opinions.

Hint
Product giveaways or exclusive news updates can act as rewards to the community for accepting and allowing sales orientated messages.

It is also possible to 'take over' a forum for a period of time to create noise for products and services. This often takes shape as a special day of offers, activities and forum events, integrated with real world goings-on. You could, for instance, provide discount codes for those who take part in discussions and provide product feedback or post details of locations where forum users can go to collect free prizes; brands often turn this into something of a scavenger hunt which is a great way to involve and excite users.

As you might imagine, hijacking a forum unannounced may be seen by its users and administrators as hostile and they are likely to react in a very antagonistic manner, shutting down all of the offending material and damaging brand perception. The way to overcome this is to understand the culture of the forum. If you have been active on the forum already, then you should already be familiar with its ins and outs and understand the inherent hierarchy. It is important to gain permission from the major forum figures – the creators and admins – through an email or private message and to also publicise the event to the rest of the users and only proceed if the go-ahead is granted. If consent is not given then it is always worth making another attempt, perhaps with a slightly more diplomatic or sugar coated approach but it is important to know when to accept that permission is not going to be forthcoming.

Once a brand has made its mark on a series of forums and message boards, it will receive a huge boost to customer loyalty, brand perception and the all important trust that needs to be present in every campaign if it is to succeed.

I think that forums are great places to ask questions, gain knowledge and share my thoughts

So do I!
Let's create a forum where we can discuss this

Crowdsourcing

Crowdsourcing is a huge movement in research and development and can be used across a huge range of disciplines, from the world of science to politics and obviously marketing. It is the practice of posing a problem to the public forum in order to employ the manpower needed to tackle issues that would be otherwise impossible. It has been used to help map the galaxy, label and archive historical documents and translate websites into a range of languages. The old adage of many hands making light work is epitomised through crowd sourcing and provides a great opportunity to marketers as it not only solves problems but also makes people feel that they are part of the brand; it gives an element of 'for the people, by the people' and demonstrates that the brand is interested in what the public has to offer.

One of the best opportunities for crowdsourcing is creative design, where the public submit ideas for a new product aesthetic, advert, slogan, etc. with the best entrant going on to be utilised in further marketing. **Doritos** made a TV advert by asking people to make and submit their own ad and then rewarded the winner for their efforts, while the online clothing company **Threadless** relies almost entirely on crowdsourcing for the t-shirt designs that it sells.

Starting a crowdsourcing movement should utilise all current brand channels to direct the public to a centralised hub – usually a page on a social network or the brand's site – where individuals can receive their tasks, discuss them and submit their solutions. Most marketing crowdsourcing will take a form similar to those mentioned above and will require a manner by which a winner can be picked, and a reward for that winner.

Media Sharing

Media sharing sites allow users to upload videos, photographs, **PowerPoint** presentations and other media to share and discuss with their friends and the wider world. Sites such as these are enormously popular and have already had a significant impact on politics, business and society. For example in 2006 Tom Dickson, CEO of blender manufacturer **Blendtec** began posting a series of videos to his site **WillitBlend.com** and **YouTube** in which he tested his blenders against such items as golf balls, hockey pucks, and iPods, and in the first six weeks the videos had received more than eight million views and generated massive publicity for his company. But the viral power of social media sharing creates dangers as well as opportunities. When **United Airlines** broke little-known Canadian musician Dave Carroll's $3,500 Taylor guitar and then refused to offer compensation he recorded a humorous, catchy song about his experiences entitled 'United Breaks Guitars' which within a few weeks had received millions of views on YouTube and was being widely reported by the mainstream media, resulting in terrible publicity for United Airlines. The influence that media sharing has on the world of marketing, business and brand is clearly too great to be ignored.

Video

The subject of any videos that you produce will, of course, depend on what you are trying to achieve and the nature of the business that you are marketing; if you are trying to increase brand exposure then an entertaining video with the potential to become viral might be the best option, whereas if you are focusing on improving the brand perception of existing customers, you could provide a series of instructional videos to offer solutions to common problems. This would serve to demonstrate the company's expertise and can give them a human face by featuring different employees – or actors playing employees – in the videos.

Hint
You should make sure that videos are not too overt in their marketing message, as an explicit advertisement will deter people from forwarding the video to their friends. A better option is to simply mention the brand at the very end of the video, and perhaps link to an affiliated site in the description field.

To ensure that videos receive as many viewings as possible, each video should be given a title and file name which clearly signposts its content to users and search engines and add a description that builds on the information provided in the title and gives people a reason to keep watching the video through to the end. Think carefully about the tags to attach to each video – these are important as they help determine which 'related videos' they will be linked from. Tags should be individual words or very short phrases that are relevant to the video and company; there is no limit to the number of keywords so include anything relevant that you can think of.

Photographs
Media sharing isn't all about videos. You can also look to engage with sites such as **Flickr** or **Photobucket** where you can share photographs or **Slideshare,** where you can share presentation slides, in order to gain maximum exposure across the social web. For example, on Flickr you can post a lot of high quality photographs related to a company's

build and maintain relationships

work, comment on other people's photos, and join and engage with groups relevant to the industry that allow you to join discussions with other users. If you use the company's website URL as your username then every time that you interact with other users in this way you will be increasing brand exposure.

Streaming

With the prevalence of high-speed broadband, live streaming – provided by sites such as **Ustream** – has also become a popular method of viewing video content. In the world of on demand video, where viewers can watch TV programmes, films and the like whenever they want, live streaming sites show that scheduled programming still has an audience. Marketing can be applied to these live streams through sponsorship and advertisement, though they have to be fairly unobtrusive as users generally have a much smaller tolerance for advertising interruptions. This is mostly due to the fact that, unlike most of the video content on the internet, streaming video cannot be skipped forward. It is, therefore, a great but risky marketing opportunity as anybody wanting to watch the content is forced to also view any integrated adverts and sponsor messages. To find the balance between advertising the brand and not frustrating the viewer, the advert should be short, succinct, in keeping with the tone of the accompanying stream and strategically positioned – usually at the beginning – so as to minimise interruptions to the content.

Tagging, Bookmarking and News Aggregation

News Aggregation and Social Bookmarking Sites

News aggregation sites such as **Digg**, **Sphinn**, and **Reddit** enable users to submit links to news articles on the internet and to vote and comment on them; articles with the most positive votes will get the most prominent positions within the site. Bookmarking sites such as **Del.icio.us** are similar but operate in a slightly different way in that users create bookmarks for their favourite websites so that they can access them on any computer simply by logging on to the site, and these bookmarks are shared with other users. The bookmarking site can then analyse people's bookmarking choices and rank sites and pages in order of popularity.

Users can simply look at the most popular content displayed on the front page or within particular categories such as sport, politics, etc., or they can use the search facility to look for specific information. It is this latter function that makes these sites really interesting as the search results that they provide will – at least in part – be based on the number of recommendations that they have received from other users and by categorisations assigned to them by people who have actually read the page. This is in contrast to the traditional search engines which use computer programs to determine the subject matter and quality of particular pages and which, however technologically sophisticated, will always be to some extent flawed. These sites will therefore often return more valuable results than the search engines and they attract large numbers of visitors as a result. Just as with traditional search engine optimisation, if you can get a site onto the results pages of these sites, you could potentially attract a large amount of highly-targeted traffic.

The first step to gaining a presence on these sites is to become a member of several of the major bookmarking services, bookmark the company's web pages and tag them with appropriate keywords, as well as submitting relevant, newsworthy articles to news aggregation sites. You should concentrate on producing content which visitors will find valuable and compelling, that they will want to bookmark or submit to news sites and remember to provide links to the most popular services such as Digg and Del.icio.us at the bottom of appropriate pages on sites to encourage visitors to do so.

Spend some time researching the type of content which is proving to be most popular and determine what you can learn from them to help you to replicate their success; the comments section can be useful for this purpose as users will often explain exactly what it is that they like or dislike about certain sites or pages. This will not only ensure that pages appear in the search results on these sites thereby helping to direct traffic towards your pages, but it will also help SEO efforts by aiding the search engine robots - which regularly crawl bookmarking and news aggregation sites - in understanding the content and function of the site. More generally, by consistently submitting high quality content and engaging intelligently and helpfully in the discussions that take place on these sites you can improve brand reputation.

Social Networking

It is almost impossible to have missed the rise of social networking; it is so prevalent in modern life, news and popular culture. As such, we have decided to take something of a liberty in this section by

assuming that you are familiar at least with what social networking sites do. We have, therefore, devoted this section to the practice of using social networks – for marketing activities and kept explanations of the basics of the sites – such as setting up accounts – to a minimum because this will change as technology improves. If you are one of the few people that we have misrepresented who are completely unfamiliar with social networking sites, then we would suggest heading to the homepage of any of the big social networks, such as facebook.com, where getting set up is really very self-explanatory and after an hour of exploring you should be up to speed.

Social networks are websites that allow users to develop a group of friends to whom they can send messages, share common interests, connect with old and new friends and most social networks also allow users to play games, share videos, music and other media with their friends and monitor the latest goings on in almost any topic that they could wish. As such, they cover much of the same ground as the other social media sites that we have mentioned, though importantly they present all of these services in one place. In fact, they have become something of a meta-internet within the web as people are provided with ever more applications that perform the fundamental actions that would usually be catered for by the wider web. For instance, **Pizza Hut** have added an application to their Facebook page, which allows users to find their nearest restaurant, book a table or even order a pizza. These sites may not be able to provide each individual service to the same quality as specialised sites, but are often more popular amongst general users who appreciate having everything 'under one roof'.

Once you have set up a brand's account and created its page you will want to start attracting people to view it and become members, friends or fans. A great way to do this is to link to the page from the company website and emails. Importantly, you can directly link to one of the specific tabs on the page which means that you can have different target pages for different links in order to increase the conversion rate of people becoming fans. So, for example, if there is a discussion forum on the company website, you could invite users to go and join the debate on the Facebook page and link to the **Discussion** tab, or if you are sending an email offering advice on a particular topic you could link to the **Resources** tab where they can find additional help. Of course you should be careful not to create too many different tabs in order to avoid creating a page that is overly large and complicated, but by targeting links according to audience you could significantly improve conversion rates. Generally speaking, it is best not to link to a wall as you are unable to control the content that fans are posting, so it is usually better to direct new visitors to a section that can be optimised to maximise conversions.

In order to get the most out of a page you should utilise the aforementioned applications to help create customised and engaging content. There are thousands of applications available and some of them could prove invaluable to the success of a page. For example, the **Static FBML** application for Facebook can be added to integrate

HTML or FBML – **Facebook Markup Language** – directly onto the page, which enables greater customisation and functionality without having to go through the more complex process of creating a custom application on **Facebook Platform**. The **Flash Player** application allows you to upload Flash files to enable fans to play any Flash videos or games that you have developed, which can be a great way of encouraging fans to engage with the page. There are also a number of applications that will automatically publish a company's blogs or feeds to its page, which helps to keep the page populated with new content and makes sure that the consumer has as many avenues as possible to see it. There are an ever-growing number of applications that can help to make a page more compelling and easier to manage and we advise that you spend some time researching which applications might best suit your own particular needs and experiment to see which work best.

Hint

As well as gaining a presence in the big social networks, it is worth reviewing the more niche social networking sites – such as **Mumsnet.com**, a social site aimed at parents – as these can be a lot less competitive for marketers and allow for a very engaging and targeted approach.

Many of the social networking sites include utilities – such as Facebook's **Insights** – that allow you to measure a page's performance across a number of different metrics in a similar way to **Google Analytics**'s function for web pages. You should keep an eye on these measurements to identify ways in which pages can be improved. The following are the metrics by which you can monitor usage of a Facebook page through Insights:

Interactions – Insights measures the number of times that fans have interacted with a page – by writing on the wall, commenting on a post, etc. – and displays the total number over a seven day period. The interactions metric is a key indicator of fans' engagement with a page and is important in increasing exposure on Facebook as the more that fans interact with a page, the more stories will be published about it in their friends' News Feed. A low level of interaction suggests that you are failing to create compelling content for the page, and if you find yourself in this position you should make sure that you are posting frequently and that the content is relevant, useful and interesting to fans.

Post Quality – the Post Quality score measures engagement levels of fans over a seven day period and compares the level of activity on a page to similar pages with a similar number of fans. The score is calculated with an algorithm and is affected by factors such as the number of fans, the number of posts, the number of fan interactions, and other factors. A page's Quality Score will be higher if it has a smaller number of posts each attracting a reasonable number of responses rather than a large number of posts with relatively few responses. This is an important reminder that you should avoid overwhelming fans with useless information and to instead focus on providing regular, high quality content.

The Fan Dashboard Graph – the Fan Dashboard Graph provides information on the number of people who have become a fan of a page, the number of people who have stopped being a fan, the number of fans who have chosen to hide the page's posts in their News Feed – unsubscribers – and the number of unsubscribers who have subsequently re-subscribed to posts. Clearly if there are a high number of people cancelling their fan-ship then this may indicate that you are failing to provide engaging content, and a high unsubscribe rate suggests that posts are low quality or too frequent. The unsubscribe rate is particularly important as posts to fans' News Feed are your main means of communicating to them.

It is even possible to create your own social network through sites such as **Ning**. These sites are mostly used to create networks within academic circles or for a school's alumni but they can also be used effectively by brands. If you create a network for a brand then you have a much greater degree of control over it and the members that inhabit it than you would with a page on a third-party network. This extra control needs to be sold to the consumer as exclusivity, as an elite club to which they can belong as VIPs; everybody likes to feel special.

CROSS MEDIA

Primal Fears

When you are putting together a social media campaign, it is important to get people involved, and a great way to achieve this is through engaging imagery. There are, however, a few images that do not sit well with the human psyche, causing our skin to crawl and an uncanny feeling of unease to permeate through our very being. Falling, wolves, big hairy spiders, drowning and dark and narrow spaces; these images tap into our primal fears and are worth steering clear of if you want people to feel comfortable sharing your content. In fact, it's not just explicit representations of these innate fears that should be avoided, but also the suggestion of them. This also holds true across most of the rest of direct marketing media as the fears remain the same no matter which medium they are presented in.

Selling stair lifts? Make sure that all of your pictures and video across all media show them going up the stairs rather than down, to sidestep the fear of falling. Marketing beach holidays? Show the family having fun on the sand rather than splashing around in a deep sea, so as not to evoke any drowning imagery.

Conversely, if you are running a campaign where you want to get people's hearts beating and adrenalin pumping, to elicit a feeling of excitement, then including one of these fears might be the exact right thing to do. If you are marketing adventure holidays, theme parks or fast cars, then try using some primal fear imagery to capture the thrill of the product.

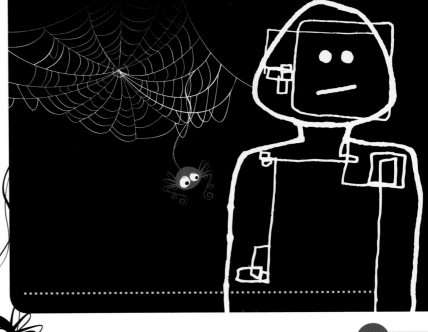

social media case study

social media feeds

Your social media presence needs to be ubiquitous across everything you do. Bring people into your social community by populating all your media with links, mentions and excerpts.

facebook link

twitter link

live twitter feed

video and blog

Social media needs to be updated regularly with interesting and varied content. Be creative and utilise media and channels that your target audience are most engaged with.

show first few lines of words –
click 'more' for full blog

clear headlines
create interest

clear link back to
previous page

details of
author

maximum
viewing size

category
filtering

playback/
viewing
functions

integrated
video footage

opportunity to
comment

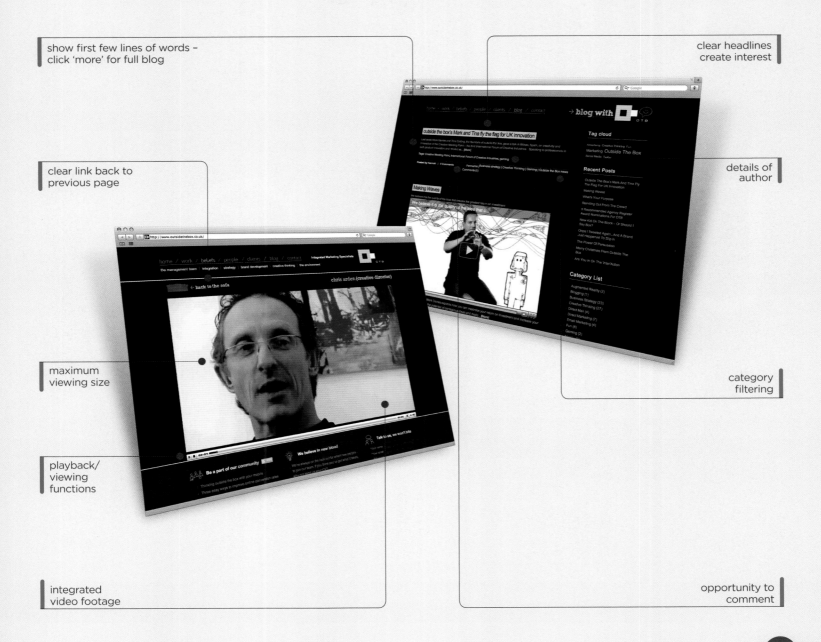

? testing

Without a great test strategy, campaigns can become stagnant very quickly

Throughout this book, we have used the phrase,
'this will be dependent on demographic, product and purpose'—
or words to that effect — fairly regularly.

This is symptomatic of the fact that, although we have tried to provide a reliable overview of the truisms and best practises inherent to each aspect of direct marketing, the variables of a campaign are near-infinite and must be chosen on a case-by-case basis. Even some of the most reliable maxims are not always applicable; for example, the adage that a lower price leads to more sales is not always valid, especially with a luxury or elite brand or product.

The deluge of choices that need to be made for a campaign – both new and ongoing – can appear daunting and, through our assertion that the overabundance of choice makes it impossible to provide definitive answers, it may seem as though we have passed the responsibility back to you.

This is because you will need to test any marketing activity you do.

testing

Most of the choices that you make when marketing should depend on thorough testing as, alongside personalisation, testing is one of the greatest strengths of direct, narrow-cast, marketing as it is relatively cheap to perform – especially with online marketing – and can produce convincing, credible results on **real** customer behaviour.

Despite this, testing is an aspect of marketing that is too often neglected by many companies claiming that it is too expensive, protracted or complicated, with the most prevalent excuse being that testing is simply not needed as people in the company 'know the market'. Even if testing does occur, in some cases the testing will focus on the wrong features, be sent to too small a sample, or will not be pursued far enough.

At the most basic level, testing does not have to be expensive or time-consuming; though choosing to invest larger amounts of resources, will often result in better returns. Even the smallest test is better than none and can provide exponentially extraordinary profit.

A well-known example of this is that of **Amazon** who tested a form with two fields, – **email address** and **password** – two buttons, – **login** and **register** – and one link – **forgot password?**. The tests found that labelling one of the buttons **continue**, rather than **register** provided better returns as customers found registering to be confusing or irritating. When this change was implemented the number of customers purchasing went up by 45%, generating an additional $300m over 12 months.

Still unsure of the importance of testing? Then we suggest that you follow the next section of this chapter so that you can allow testing into your life. If you are already a testing convert then feel free to skip it.

T.A.P. – The Two Step Programme
There are only two steps to the **outside the box Testophobics Anonymous Programme – T.A.P.** – making it much more efficient than most other self-help programmes out there:

Step One
Accept the Customer's Unreliability
Most of those in favour of testing will tell you that if you believe that you know a market well and that, consequently, your ideas don't need testing, then you are being either naive or arrogant. They will claim that we live in a world of 'I reckon' fallacy, heavily biased by our own views and experiences which are rarely indicative of those of our potential customers or clients. You do not know your customers inside out; believing that you do will only lead to potentially expensive surprises.

However, it is not arrogance to think that you can put yourself in the customer's position. Every man is not an island; there is such a thing as empathy and, as stated in our **Strategy** chapter, you should be following a customer-empathetic path throughout every stage of a campaign. You may even be exactly the type of person that you are marketing to.

We therefore approach testing's importance from a different angle: the public don't know what they want, so how are we supposed to? Taken as individuals, customers can be understood to a reasonable degree; their behaviours can be mapped and predicted. However, en masse, customers become a wholly different creature with the most unreasonable behaviours and buying habits. There is an abundance of anecdotal evidence that demonstrate just how unenthusiastically customers can react to sure-thing campaigns or, conversely, how they can react positively to the most mundane promotion.

In short, be confident in your abilities but understand that you have to test anyway because **the general public are not to be trusted.**

Step Two
Start testing
It's as simple as that.

The Control
Before any tests can begin, you must identify a control. This is easily done as a control is generally the existing incarnation of the website, mailing package, email, etc. that you wish to test. If, however, you are providing marketing for a fledgling business and have nothing to appropriate for a control, you must make sure that any test is carried out with multiple test subjects so that each takes the position of the control for the other.

In all other cases, a control is vital and should never be lost sight of. If a new campaign seems to work well, a control allows you to quantify the degree to which it has improved and, more importantly, without a control there is no way to ascertain whether the upturn in performance can be attributed to the new campaign or another factor; the old campaign might have worked just as well or even better. There are clever ways to make the use of a control more efficient, such as the application of multivariate testing, but at no point should it be absent from a test.

Hint
A quick word of warning. When performing tests on offers, you need to be aware that the proliferation of consumer social networking can lead to people who are being tested on cross-referencing their offers with one another. This can damage brand if managed improperly, but if you are proactive, it can actually drive footfall. For instance, an 'if you see a better offer elsewhere we'll match it' message can be included.

The Tests

A/B Split Testing
A/B testing is the most basic form of reliable test in marketing and is also the most simple to carry out and analyse. A/B testing's only downfall is the time that it takes to fully optimise a campaign as only a single aspect of the campaign can be tested at any one time. To perform an A/B test, you take a control, change a single element of it that you believe may have an impact and then run both the control and the new version simultaneously. If the new incarnation outperforms the control then you can be reasonably confident that using it in the campaign in the control's stead will provide better returns. At this point, the new version can become the control which can have a further element changed for the next test.

Multivariate/Multivariable Testing
In an environment where speed and efficiency is paramount, the simple A/B tests do not always measure up. The answer to this lies with **multivariate** or **multivariable testing – MVT**. MVT is the practise of testing a range of modifications on the same campaign simultaneously. It is ideal for online marketing where media are likely to have multiple links, images and buttons that are prime for testing.

In the offline camp, it can be difficult and expensive – though far from impossible – to perform MVT on the actual literature of the campaign to the same degree as online. However, as described in the **Database** and **Where and When** sections below, you can introduce extra variation by testing different times of year or different target audiences; by profession, geography, etc.

As well as the obvious benefits to efficiency, MVT can also aid in optimisation by allowing you to take more risks with the aspects of the campaign that you choose to test. If, for example, you decide to test ten elements of a landing page, then you should have room for at least two wildcard variables once the key variables – refer to the hierarchy of variables below – are addressed. Without the pressure

of having to select only the obviously important aspects of a page to test, you can uncover a range of obscure but surprisingly significant elements; and even if you don't, you will have still managed to test all of the essential elements in the process.

Analysing the results of multivariate testing manually can be very taxing. Even some of the most mathematically gifted members of the **outside the box** team would run crying to their mothers if presented with the prospect of manually tackling MVT analysis. There are, however, programs that can be employed for most of the heavy lifting or you can turn to an analytics company who will convert MVT data into a simple, easy to digest report.

The What and The Who
In the early days of **outside the box**, we produced a piece of direct mail for a delivery company and tested the font, offers, timing and everything else that we thought needed testing. Throughout five iterations we optimised the mailing to what we thought was the peak of perfection. However, after a year somebody pointed out that there was an aspect of the mailing that hadn't been tested: we had used a picture of a delivery person on the front and throughout each iteration the picture was of a male model. This was because, in our experience, most delivery personnel were men, and we assumed that customers would have the same experience and feel comfortable with a male figure. The decision was made to test a female picture to see if it made any kind of difference and the results were a revelation. Responses rose substantially with the female picture as, we can only assume, customers must feel far more comfortable with the idea of a female delivery person. We could have been making far more money for our client for a whole year if we had performed the right tests.

When it comes to deciding what to test, therefore, we at **outside the box** believe that **the only rule is that there are no rules**... except for that one... and a few others:

Major not Minor
To determine which elements of a campaign to test, and in what order, the following lists are generally accepted as the hierarchy of key variables when testing campaigns.

Offline
- Product/service
- Audience
- Offer
- Format
- Creative
- Timing
- Response Mechanism

Online
- Product/service
- Audience
- Offer
- Usability
- Penetration
- Creative
- Timing
- Response Mechanism

It may be obvious that the major variables are the ones to test first. They are, after all, the easiest to identify and are likely to provide the largest returns. This does not, however, seem to stop companies from performing tests on the colour of a button or the size of a logo before they test their offer.

That is not to say that there will not come a point where you will be testing a button colour as, ultimately, testing the most important factors will become stale, providing less return for the effort and cost of the testing as these elements become refined to their optimal composition. The time may, therefore, eventually come for testing the colour of buttons, but only once the law of diminishing returns has taken hold of all of the elements above it on the hierarchy. Alternatively, as mentioned above, MVT can allow for the testing of elements from the lower end of the hierarchy or, once you have reached a point where button colour is the only thing to test, it may be time to completely revamp a campaign.

Evolution or Revolution

A long-established general rule of testing is that you should take either an **Incremental** or **Radical** approach; testing either a single element of a campaign or an entirely new campaign. Using an incremental approach allows for greater accuracy as the changes that provide the best results can be easily pinpointed and isolated. Eventually, testing incremental changes will become something akin to dead horse flogging and it will be time to start a revolution and test an entirely different campaign. It may even be worth doing some radical tests while the incremental ones continue to provide returns, so that you are prepared for the day that the incremental approach grinds to a halt.

The Mathematics — Sample Size

When testing, it is important to ascertain the optimal sample size. Tests need to be as cost-effective as possible, and an overly large sample will only serve to waste funds whilst a sample that is too small cannot be relied on to accurately represent the whole customer base. To determine your sample size, you must first decide on the values to apply to the following three criteria:

The confidence level required — this is a representation of how faithful the test will be to the entire market and is best kept above 90%, with 95% being the standard. Any lower than 90% is liable to reduce the reliability and, consequently, the value of your results.

The tolerable percentage variance above or below the observed test result — this is the acceptable number by which a result can be allowed to vary; try and keep this as low as possible.

The expected response rate — to ascertain this value, you can look back at past campaigns and determine an average response rate, expressed as a percentage.

Once you have established the above values, you can ascertain your sample size by applying them to this formula:

$$Sample = 3.8416 \times c\,(100 - c) / b^2$$

With **b** as the tolerable variance and **c** as the expected response.

Or you can simply use the table below which gives an approximate sample based on your tolerable variance and a 95% confidence level:

Anticipated response	Anticipated plus or minus error on anticipated response											
	0.1	0.2	0.25	0.3	0.4	0.5	0.6	0.7	0.75	0.8	0.9	1
0.5%	19,100	4,800	3,100	2,100								
1.0%	38,000	9,500	6,100	4,200	2,400							
1.5%	56,800	14,200	9,100	6,300	3,500	2,300						
2.0%	75,300	18,800	12,000	8,400	4,700	3,000	2,100					
2.5%	93,600	23,400	15,000	10,400	5,900	3,700	2,600					
3.0%	111,800	27,900	17,900	12,400	7,000	4,500	3,100	2,300	2,000			
3.5%	129,800	32,400	20,800	14,400	8,100	5,200	3,600	2,600	2,300	2,000		
4.0%	147,500	36,900	23,600	16,400	9,200	5,900	4,100	3,000	2,600	2,300		
4.5%	165,100	41,300	26,400	18,300	10,300	6,600	4,600	3,400	2,900	2,600	2,000	
5.0%	182,500	45,600	29,200	20,300	11,400	7,300	5,100	3,700	3,200	2,900	2,300	
5.5%	199,700	49,900	31,900	22,200	12,500	8,000	5,500	4,100	3,500	3,100	2,500	2,000
6.0%	216,700	54,200	34,700	24,100	13,500	8,700	6,000	4,400	3,900	3,400	2,700	2,200
6.5%	233,500	58,400	37,400	25,900	14,600	9,300	6,500	4,800	4,200	3,600	2,900	2,300
7.0%	250,100	62,500	40,000	27,800	15,600	10,000	6,900	5,100	4,400	3,900	3,100	2,500
7.5	266,500	66,600	42,600	29,600	16,700	10,700	7,400	5,400	4,700	4,200	3,300	2,700
8.0%	282,700	70,700	45,200	31,400	17,700	11,300	7,900	5,800	5,000	4,400	3,500	2,800
8.5%	298,800	74,700	47,800	33,200	18,700	12,000	8,300	6,100	5,300	4,700	3,700	3,000
9.0%	314,600	78,700	50,300	35,000	19,700	12,600	8,700	6,400	5,600	4,900	3,900	3,100
9.5%	330,300	82,600	52,800	36,700	20,600	13,200	9,200	6,700	5,900	5,200	4,100	3,300
10.0%	345,700	86,400	5,300	38,400	21,600	13,800	9,600	7,100	6,100	5,400	4,300	3,500

You can also find a program on **www.outsidethebox.co.uk/marketing** that will determine your sample size for you.

Database

The perfect pool of subjects from which to take a sample is a database of previous customers/users. These individuals have already shown their interest in the product or service and can therefore be relied on for a larger response to the tests. As explained above, the number of responses is vital to a statistically significant test so the more that you can rely on, the better the results.

The database itself is also a prime candidate for testing as it can be segmented into different types of individual – by age, profession, and so on – and then these segments can be tested to ascertain which variations of a campaign perform best with them.

Don't Forget the When and Where

As well as testing Email A against Email B, it is also worth taking into account the time of year and the geography of your campaigns. To do this, you could simply test your current campaign at different times of year or test whether your direct mailings are as effective in the North East as they are in the North West. We would, however, suggest that you go further and complicate things slightly by integrating your geographical and temporal tests into your other tests. For example, you could run Mailing Package A in the North and Mailing Package B in the South and then swap the following month so that A is now being run in the South and B is being received by the North. Continue to rotate your geography multiple times to create increasingly more reliable results.

Offline Testing

When testing the offline media of catalogues and direct mail, there are some considerations that need to be made that are exclusive to offline. Most of these are, unsurprisingly, results of the media's physical nature which allows for great opportunities for a vast array of shapes, finishings and materials, while presenting limitations concerned with delivery and printing costs.

Hands On

If you are putting together an offline campaign or a campaign that incorporates offline, then you should be taking full advantage of the sensory engagement that offline elements afford. For a deeper examination of the various options available when creating an offline marketing package look to our **Direct Mail** chapter, but the primary variables are material, – paper, plastic, foil, etc. – finish, – scents, textures, sounds, etc. – size and 3D components. Adding any of these to a package is going to make it more engaging to the recipient but the costs will also increase, causing a potential risk to ROI; this is the point at which testing becomes important. When putting a direct mail package together for **Direct Holidays**, **outside the box** created a mailing which, when opened, presented the recipient with a 3D cardboard cocktail. This simple pop-up book addition created a 30% increase in response.

Whether you are marketing chocolates, curtains, cars or constitutionals, there will be ways of making your package reflect and evoke the product – perhaps a chocolate scent, fabric cover, new-car smell or sound of the sea, respectively – and testing will help you to identify which is most successful and cost effective.

Printing Techniques

When it comes to printing the test literature, there are a number of methods that can be used to produce two or more versions in the same printing run. If carrying out a simple A/B split, then most printers can create a set up where the different versions of a mailing are placed on the same plate and printed simultaneously. There are, however, other methods that can be employed to keep the test costs down or to allow for MVT.

One of the simplest, and cheapest, ways to test is through **Black-Plate Change** where, of the four colour plates in the printing process, the black plate is changed to include different offers, copy or anything else that has been printed in black, while the rest of the layout remains exactly the same.

The most common printing method used when a mailing needs to be personalised is **Laser Printing**. This method of printing a large batch of identical mailings and then adding detail later can also be used to split mailings into sections that can be tested against one another. In this way, MVT can be achieved as a variety of variables can be applied to a range of mailings in different combinations.

As mentioned in the **Direct Mail** chapter, **Digital Printing** allows for each individual mailing to include pictures and text unique to the recipient which are likely to make a mailing far more engaging. When testing, digital printing provides near-complete freedom with the amount of variables that can be placed on a mailing as well as their positions on it. In theory, this would allow for MVT on a par with online, however, printers will usually only print a small amount of digitally printed mailings – under 10,000 – and splitting these into too many segments will mean that statistical significance takes a hit. Digital prints can, therefore, only be split into a small number of variants, severely decreasing their usefulness for MVT.

Hint

A printing of 10,000 may seem small when you need to split it into testable segments, but you can test all 10,000 personalised mailings against a control mailing with no personalisation to ascertain if the level of personalisation afforded by digital printing delivers sufficient returns.

Patience

Finally, all testing requires an element of patience as you wait for results to become significant and offline media requires the most. The time between sending out a mailing or catalogue, and a batch of significant, actionable results is longer than most are willing to wait. You can look at **The Mathematics** section above for instructions on how to tell when a test becomes statistically significant, but this will not make the responses arrive any faster so exercise plenty of willpower so that you do not become impatient and take action prematurely as this could render the tests completely useless.

Online Testing

Tools

When it comes to testing emails and web pages, there are plenty of measurement tools that can be utilised. These tools allow you to follow bounce rates, conduct bail-out surveys and review individual customer journeys and the good news is that there are some very good ones that can be obtained for free. **Google Website Optimizer** is one of the best of the free tools and is a good place to start.

Website

We have already stated that it is important to test the major aspects of a campaign first, and this is best applied to a website by focusing on the pages that can produce the best returns. Pick the pages that aren't living up to expectations – Google Website Optimizer will give you a good idea of the offending pages – and make them the focal point of the next round of tests. You should also run customer surveys to find which pages or site functions are causing problems for users and start tests that aim to address this.

Email

The test everything rule arguably applies to email to a greater extent than all other media. From a design perspective, you can test different lengths, layouts, images, colour schemes and so on, and you can also try different incentives and product descriptions. You can also try sending emails on different days, at different times, and at different levels of frequency. As mentioned in the **Multivariate Testing** section, emails are prime candidates for MVT, where you can test up to approximately twenty permutations of the same campaign, simultaneously. If you are investing the time and/or money into MVT and its analysis then the price to test each individual element will be negligible and you should, therefore, leave no testing stone unturned.

Testing on a Shoestring

Testing should have a significant budget applied to it, but those without the funds shouldn't despair as there are avenues of testing that can be very cost effective. If the finances are not available for a large series of thorough tests, then start testing small. Your tests should result in more revenue which, in turn, will lead to bigger budgets becoming available as the bosses realise how good the returns are; a portion of the returns can even be used to fund the next round of testing. Testing should never be abandoned, as it is easily scalable to budget and is always useful. Here are a selection of possible directions that the **outside the box** team have come up with:

Cheaper Mailings

The first variable that you could test is the size of mailings. Remember that the goal is to make as much net profit as possible and this does not always equate to more customers if the overheads negate the larger customer draw of a large advert. Similarly, elements such as the quality of materials can be tested to determine whether savings can be made without affecting response.

Smaller Tests

We would rarely suggest it, but if you feel that the sample confidence level can be compromised, then a smaller scale of test could be viable. Remember that the more compromises that you make on the confidence level, the less reliable your results will be, until the test becomes completely irrelevant.

Choose your media

Emails are much cheaper to produce than mailings, and the testing of these media follows suit. So why not start your testing online?

Common-sense Evaluation

Don't be lead blindly by results. Keep sight of the reason for the campaign – usually conversion value/return on investment, rather than conversion rate. To ascertain return on investment, use the following formula:

(revenue generated from campaign /total cost of campaign) x 100%

Your overriding goal in business is to make money. Even if every other KPI is showing positive results, a low ROI suggests that too much money is being spent and a new, more cost efficient, approach is needed.

Coupons and Codes

It is impossible to identify which test subject is most successful if there is no way to ascertain which version acquired the most – and most valuable – responses. In certain cases, the medium will allow for this information to be garnered fairly easily; emails or web ads with links are a good example, as every response can be followed back to the respective link that the respondent clicked on. However, for offline media or cross-media marketing, codes need to be placed on the literature that can be quoted at some point in the response process so as to identify that individual as a recipient of, for example, Mailing A rather than Mailing B.

Hint
Codes can also be placed on vouchers or coupons that act as the response mechanism and have the benefit of not having to make it clear to the recipient that the code is an important part of their response.

The What but not the Why

For all of our preaching on the Tao of the Test, we at **outside the box** must admit that testing is not the answer to every problem. A particular short fall is that testing generally indicates **What** works, but it cannot explain **Why** it works; the why requires research.

There is, of course, the argument that the why is irrelevant and something to be pored over by the scientists and sociologists, while the marketers get on with selling their product. However, ascertaining the reason for the success of a specific variable over another could provide valuable insight into the next direction for a company to take. For example, through testing you might find that one of your advertisements for a male-skewed product performs surprisingly well on a female-skewed website. This could be due to women buying the product as gifts for men; it could mean that there are a significant amount of men browsing websites with a traditionally female readership; or there could be another, entirely different, reason. The only way to determine which is the actual reason is to perform research. If, through research, it becomes obvious that women buying gifts for men are the culprits, then this information could be used to change a company's strategy so that a heavier focus is put on male products around the major gift-giving times, such as Christmas or Valentine's Day.

Record Keeping

Direct marketing should be a conversation with the customer, and the trick to getting this dialogue right is to have a good memory. As anybody in a relationship can tell you, it is easy to get into trouble if you don't pay enough attention and remember what the other person says. As it is with loved ones, so it is with customers – don't take this analogy too far though as **outside the box** cannot be held responsible for any harassment cases.

We mentioned earlier that testing provides an insight into real customer behaviour, making the results of a test equivalent to the customer's side of the conversation and, as the number of customers usually outnumbers loved ones, it becomes imperative to keep thorough, accurate and organised records to bolster your biological memory. Otherwise, it is easy to forget that Customer Type A prefers Offer B on Product C in February, while Customer Type B prefers Offer A on Product D in June, and then there's Customer Type C, D, E, F...

What to record checklist:

- A record of the campaign literature
- The when and the where
- Daily results and conversion rates
- Cumulated final results and conversion rated
- News, weather or political events that could have affected performance

What's more, using records to create campaigns that are tailored to the customer, and making it obvious that their opinions have been taken onboard, will nurture a reassuring bond of trust between business and consumer.

Rinse and Repeat

Testing needs to be a continuous process, to refine current practice and uncover the next one. Every successful test should create a new control from which to start a fresh batch of tests and until you achieve 100% conversion, there is room for improvement.

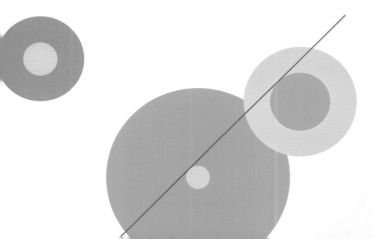

targeting—couples

When testing, focus on the things that matter. Know what you want to test and don't overcomplicate things. The two mailers on this spread were tested against one another, with the first focusing on couples, and the second on families.

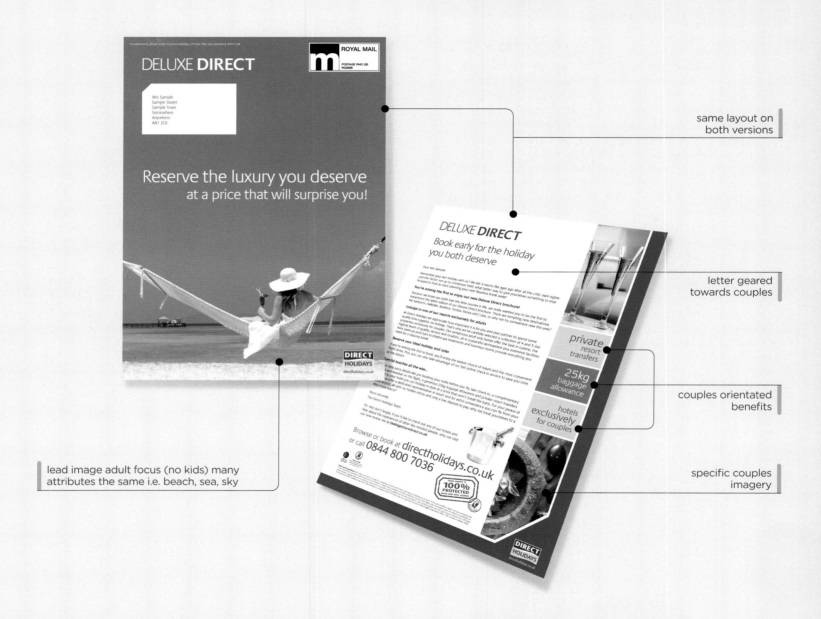

same layout on both versions

letter geared towards couples

couples orientated benefits

specific couples imagery

lead image adult focus (no kids) many attributes the same i.e. beach, sea, sky

targeting—families

Bigger, more interesting marketing communications will often gain more responses, but will the extra responses justify the extra expenditure? Test against a cheaper alternative to find out.

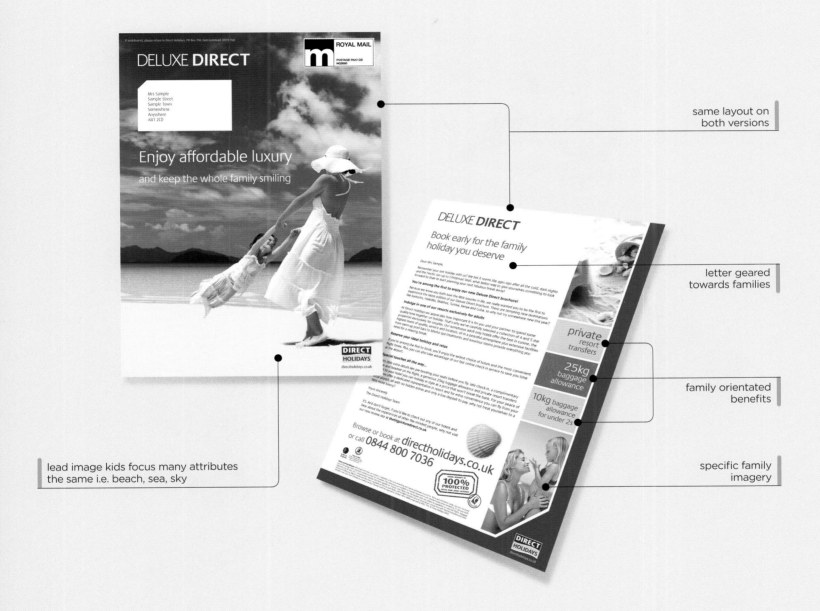

same layout on both versions

letter geared towards families

family orientated benefits

specific family imagery

lead image kids focus many attributes the same i.e. beach, sea, sky

format—postcard v larger pop up mailer

Testing gives you facts. Marketing is not a place for assumptions and hunches.

postcard
front

postcard
reverse

pop up
mailer inside

front
cover

offer—free p&p v 10% off

call to action
quoting code

different
stationery codes

t's & c's

different call to action
quoting codes

t's & c's

and finally...

...well there is no 'and finally'.

Making Waves is a cyclical process with each **Wave's** dissipation serving as the beginnings of the next one in an ongoing iterative progression. The cycle never stops, but the keywords here are 'iterative progression'. Learn from the mistakes and successes of the past and aim for innovation going forward, rather than falling into a stale mire of repetition, as new waves need new ideas; new hooks to excite and engage the masses.

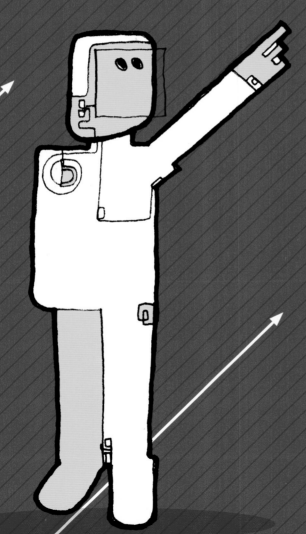

The world of marketing moves fast, and although there are many broad constants that are unlikely to change for many years, the particulars move quicker than we could hope to keep up with, even if we reprinted this book daily. To allow us to continuously iterate, amend and improve on the content of this book, we have created a website, www.outsidethebox.co.uk/marketing which will be updated with the newest marketing trends, techniques and information and will provide a forum for questions and discussions so be sure to pay a visit and join in.

All that is left now is to take what you have learned and start again...

From guerilla warfare in the Ryvita Inch War campaign of the seventies, to a gorilla outdoing Phil Collins on drums for Cadbury at the end of the noughties, big disruptive creative ideas have been the hallmark of all that is great in advertising. However, a big idea can't produce even the tiniest ripple on the public consciousness by itself. To really make waves, an idea needs to be delivered to its audience through the right channels, and these days, the channels themselves are just as important, varied and exciting as the ideas they deliver.

Great ideas flow through people, and the connections that they have with one another, be it through the latest advancements of technology, or simple word of mouth. This is changing the way professional creative thinkers think. Technology has also enabled greater freedom, a wider perspective and helped to inject pace into the way marketers work and think. The tables can even be turned, with creativity driving changes in technology, providing almost limitless marketing opportunities across every form of media; if the means to deliver a message in the manner that you want doesn't exist, you can now invent it.

Our creativity-centric world also provides a huge range of cross-media opportunities as digital components can be integrated with offline and vice versa in a variety of ways, some of which haven't even been imagined yet. For example, a sim card, battery, sensor and transmitter could all fit inside the cover of a catalogue or the envelope of a direct mailing and, on sensing that the literature has been opened, could be used to register the recipient on a corresponding website and set up a pre-populated online order form. The opportunities are immense. A widely used but simpler approach is to supply codes with literature that can be submitted via SMS or a website for a number of outcomes, such as discounts and free gifts. Media amalgamation sells by flooding and percolating the public consciousness and by being impressive, innovative and easy to engage with.

The way that people now interact with technology has led to the development of new patterns of behaviour. Individuals hold the key to a huge source of power through the explosion of social networking, message boards, forums and a huge range of other social media. They now have the opportunity to make their voices heard by millions of others, who can then engage with, react against or, most importantly, share the experience. Once an idea catches the interest and imagination of a community it can become almost like a force of nature, spreading the message from person to person.

Is this reference still relevant to our target audience?

Should we wait until further in the chapter to reference 'making waves'?

ould we make this guy do a Mexican Wave?

marketers or marketeers?

Can we add a more high tech example?

Are we taking too long to introduce the 'making waves' concept?

dedication
to the teams at **Think**
and **outside the box**